PRAISE FOR
The Spirit of Justice

The Spirit of Justice taught me how important it is to continue the work that so many before have done—to keep advocating for us! As a woman who is a part of the movement, this book's key points show me how I can continue my work to pursue justice. Readers will learn why it is important to make sure our voices are being heard. In *The Spirit of Justice*, you will learn about the strength of many everyday women pursuing justice and the courage it took to push their work to the forefront. Women must continue to show up even though our work is always so underplayed. I took pride in learning about the women before me and learning how the points and concerns I have are not mine alone!

—TAMIKA PALMER, mother of Breonna Taylor,
founder of the Breonna Taylor Foundation

In *The Spirit of Justice*, Dr. Tisby navigates through US history, spotlighting the unwavering spirit of justice. Focused on Black Christian resistance to racism, this book showcases diverse individuals who, despite imperfections, championed racial justice. Tisby's work emphasizes that embracing the spirit of justice is about progress, not perfection, urging each generation to continue the fight for positive change. This book is not just a historical survey; it is a call to action. In a world prone to historical appropriation, *The Spirit of Justice* serves as a poignant reminder to honor and learn from the past without distorting its truths.

—LATASHA MORRISON, author of the
New York Times bestselling *Be the Bridge*

The history of our country can provide us with countless reminders of how oppression, injustice, and racism tried to break us. In *The Spirit of Justice*, Jemar Tisby reminds us of a people who could not be broken. Reading this book strengthened me in my advocacy for racial justice and encouraged me in my identity as a Black Christian woman who will not break in the face of injustice—fueled by the power of the Spirit and the resilience of those who came before me.

—**DANIELLE COKE BALFOUR**, illustrator, advocate, and author of *A Heart on Fire: 100 Meditations on Loving Your Neighbors Well*

A bold, incisive, and compelling account of how Black antiracist leaders of the past drew on their Christian faith to challenge inequality and injustice. *The Spirit of Justice* is necessary reading for anyone determined to build a better world.

—**KEISHA N. BLAIN**, coeditor of the #1 *New York Times* bestseller *Four Hundred Souls: A Community History of African America, 1619–2019*

If you've been asking what keeps one's soul going in the face of white supremacy that threatens the very existence of those who have been marginalized and discriminated against, while navigating a world that seems apathetic toward the struggles and sufferings of others, then I believe Dr. Jermar Tisby has an answer in this timely work—it's the strength of God and the spirit of justice. His words carry the spirit of those who fought injustice with nonviolence and resistance, revealing the enduring power of faith in overcoming centuries of systemic oppression. Dr. Tisby's work offers hope and a call to action for all who seek to embody that same spirit to keep the work of justice alive.

—**DR. TERENCE LESTER**, founder of Love Beyond Walls, author of *I See You*, *When We Stand*, *All God's Children*, and *Zion Learns To See*

When one considers the centuries-long list of unspeakable atrocities endured by Black Americans, the question of how a people were bent but not broken defies explanation. But in *The Spirit of Justice*, Dr. Jemar Tisby offers the historical record as proof that their strength was drawn from the supernatural well of faith in an unfailing God. This book is eye opening, heartwarming, and hope igniting.

—**NONA JONES**, founder, Faith and Prejudice

THE SPIRIT OF JUSTICE

THE SPIRIT OF JUSTICE

TRUE STORIES OF FAITH, RACE, AND RESISTANCE

JEMAR TISBY

ZONDERVAN
REFLECTIVE

ZONDERVAN REFLECTIVE

The Spirit of Justice
Copyright © 2024 by Jemar Tisby

Published in Grand Rapids, Michigan, by Zondervan. Zondervan is a registered trademark of The Zondervan Corporation, L.L.C., a wholly owned subsidiary of HarperCollins Christian Publishing, Inc.

Requests for information should be addressed to customercare@harpercollins.com.

Zondervan titles may be purchased in bulk for educational, business, fundraising, or sales promotional use. For information, please email SpecialMarkets@Zondervan.com.

ISBN 978-0-310-14489-2 (audio)

Library of Congress Cataloging-in-Publication Data

Names: Tisby, Jemar, author.
Title: The spirit of justice : stories of faith, race, and resistance / Jemar Tisby.
Description: Grand Rapids, Michigan : Zondervan, [2024] | Includes index.
Identifiers: LCCN 2024011366 (print) | LCCN 2024011367 (ebook) | ISBN 9780310144854
    (hardcover) | ISBN 9780310144878 (ebook)
Subjects: LCSH: Social justice—Religious aspects—Christianity. | Anti-racism—Religious
    aspects—Christianity. | Christian life—United States. | BISAC: RELIGION / Christian
    Living / Social Issues | HISTORY / United States / General
Classification: LCC BR115.J8 T58 2024 (print) | LCC BR115.J8 (ebook) | DDC 261.8—dc23/
    eng/20240412
LC record available at https://lccn.loc.gov/2024011366
LC ebook record available at https://lccn.loc.gov/2024011367

Cover design: Gearbox Studio
Cover photos: Shutterstock, Getty Images, public domain
Interior design: Kait Lamphere

Printed in the United States of America

24 25 26 27 28 LBC 5 4 3 2 1

To all those who are weary and heavy laden,
be encouraged

CONTENTS

CHAPTER
ONE

THE SPIRIT OF JUSTICE

Myrlie Evers-Williams had salt-and-pepper black hair cropped short, and she wore a patterned red and black scarf draped across her shoulders like a queen's robe. She held herself with such regal dignity that the wheelchair she sat upon seemed to become a throne. She spoke with a deliberateness and profundity that made us all lean forward to catch every utterance.

We were in Jackson, Mississippi. I was part of a group of journalists and writers who had been granted a private audience with this legend of the civil rights movement on the grand opening day of the Mississippi Civil Rights Museum on December 9, 2017.

Mississippi Civil Rights Museum

The occasion was packed with political baggage. The president at the time, Donald J. Trump, had hinted that he might attend the grand opening of the museum. His presence there, as a man who had often trafficked in racist tropes and prejudices, represented an affront to the museum's mission to accurately tell the racist history of the state of Mississippi and be part of the effort to move beyond it. Notable invitees such as Congressmen Bennie Thompson of Mississippi and John Lewis of Georgia declined to attend because of Trump's presence. Myrlie Evers-Williams, however, still spoke at the event.

Myrlie Evers-Williams
Jemar Tisby

At eighty-four years old, Myrlie Evers-Williams still sounded a note of hope in her public remarks. "Going through the museums, I wept because I felt the blows, I felt the bullets, I felt the tears, I felt the cries. But I also sensed the hope that dwelt in all those people," she said.[1]

Her dedication to justice and interracial fellowship was improbable given what she had experienced. Most people know Myrlie Evers-Williams as the widow of Medgar Evers, the NAACP field secretary of Mississippi who was gunned down in his driveway by a white supremacist.

Born in 1925 in Decatur, Mississippi, Medgar Evers became the first field secretary for the Mississippi branch of the NAACP in 1954.

The Mississippi movement had been persistent but lacked unified leadership until Evers came to the helm. Evers helped organize Black people in the wake of the *Brown v. Board of Education* decision. After the lynching of Emmett Till in 1955, Evers dressed up as a field hand to blend in and put people at ease as he gathered eyewitness accounts. He championed people like James Meredith, helping Meredith get admitted to the University of Mississippi, and organized economic boycotts.[2] Medgar and Myrlie met at college in Mississippi, and they became colaborers in the NAACP and civil rights activism. Both of them shared a strong sense of justice, a deep affection for one another, and an abiding faith in God.

In the aftermath of her husband's death, Myrlie Evers-Williams became a renowned activist in her own right. She moved her family to California, where she twice ran for Congress. She led the NAACP as the chairperson of their board of directors for several years. She delivered the invocation at Barack Obama's second presidential inauguration and received numerous accolades for her contributions to civil rights along the way.

Now she was back in her home state of Mississippi, addressing crowds at the museum that exhibited the same gun used to murder her husband more than half a century prior.

After the public portion of the grand opening, she took time to answer our questions in a smaller gathering. One journalist asked her about the state of race relations today. I'm glad I was recording because her words helped inspire this book.

"I see something today that I had hoped I would never see again. That is prejudice, hatred, negativism that comes from the highest points across America," she told us. Then, with the candor that comes with old age, she said, "And I found myself asking Medgar in the conversations that I have with him: Is this really what's happening again in this country? And asking for guidance because—I don't mind admitting this to the press—I'm a little weary at this point."

At that moment, I fully expected her to expound on the weariness of fighting for racial justice for decades. To vent about her frustrations with people who still oppose the laws and policies that would move us closer to racial progress. To say that she was passing the torch to another generation and that she had earned her rest. But she took her comments in a different direction—one that pointed to the strength and resolve of the staunchest defenders of justice.

"But it's something about the spirit of justice that raises up like a war horse. That horse that stands with its back sunk in and hears that bell—I like to say the 'bell of freedom.' And all of a sudden, it becomes straight, and the back becomes stiff. And you become determined all over again."

Here was a woman who had endured decades of exclusion and injustice, punctuated by the assassination of her husband. She had fought and labored her entire life for change. Yet even in the ninth decade of her life, she still had the resolve to continue the struggle for racial justice. I couldn't fathom it. I couldn't make it make sense.

My mind lingered on a phrase she used: the spirit of justice.

THE SPIRIT OF JUSTICE

In the years since I heard Myrlie Evers-Williams speak those words, I have often pondered their significance. As I've studied history, I've found a pattern of endurance not only in her life but in the centuries-long struggle for Black freedom. Time and again, people endured the most horrendous results of racism, but somehow they kept going. They kept working, loving, fighting, and moving toward a better future.

How? How do people see the worst of humanity, experience the most demoralizing setbacks, and still find the resolve to work for change? How do they not give up? What keeps them going?

There is a relentless drive in human beings, both inward and transcendent, that demands dignity and propels our progress—it is the spirit of justice. It is the conviction to continue the struggle no matter the odds or the obstacles. It is the heartbeat of people who hunger and thirst for righteousness. It will not concede. It will not let the evil of racism and inhumanity prevail. It will not quit until justice rolls down like a river.

This book probes the depths of history and asks: What manner of people are these who courageously confront racism instead of being complicit with it? And what can we learn from their example, their suffering, their methods, and their hope?

The spirit of justice is a force for liberation. It inspires strength in those who understand that they must play a part in making the world kinder and more equitable. The spirit of justice animates action. It molds hearts and strengthens hands for the work of correcting oppression. It keeps weary feet moving on the protest path. It uplifts the souls of those persecuted for the sake of righteousness. It is finding your second, third . . . fiftieth wind as an aged activist, pushing further for just a bit more progress.

The spirit of justice is reflected in the human spirit, the indomitable will of oppressed people everywhere to rise up and throw off the burden of injustice. The spirit of justice is found in every culture, continent, and community. We see it expressed in those who struggled for freedom against apartheid in South Africa, colonialism in India, and labor exploitation in Mexico. It is the irrepressible instinct that says, "I will not endure indignity. I will make you see my worth, and you will treat me accordingly."

For those who claim the Christian faith, one might understand the spirit of justice as the Holy Spirit. The indwelling Spirit empowers the believer to do the work of loving God and loving neighbor. This struggle for justice encompasses both material and spiritual dimensions. As the apostle Paul once wrote long ago, "For our struggle is not against flesh and blood, but against the rulers, against the authorities, against the powers of this dark world and against the spiritual forces of evil in the heavenly realms" (Ephesians 6:12).

With the eyes of faith, one can see that the Spirit of justice is not an impersonal force detached from the human experience but the Holy Spirit of God, who lives within the hearts of those who follow Jesus. This is not to say that the work of justice can be accomplished only by Christians. People of any religion or none at all can and do pursue the common good from common grace—a blessing bestowed upon all of humanity. For followers of Jesus, the Spirit of justice grants them spiritual gifts to equip them for their work of redemption in the world. The Spirit supplies believers with spiritual armor to fight injustice (Ephesians 6:10–20). The Spirit enlivens and motivates the pursuit of all forms of justice because God hates injustice and seeks to correct oppression (Isaiah 1:17). The Spirit of justice is always at work to inspire followers of Christ to undertake acts of liberation and bear witness to the good news of their Savior.

At the inauguration of his public ministry Jesus said, "The Spirit of the Lord is on me." That Spirit empowered Jesus for his mission "to proclaim freedom for the prisoners and recovery of sight for the blind, to set the oppressed free, to proclaim the year of the Lord's favor" (Luke 4:18–19). That Spirit abides in all who, because of their faith in Jesus, seek to follow his example and continue his mission. "Where the Spirit of the Lord is, there is freedom" (2 Corinthians 3:17).

However, the work of the spirit of justice is not confined to the past. Nor is it the privilege of a single group or individual. The spirit of justice belongs to all of us. We must learn to recognize the work of the spirit of justice so we too can continue the struggle against racism in our generation.

WHAT HISTORY TEACHES US ABOUT THE SPIRIT OF JUSTICE

This book, *The Spirit of Justice*, is a historical survey marching you through US history from the colonial era to the present day. A historical survey provides an overview of a long period, necessarily moving briskly, in order to spot trends and patterns. Since history is so dense, it is impossible to include every single relevant event in a single work, which is true of any historical study. But the historical data presented here is representative of the subject of this book—the spirit of justice. The people and their stories demonstrate that in every period of US history the spirit of justice has been present among those who had the courage and imagination to pursue a better future.

Most of the stories you'll read about focus on Black Christian resistance to anti-Black racism. Throughout the history of white supremacy, Black people have been motivated by their faith to resist dehumanization. They have understood their divinely bestowed dignity and asserted their equality in the face of crushing oppression: "As one of the few totally black controlled and independent institutions, black churches played a major role in resistance."[3] The Black church itself is, in many ways, a direct response to the racism embedded in many sectors of predominantly white Christian traditions that arose in the United States.

This focus on Black Christian resistance to racism should not suggest that other groups do not have their own stories of resistance that are worth telling. Indeed, people across the racial and ethnic spectrum, including white people, have demonstrated solidarity in movements to oppose anti-Black racism. Some of them will be part of this book. Any historical survey of the resistance to racism reveals that anyone— whatever their race or ethnicity—can join the cause of racial justice.

The people featured in this book are not perfect. Far from it. In fact, some are problematic in what they believed or what they said or did. They may have had harmful ideas about gender and sexuality. Their efforts to fight racism may have been tainted by paternalistic notions. They may have had abrasive personalities or big egos. Some of their ideas about fighting racism may seem antiquated by today's standards. No one in this study is meant to be a model of exemplary behavior in every way. From a Christian standpoint, there is only one perfect person. His name is Jesus, and not one of the figures profiled in this book is him.

Even the lives of imperfect people can be instructive though. Flawed as they are, they still took bold and meaningful stances against racism. I've tried not to include people whose harmful actions overshadowed the good they did and made them into notorious figures. But because my knowledge is not all-encompassing, I may not have been aware of some pernicious acts perpetrated by the people presented here. If an oversight of this kind occurred, as the saying goes, "credit it to my head, not to my heart."

In any case, we should always remember that all human beings have proverbial feet of clay. We are all subject to flaws, failings, and shortcomings. The same is true with these historical figures. Even as they displayed courage and creativity in pursuing racial justice, they may have fallen woefully short in other areas. The goal of *The Spirit of Justice* is not to present perfect people who never did or said anything objectionable; it's about learning from the past work of those who pursued racial progress and seeing what we can emulate, or avoid, based on their examples.

It is also important to remember that resisting racism is about progress, not perfection. As we survey US history, we will find that even the most well-regarded figures and their efforts had short shelf lives. Organizations folded. Funding dried up. Activists moved on to different seasons in their lives. Well-intentioned efforts came to be regarded as missteps.

The partial progress of so many who resisted racism reminds us that growth is fragile. The gains of the past are not guaranteed to persist into the future. Victories can turn into losses. Rights can be rolled back. Time is not an inevitable march toward greater freedom and equality. Instead, each new generation must take up its responsibility to embrace the spirit of justice and maintain the struggle for positive change.

BEWARE OF HISTORICAL APPROPRIATION

Every year at the end of October, kids and adults alike cover their faces in paint, search the internet and pop-up stores for outfits they wouldn't wear any other time of year, and pretend to be someone or something else for Halloween. In years past, people thought nothing of smearing their faces with brown or black paint to pretend to be a Native American or a person of African descent. They wore clothes, teeth, noses, and makeup in garish caricatures of actual people and cultures. These costumes often played on racist tropes and perpetuated harmful prejudices. Insensitive choices for Halloween costumes is just one example of cultural appropriation. Cultural appropriation means claiming aspects of a culture other than your own without offering the respect, dignity, and understanding due to the people who inhabit that culture and its practices.

Just as there is cultural appropriation, there can also be historical appropriation: the attempt to claim the heroic historical actions of the few to downplay the atrocious actions of the many. As cultural appropriation selectively adopts the most visible or celebrated parts of a culture one cannot rightfully claim, historical appropriation involves picking and choosing which historical figures and events to claim in order to create a more valorous version of the past. You try to make the struggles and triumphs of people who fought against racism and white supremacy your own, even if your community had no part in that resistance. In fact, historical appropriation is most tempting to those whose political, theological, and economic lineage not only ignored racial justice but actively supported racist beliefs and actions.

Many Christians like to claim John Newton, the British pastor and songwriter who wrote the hymn "Amazing Grace," as part of their spiritual heritage. Newton was a slave-ship captain who became a Christian and eventually became an outspoken abolitionist. Christians today point to Newton as an example of how Christianity redeems and reforms individuals and serves as a force for racial justice. Yet they fail to acknowledge two realities. First, Newton remained a slave-ship captain for years after his conversion. He did not immediately see his profession as a contradiction to his faith because it was far more socially acceptable for him to be a proslavery Christian than an antislavery one. Second, people who claim Newton today fail to follow his example. After he eventually changed his views on slavery, he was not quiet about it. Newton wrote an entire public pamphlet in support of *changing laws* to promote racial justice and abolish the slave trade. Historical appropriation occurs when you celebrate John Newton's redemption arc of moving from slave-ship captain to abolitionist and yet refuse to emulate his public support of racially progressive policies.

Oftentimes, people who point to historical actors such as John Newton are trying to claim that the preponderance of Christian history in the United States shows Christians resisting racism. Yet while the historical record reveals that many Black Christians and other exploited groups stood up for justice, most white Christians demonstrated compromise and complicity with racism.[4] Those who courageously confronted injustice were the exception, not the norm.

In a book like *The Spirit of Justice*, which discusses people who struggled against racism, it would be easy to say, "See! Christians aren't all bad. Sure, some of them were racist, but most were decent folks who did the right thing. Let's just celebrate them and not focus so much on a few 'bad apples.'" Such sentiments ignore the host of Christians who looked the other way or actively participated in racism. Do not claim the historical legacy of antiracists if you are not also willing to claim and contend with the legacy of racists in your own tradition.

The best way to celebrate the struggle of those who came before us is to acknowledge the truth, learn from it, and act on it. If your Christian tradition has historically supported slavery, segregation, and racism, then admit it. You cannot claim the antiracist actions of historical actors if you refuse to acknowledge the many others in your faith tradition who were the source of racist ideas and behaviors. Beware of historical appropriation.

DISTINGUISHING BETWEEN RESISTANCE, ADVOCACY, AND ACTIVISM

In describing how the spirit of justice manifested in various eras and individuals, it is helpful to distinguish between resistance, advocacy, and activism. Usually when we think of resistance, we think of conspicuous endeavors such as marches or sit-ins. In *The Spirit of Justice* we'll look at a variety of antiracist actions that range from starting schools to boycotting segregated businesses to writing books. Actions of any kind, from the everyday to the extraordinary, can be motivated by the spirit of justice, and they all deserve consideration.

Resistance is defined as any action taken for spiritual, emotional, and physical survival and in pursuit of joy and thriving. Acts of resistance may not be consciously conceived of as such, and they may not be directed at a particular person, policy, or institution. These works may not change the mind or practices of the oppressor, but they help to sustain the oppressed. Resistance often takes the form of the commonplace and the quotidian. Examples of resistance include raising a family, starting a business, going to therapy, or attending church. Absent of context, such actions seem unremarkable. But since racism is so widespread and varied, there are always conditions that must be taken into account. In a white supremacist society, any action or attitude that asserts one's full humanity despite ongoing attempts at dehumanization can be considered resistance.

Advocacy is an intentional action taken in support of a specific justice cause. It often includes efforts to increase awareness about an issue through verbal or written communication. Advocacy can take the form of writing or sharing articles, using a hashtag to amplify a movement, or having conversations to build bridges of understanding.

Advocacy often involves supporting individuals and organizations that are dedicated to a justice cause full-time. Advocacy is the intentional effort to raise awareness about a particular cause in the hope of encouraging positive change.

Activism involves actions that purposely and directly challenge injustice to change opinions, policies, and practices. Activism is most often public and visible, such as marches, sit-ins, and the blocking of highways. Activism is designed to draw attention to an injustice and usually entails some form of demonstration designed to provoke a response. Thus, activists put themselves at risk of retribution, whether through imprisonment, loss of employment, or even death. An activist dedicates a significant portion of their time and energy to bringing about justice in a particular area. They may work for a nonprofit or similar entity. Not all people who experience oppression engage in activism, but many do, if even briefly, at some point in their lives.

The lines between resistance, advocacy, and activism are not always clear. When an enslaved person broke custom and learned to read, was that an act of resistance or activism? Would starting a Black-owned newspaper in defiance of the lies promulgated by white outlets constitute advocacy or activism or both? These distinctions are not meant to neatly categorize what people did to protest injustice. Rather, they help us better understand why such varied acts deserve attention. The spirit of justice takes many forms.

WHITELASH AND COUNTING THE COST

In my first book, *The Color of Compromise*, I opened with the story of Charles Morgan Jr. He was a young white lawyer in Birmingham when a white supremacist bombed the 16th Street Baptist Church and killed four young girls—Carole Robertson, Denise McNair, Cynthia Wesley, and Addie Mae Collins—during church on Sunday, September 15, 1963. The next day, Morgan took to the podium at a meeting of the Young Men's Business Club of Birmingham and gave a shocking speech, shocking coming from a white southern man at that time.

"Who did it? Who threw that bomb?" Morgan asked. "The answer should be, 'We all did it.' Every last one of us is condemned for that crime and the bombing before it and the ones last month, last year, a decade ago. We all did it."[5] Morgan was not speaking to a group of Ku Klux Klan members. The most strident prosegregationist personnel were not in the audience. The members of this club were rising leaders in Birmingham who had made gestures at school desegregation and attempts to blunt the brutality of the infamous Eugene "Bull" Connor. These were the moderate, levelheaded, unity-minded voices of reason in the city.

It would have been easy to condemn the white supremacist extremists alone for the bombing, but Charles Morgan Jr. did something far more hazardous—he blamed the "good white people" for their silence and inaction. He even included the good white Christians. "It is all the Christians and their ministers who spoke too late in anguished cries against violence."

What I did not write about in my first book was what happened after Morgan's speech. Four young Black girls had been murdered at church on Sunday. But instead of directing their ire toward white supremacists and the rampant racism in the city, Morgan's listeners reserved much of their anger for him and his family. The next morning at 5:30 a.m., Morgan received a call at his house. "Is the mortician there yet?" a voice over the phone asked. "I don't know any morticians," Morgan responded. "Well, you will, when the bodies are all over your front yard." The caller hung up.

Morgan received many more death threats, and his opponents even threatened his wife and young son. Within a few weeks, Morgan and his wife decided to leave the city permanently. Morgan closed his law practice. He gave away his law books and furniture. Their son gave away his dogs. "There was no way for us to remain in the city of which I had been a part yet from which I had grown apart."[6]

Morgan went on to have a notable career in civil rights law. He helped represent Muhammad Ali when the champion boxer refused the Vietnam draft because of principled opposition and religious beliefs. He sued to desegregate the University of Alabama, his alma mater. As a leader in the American Civil Liberties Union (ACLU), Morgan helped defend Julian Bond after the civil rights organizer was denied his seat in the Georgia legislature because of his anti–Vietnam War stance.[7]

But Morgan would never again live in the city where he had so boldly denounced racism.

This is a book about resistance to racism, but it's also about resistance to the resistance. It's about the backlash—some would call it "whitelash"—that occurs every time a movement for racial justice takes place. "It is not the mere presence of black people that is the problem. . . . It is blackness that refuses to accept subjugation, to give up," wrote Carol Anderson in her book *White Rage*.[8] It's like a social version of Newton's Third Law: for every antiracist action there will be an equal (or disproportionate) and opposite reaction. What happened to Charles Morgan Jr. and his family is an example of the backlash that almost invariably befalls those who pursue the spirit of justice.

Telling stories of faith-motivated resistance without also acknowledging the extent to which the forces of regression fought back would be telling only half the truth. The full truth is that any substantive initiative for racial progress will face vocal, targeted, and even violent obstruction. This happened after every revolt of enslaved people. It happened after the Civil War and Reconstruction. It happened in response to the civil rights movement. It happened in the wake of the Black Lives Matter movement and the racial justice uprisings of 2020. Racist backlash follows every gesture toward racial justice.

Martin Luther King Jr. put it this way in his final book, *Where Do We Go from Here: Chaos or Community?*: "He remembers that with each modest advance the white population promptly raises the argument that the Negro has come far enough. Each step forward accents an ever-present tendency to backlash."[9]

In the Bible Jesus shares an illustration: "Suppose one of you wants to build a tower. Won't you first sit down and estimate the cost to see if you have enough money to complete it?" He then explains the consequences for failing to anticipate the burden of an ambition. "For if you lay the foundation and are not able to finish it, everyone who sees it will ridicule you, saying, 'This person began to build and wasn't able to finish'" (Luke 14:28–30). In a similar manner, saying that one is for racial justice without counting the cost is a recipe for retreat.

Many people prematurely proclaim themselves allies and activists before considering what such stances may require of them. But even as the spirit of justice moves people to challenge existing norms that oppress and exploit people, others will be moved to oppose those efforts. In every instance, some people benefit from trampling the rights and denigrating the humanity of others. They will not surrender their power willingly. As I have written before, white supremacy never goes down without a fight.

The stories in this book reveal the price of racial progress. People were whipped, limbs were cut from bodies, churches were burned down, their property was stolen. Some were fired from jobs, strung up from trees, burned alive, sold away from their family members, or unjustly imprisoned. Others simply had their good names smeared. While the methods of retribution may change, the principle remains: there is a steep cost for investing in racial justice.

Most people are not willing to give up their comfort, status, time, or treasure to truly devote themselves to the cause of racial justice. But as this book shows, there has always been a small but stalwart group of people who have been gripped by the spirit of justice, who cannot and will not give up. To learn from them is to learn our own potential and power.

Have you considered the price? Are you truly prepared to sacrifice as much as or more than the people in this book? Count the cost before you claim to be inspired by the spirit of justice.

DETERMINED ALL OVER AGAIN

In her remarks at the grand opening of the Mississippi Civil Rights Museum, Myrlie Evers-Williams confessed that she felt "weary." She had already devoted long decades to overcoming racism, and now she looked upon a national landscape that seemed mired in the same injustices she had faced her whole life.

People today may likewise feel deflated at the lack of racial progress. The international uprisings in support of racial justice that held so much promise in 2020 seemed to evaporate as the calendar turned from one year to the next. Police brutality continues to trample over Black life in events as "routine" as traffic stops. Voting rights, the forefront of the civil rights movement more than half a century ago, are nearly as in peril now as they were then. A resurgence of white Christian nationalism—an ethnocultural ideology that uses Christian symbolism to create a permission structure for the acquisition of political power and social control—proudly displayed its willingness to destroy democracy on January 6, 2021.

We might echo Myrlie Evers-Williams's understated sentiment—we are a bit weary. Despite acknowledging the feeling of exhaustion, Evers-Williams said she became "determined all over again" to continue the struggle for freedom. However, she heard the "bell of freedom" and rose to face the battle against racism once again. You have access to the same determination and gumption that characterized every historical figure who ever dared to fight against racism. You can also resolve to move forward amid opposition. Let these true stories of faith, race, and resistance inspire you to draw on the spirit of justice as you continue the struggle for justice today.

CHAPTER TWO

BECOMING AFRICAN AMERICAN

Remember that rhyme you may have learned in school? "In 1492, Columbus sailed the ocean blue." Someone should write a rhyme about the next year—1493—because what happened then shaped the contours of the Atlantic world for centuries to come. On May 4, 1493, Pope Alexander VI, head of the Roman Catholic Church, issued a papal bull (official decree) called *Inter Caetera* that further articulated the "doctrine of discovery" as it related to the Americas. As Mark Charles and Soong-Chan Rah explain in their book, *Unsettling Truths*, "The pope offered a spiritual validation for European conquest."[1]

Understanding the vast wealth and geopolitical advantages that would come their way if they laid claim to these "new" lands, European rulers were eager to create a justification for their colonial endeavors. Spanish rulers were the first beneficiaries of a new policy for expanding their territory. The doctrine of discovery established a line "a hundred leagues towards the west and south from any of the islands commonly known as the Azores and Cape Verde." This meant that any lands within that line of demarcation would be considered the territory of the Spanish empire. This declaration afforded no rights or respect to the indigenous persons who already inhabited the land.[2]

Coming from the pope, the doctrine of discovery gave the

impression that none less than the divine Creator of the universe consecrated the imperialistic plans of European nations. Indeed, this declaration sanctified European expansion as a method of spreading the gospel. The pope, as Christ's representative on earth, blessed the efforts of the explorers that they "may be enabled for the honor of God himself and the spread of the Christian rule to carry forward your holy and praiseworthy purpose so pleasing to immortal God."[3] Thus, the project of European imperial expansion into the Americas became not merely one of nation-building and resource-hoarding, but rather the doctrine of discovery made the effort into an unequivocal good for the glory of God. But the reality that some indigenous and African people were also Christian complicated an emerging system of racial and ethnic oppression in the colonies.

EARLY AFRICANS IN THE ATLANTIC WORLD

Even before British colonists traded goods in exchange for "20 & odd. Negroes" in 1619, Africans already had a long history in the Americas. Africans were among the sailors on Columbus's first voyage in 1492. An African, Pedro Alonso Niño, is even said to have been the captain of *The Niña*, one of the three vessels on that voyage. Dental records from one of Columbus's early settlements in the Caribbean also reveal that several settlers may have been of West African descent.[4]

In subsequent years, Africans in the Americas labored as indentured servants just as some Europeans did. They learned trades. Some even owned plantations and enslaved other Black people. Even though they were separated from their homeland, it would be a mistake to assume that Africans abandoned their cultures or religious beliefs just because they had been forcibly shipped off to the Americas. What characterized much of the struggle during these decades was the melding or hybridization of one's African history and identity with emerging "American" identities through forced contact with colonial European society and Christianity. This chapter traces acts of Black resistance to racism from the late fifteenth century up to the mid-eighteenth century.

THE SOCIAL CONSTRUCTION OF RACE

During the initial decades of colonization, the status of indigenous people and people of African descent fluctuated. The racial hierarchy had not yet been solidified. While never having precisely equal standing as Europeans, people of color in this era constantly contested their status and fought for better positions in society. Even though Africans in America already faced discrimination simply for being non-Europeans, they also took advantage of opportunities to lead, own land, and otherwise live as if they were truly equal to any other people group, which, of course, they were.

The frantic land grabbing in North, Central, and South America by imperial powers, such as the Dutch, French, Spanish, Portuguese, and English, required a massive labor force that could extract resources for the enrichment of European leaders. This demand for labor helped give rise to the trans-Atlantic slave trade and race-based chattel slavery in what became the United States of America.

Prior to about the 1730s, many African people in the United States still had a sense of home. They still saw themselves as members of the Igbo, Fon, Yoruba, or any of the myriad peoples of Africa. A shared identity of blackness emerged through a long process of enculturation and reculturation in North America.[5] African-descended peoples clung to a sense of their African heritage while simultaneously attempting to carve space in an emerging social order far from their homelands. They reached back toward their tribal identities, spiritual practices, and freedoms while at the same time reaching forward to assert places of dignity and mobility in the Atlantic world.

Throughout the colonial era, as concepts of race were still being socially constructed, religion stood as a primary identity marker. Europeans divided the world into Christian and pagan, which was also a proxy designation for European and non-European. At the same time, Africans already came with rich religious and spiritual traditions that included Christianity among others. Africans adhered to an array of spiritual traditions such as belief in Orishas in western Africa, as well as Islam and Christianity. African understandings of religion significantly differed from those of the Europeans they encountered in the colonial era. "For starters, the word 'religion' is problematic for many Africans, because it suggests that religion is separate from the other aspects of one's culture, society, or environment," said Jacob Olupona, a Harvard professor and expert in indigenous African spirituality. "It is a way of life, and it can never be separated from the public sphere. Religion informs everything in traditional African society, including politics, art, marriage, health, diet, dress, economics, and death," Olupona explained.[6]

Given this holistic understanding of the material and ethereal, it makes sense that Africans would understand their experiences in the Americas from a spiritual point of view and enlist those beliefs in the pursuit of freedom. This integrated view of the world and events would continue to characterize African American religion, including the practice of Christianity, in the coming centuries. Throughout the early years of the emerging republic, Africans in America made various appeals for their freedom and equality with Europeans, and one of the primary tools for resisting racism came from spiritual beliefs.

WHY CHRISTIANITY IS *NOT* THE WHITE MAN'S RELIGION

In most examinations of the role Christians have played in creating and compromising with racism, the same question is asked. Sometimes it is uttered tentatively and furtively. Other times the query is accompanied by a sense of anger and indignation. But the question always has urgency behind it: Is Christianity the white man's religion?

Given the centuries-long history of white-Christian compromise and complicity with racism, it is fair to wonder whether there is something about Christianity itself that is racist. Howard Thurman, the Black Christian mystic and civil rights leader, wrote, "Why is it that Christianity seems impotent to deal radically, and therefore effectively, with the issues of discrimination and injustice on the basis of race? Is this impotence due to a betrayal of the genius of the religion, or is it due to a basic weakness in the religion itself?"[7] Thurman would ultimately see racism among Christians as a betrayal of their religion, and he dedicated his life to racial reconciliation. He understood that characterizing an entire religion as racist because of the behaviors of some of its adherents displayed a shallow understanding of how people practice faith.

The idea that Christianity is the white man's religion falls short on several counts. The first matter concerns time. Race is a social construct. As such, it has not been around forever. The category of race as we now understand it only began in about the fifteenth century. The concept of "white" or "whiteness" as a measure of melanin in someone's skin arose in relation to the imperialist efforts of European nations that resulted in the enslavement of millions of African-descended peoples. So one can only make the assertion that Christianity is the white man's religion if they ignore a millennium and a half of Christian history prior to the advent of modern concepts of race.

Christianity also cannot be the white man's religion because it is a global religion. You will find people practicing Christianity in Korea, Colombia, Kenya, and across the world. While it is true that people of color may adopt a colonized version of Christianity that smuggles in racist assumptions, they can also rethink and revise their beliefs to arrive at a truer understanding of what it means to be created in God's image and likeness—an image that includes their skin color, culture, and other aspects of identity. To claim that Christianity is mainly the purview of white people strips the religion of its global roots and its adherents of their agency.

It is also critical to note that Christianity had a long history in parts of Africa that predates much of Europe's contact with the religion. The argument that white racists introduced Christianity and eternal salvation to the "heathens" of Africa ignores the fact that much of the Bible takes place in Northern Africa, Africans feature prominently in the biblical record, and for centuries after Jesus' lifetime, Africans refined some of Christianity's core tenets such as the doctrine of the Trinity and the human/divine nature of Christ.[8]

Far from conceiving of Christianity as the white man's religion, people of African descent have historically appealed to Christianity as the basis for their freedom and equality. The overwhelming volume of information about people who performed white supremacist acts in the name of Christianity may tempt us to believe that such abuses have gone unchallenged. But Christianity, in fact, has served as a basis for resisting racism and white supremacy in all their forms.

This book focuses primarily on the beliefs and actions of Black Christians. In the United States, the Black church stands as the clearest demonstration that Christianity is not the white man's religion; it is the religion of Jesus the liberator. Highlighting Black Christians in a historical exploration of the struggle against racism makes sense because the Black Christian tradition arose as an explicit refutation of racism and white supremacy. Indeed, the Black church stands as a bold declaration that God is the God of the oppressed and the liberator of those in bondage.

To call Christianity the white man's religion gives too much credit to racists and too little credit to those who have fought for racial justice. By contrast, we will soon learn how a historically victimized people found strength, dignity, and resolve because of how they understood Christianity. Motivated by their faith in Christ, Black people chose to fight for their freedom, even against others who opposed them in the name of the very same Savior.

AN AFRICAN PEOPLE

Black resistance to white supremacy and slavery began in Africa. Long before Black people ever reached the shores of North America, they attempted to assert their full humanity against slave traders while still near the lands of their birth. Slave traders collected Africans from wide swaths of the continent, not just the coast.[9] Some Africans were captured farther inland and forced to march hundreds of miles to the coast.

Those who survived the grueling journey faced yet another ordeal before they got onto the ships. Slave ships could not leave until they were full of human chattel, a process that could take months. While they were waiting, European slave traders kept the African peoples in prisons along the coast called "factories"—prisons that became despicable sites of human suffering where Africans languished and frequently got sick and died.

After that, the slavers would load Africans up in canoes and drag them on board a slave ship. Sometimes, upon seeing an ocean many of them had never seen before and fearful of the fate that lay ahead, some Africans chose death by suicide rather than enslavement. They jumped overboard and drowned themselves rather than be taken onto the larger ships. One English slave trader in the 1690s wrote, "The negroes were so wilful and loth to leave their own country, that they often leap'd out of the canoos, boat and ship, into the sea, and kept under water till they were drowned."[10] In addition to drowning, some Africans chose to starve themselves to death by refusing to eat.

The choice to end one's life rather than live and be subject to the indignities and suffering of slavery emerged as a form of resistance to white supremacy and racism. Suicide may seem like an extreme reaction. To end one's life curtails any chance of earthly freedom. But for generations of enslaved Black people, the freedom of death was more desirable than a life of bondage. Repeatedly throughout US history, some people decided that there were ways of living that were worse than dying. In their minds, better to choose one's own demise than to live at the mercy of the whims of those who treated you as subhuman property.

Suicide, for some, also held out spiritual hope. In dying, some Africans believed they would be reunited to their families and homeland in the next life. Thomas Phillips, captain of the slave ship *Hannibal*, noted this reality. He wrote in a journal entry in the 1690s, "We had about 12 negroes did willfully drown themselves and others starved themselves to death; for 'tis their belief that when they die they return home to their own country and friends again."[11] In these instances, death was both a form of resistance and a welcome escape to a better place. The belief that one could return home and dwell eternally in a better state than on earth points to the fact that African people had their own religions and ways of understanding spirituality apart from Eurocentric conceptions of Christianity. Even when people of African descent began adopting Christianity in North America in larger numbers, they found ways to adapt their understandings of the divine in ways that honored their Africanness.

An understanding of African spirituality formed the foundation for early Black freedom struggles in the colonial era. Some of the earliest permanent settlements in the so-called New World were established by people of African descent. Communities of free and self-emancipated

Black people sprang up throughout the colonial era. These settlements were called maroon communities, from the Spanish word *cimarron*, meaning "wild [free] runaway slave." Maroon Blacks established their own communities in places such as Brazil, Cuba, Florida, and Georgia.

One of the most renowned maroon communities was that of the Windward Maroons of Jamaica. This group descended from people of the Koromanti tribe in Africa. When these Africans were taken from their homelands and shipped to slavery in Jamaica, they often escaped into the forests of the island and formed their own communities. Amid a male-dominated society, the Windward Maroons had the distinction of being led by a woman, Queen Nanny. She was known as a fierce fighter and a shrewd tactician skilled in guerilla warfare, which she used to defend her people against the British and keep her people free.

Queen Nanny
Prachaya Roekdeethaweesab/Shutterstock.com

Queen Nanny lived during the 1700s, and the Jamaican people passed down legends of her leadership. She is so revered as a symbol of Black freedom that in 1975 she was honored as Jamaica's only female national hero. She was also known as the spiritual leader of her people. Queen Nanny was likely a chieftainess who practiced a form of African spirituality called Obeah. "Maroon oral traditions attribute her military

victories over the British to her superior 'science' or mastery of meta-
physical warfare, which drove fear into her British adversaries and led to
her decisive military victories."[12] As Black people resisted enslavement
in the colonial era and beyond, they would enlist the power of the spiritual world to assist them in their freedom efforts. Thus, they looked
to leaders such as Queen Nanny not only for tactical expertise but for
spiritual guidance as well.

1619

The presence of Africans from the start of European exploration of
the Americas, as well as the existence of maroon communities in the
Americas demonstrates that the well-known group of Africans whom
Europeans brought in 1619 were not the first to arrive—they were
simply the first recorded group to arrive in a mainland North American
English colony. In this early era, the question of what social, political,
and economic position Africans would inhabit was still undetermined.

Slaves arriving in Jamestown, Virginia, in 1619.

In British colonial Virginia, both English and African people could be considered indentured servants with varying levels of freedom. Their labor was not for life, and they could eventually gain their full freedom after a number of years. Over time, however, the enslavement of Africans became the primary way to procure inexpensive labor.

It is important to note that status in the first decades of European contact in North America depended not only on physical appearance and nationality, but on religion as well. Professing oneself to be a Christian or a practitioner of another religion could determine the extent to which one was free or unfree. English common law held that Christians could not enslave Christians. From the start, this custom proved troublesome to the European colonists, who sought to place Africans in a place of bondage. But European colonists would eventually find ways around the problem of religion to create a permanent class of enslaved laborers.

Records from that group of Africans brought ashore at Point Comfort, Virginia, in 1619 show that many of the Africans had Christian names and likely had been baptized into the Catholic church before their forced relocation. Among this group were people with names (likely anglicized from Spanish) including "two Anthonys, two Johns, a William, a Frances, an Edward, and a Margaret."[13] Were these men and women enslaved for life or indentured servants? Did their Christian faith afford them advantages that non-Christians in the colonies did not have? Historians have had a decades-long debate about these questions. It is possible that these names "imply baptism" and may have contributed to the uncertain labor status of these early Africans.

The saga of the "20 and Odd. negroes" of colonial Virginia demonstrates that from the earliest days of European contact with North America, the spirit of justice would have led Africans in America to appeal for freedom based on a shared faith. They would have looked to their European captors and made the case for equality because of the spiritual reality that no matter their skin color or nation of origin, they were spiritual siblings who shared in the eternal inheritance found through faith in Jesus Christ. Their shared religion taught that all people who trusted in God for salvation became part of the same community of faith who were called to "be devoted to one another in love" (Romans 12:10) and to "value others above yourselves" (Philippians 2:3).

Of course, these entreaties, which were based on both common law and Christian teachings, failed to overcome the desire for land, laborers, and money in the colonies. In a few short decades, it would become apparent that the most lucrative and easily controlled labor force could be defined by skin color, regardless of the religious beliefs the slaver and enslaved may have had in common.

ANTHONY, ISABELLA, AND THE FIRST "AFRICAN AMERICAN" CHILD

In the context of racialized oppression, one of the most defiant acts is also one of the simplest: having a family. Broken relationships characterized the African slave trade from its early days through emancipation. Displacement from one's natural relations in slavery occurred frequently as slave traders separated husbands and wives, sold children to different slave holders, raped enslaved women, and used men as "studs" to impregnate women. In the context of white supremacy, the Black family has always been a sort of miracle.

Amid the group of captives whom British colonists purchased in Virginia in 1619 were a man named Anthony and a woman named Isabella. As their names indicate, they were likely baptized Christians in the Catholic tradition. A few years later in 1625, a census in Virginia cataloged Anthony and Isabella as a married couple and noted that they had a son.

The census taker made the notation, "Antoney Negro: Isabell Negro: and William Theire Child Baptized."[14] These nine words contain important implications about the status of Africans in British colonial America. First, none of these family members had a surname listed. While wealthy Europeans and even many indentured servants were identified by first and last name, this was not typically the case with Africans. Instead, they are identified as "Negro." It is possible those who conducted the census did not know their nation of origin, so "Negro" served as a stand-in to supplement the lack of more specific information.[15] Yet some other details about the couple were recorded. They labored in Elizabeth City for a man named Captain Tucker. While surnames for Africans were not often listed, a racial reference and an association with a European household were sufficient in an emerging Eurocentric and white supremacist society.

The census data also indicates an important if quotidian fact: they had a child and named him William. Historians surmise that young William may be the first documented African child born in the British colonies of North America.[16] Identifying William as "baptized" held significance beyond a religious identity. In the 1600s, "'Christian' had a heritable ethnic, cultural, and racial definition."[17] The term *Christian* could also indicate a social and economic status. It is possible that Anthony, Isabella, and William, at some point, obtained their freedom. Their status as *Christian* may have been a precondition to their liberty.

In addition to whatever personal convictions may have led Anthony and Isabella to have their son baptized, his status as a Christian had implications for his status as a free person. Europeans in the colonial era associated being a Christian with being free. "The baptism of enslaved and free Africans implicitly challenged the religious justifications for slavery in the seventeenth century Protestant Atlantic world."[18] Anthony and Isabella and their son could appeal to their Christian religion if the legitimacy of their freedom was ever questioned. Under such circumstances, they may have hoped to fare better than being considered "heathens," which not only had ethnic connotations but also could increase the possibility of being held in bondage.

It is impossible to know whether Anthony and Isabella considered having a child a deliberate act of defiance against their capture and exploitation. But there is no reason to think that they responded to their child differently than most parents would. As they gazed upon their son, Anthony and Isabella would have wanted to raise him to be a person of character, with a solid education and the opportunity to choose the path best for him. Forcibly divorced from their homeland and heritage, Anthony and Isabella would have done everything in their power to make sure he had a sense of his own dignity and pride in his culture.

At the same time, Anthony and Isabella would have to forge a new culture in a new land. They faced many obstacles in growing a family in a place and among a people strange to them. Early African families in America began developing a distinctly African American form of Christianity and faith. Even in the early days of the colonies, people of African descent were learning to resist bondage in any way they could—including by having children and raising them to respect themselves even if society did not.

As the society they lived in developed an anti-Black racial ideology, the Black family became one of the most common and critical means of resistance. Growing a family requires considering your future and your legacy. Nurturing a Black family required working for a freer tomorrow and faith that such a reality was possible. Children represent the hope and humanity of all people who experience injustice, an aspiration that the spirit of justice will be passed down from one generation to the next.

THE CURIOUS CASE OF JOHN PUNCH

From a historical perspective, the concept of race emerged over time. There is a chronological process we can study to learn how race has been crafted. In the early days of colonial America, the status of people of African descent had not yet been determined. Some Africans in this era lived as free people. They worked jobs and got paid. They got married and owned property. Others labored as indentured servants. An indentured servant was a person bound to a "master" as a laborer for a set amount of time, and this arrangement was often made as punishment for a crime or to pay off a debt. Indentured servitude was not a pleasant existence—these women and men endured whippings, near nakedness, food deprivation, unrelenting labor, and sufferings of many kinds. In daily practice, one might not be able to tell the difference between indentured servitude and subsequent forms of slavery in the United States.[19] However, indentured servitude had an end date. It was not a lifelong sentence—unless you were Black.

A man named John Punch is believed to be the first person *legally* considered Black. A declaration by the courts put Punch, a man of African descent, in a legal and economic category that differed from people of European descent. Here's what happened.

John Punch's exact birthdate is unknown, but he entered the

historical record in 1640. Punch labored as an indentured servant under a Virginian planter named Hugh Gwyn. The conditions under Gwyn must have been insufferable because Punch, along with two other indentured servants, James Gregory and Victor, attempted to run away. Within a few days they were all caught and taken to the Virginia General Court to receive punishment for their attempted escape.

The court rendered its verdict. All three men would receive whippings, and in addition, James Gregory and Victor, the former identified in court records as a Scotsman and the latter as a Dutchman, had four years of servitude added to their original terms. John Punch, however, received a different sentence. Instead of having a few more years added to his labor, he was sentenced to a lifetime of bondage. Even though he was on trial for the same crime as the other two men, the court decided, "That the third, being a negro named John Punch shall serve his said master or his assigns for the time of his natural life here or elsewhere."[20] The only reason given for the discrepancy in punishment between Punch and the other two was that John Punch was a "negro."

By the mid-1600s, the status of people of African descent had already begun to harden into an oppressed racial class. There could have been several reasons for the court's decision to enforce lifelong bondage on John Punch and not his European coconspirators. The ideology of racism may have already crept into legal jurisprudence. Or the court personnel may have been aware of the practice of enslaving African people for life in places such as Barbados. English common law also may have played a role. Traditionally, one would not enslave a fellow Christian, but since Punch was from Africa, the court may have assumed that he was not a Christian and not subject to those common-law protections. Therefore, he could be enslaved for a lifetime.[21]

The historical records do not indicate how John Punch reacted to his sentence of lifelong slavery. It is not difficult to imagine, however, that with his hope of freedom forever extinguished he would have been despondent. To cope, perhaps he resolved to attempt another escape. What more could they do to him? Maybe he succumbed to depression and hopelessness. Or he could have attempted to find a way to accept his new condition with as much determination as possible.

While we don't know how Punch and others like him responded, what is beyond speculation is the growing legal and social sentiment that people of African descent were subject to a different status than Europeans based on a created racial category. Court cases like John Punch's were another step toward the eventual oppression of millions of African peoples in what would become the United States. Yet despite this oppression, the spirit of justice would live on in the hearts of those who refused to accept a human-made subordinate status based purely on the color of their skin.

CONCLUSION

The colonial era was a world of fluid demographic divisions—ethnic, national, religious, and increasingly racial divides. These categories were used to justify exploitation. If people could be separated into superior and inferior groups, those at the top of the social hierarchy had the ability, and in their view the right, to exercise authority over others. Yet at the same time we see the earliest stirrings of the spirit of justice. Black people have never been passive victims of white supremacy, and even in these early colonial days there were those who fought for their own dignity and on behalf of others experiencing racial oppression.

While skin color and nationality played a role in the emerging social hierarchy, being a Christian and African complicated easy racial categorizations. How could wealthy white people justify enslaving brothers and sisters in Christ? Conversely, how could Africans appeal to a shared religion to promote their own liberation? While such questions were being debated and contested in this era, people of African descent resisted racism by simply finding ways to survive, even ways as simple as having a family. Finding themselves in a strange new land, uprooted from their African home, they sought to gain their bearings and forge a new way of life. For those who were Christians, they referenced their shared Christian faith to make their case for freedom. As we will see, similar questions of status and identity will show up time and again in unfolding centuries of Black life in North America and the United States.

CHAPTER
THREE

THE LANGUAGE
OF LIBERTY

Momentous historical events often turn on seemingly small decisions. As a case in point, consider how if just one paragraph in the original draft of the Declaration of Independence had remained, slavery might never have become an enduring institution in the United States.

By 1776, European colonists in North America were ready to declare their independence from England. They turned to Thomas Jefferson to outline their reasons in writing. The document that Jefferson submitted to the Continental Congress that year included a devastating indictment of the British king. Why? Because he approved of slavery.

> He has waged cruel war against human nature itself, violating its most sacred rights of life and liberty in the persons of a distant people who never offended him, captivating and carrying them into slavery in another hemisphere, or to incur miserable death in their transportation thither.[1]

In this earlier draft, Jefferson went on to call slavery an "execrable commerce" and excoriated the "Christian king of Great Britain" for approving of such a heinous institution. Such a forceful takedown of slavery written in this soon-to-be historic document likely would have highlighted the contradiction between practicing human bondage while professing the ideals of liberty and justice for all. Jefferson's antislavery sentiment directly addressed the now-perennial question of who the "all" in "all men are created equal" refers to. These few words, just several dozen total, likely would have made the perpetuation of slavery a more tenuous endeavor in the emerging United States. They might have even prevented the Civil War.

But that didn't happen. Instead, delegates from the southern states threatened to hold the Declaration of Independence hostage unless Jefferson's antislavery message was excised. Additionally, his sentiments were disingenuous. The English were not unique in the human trafficking of Africans; plenty of colonists participated in and benefited from the practice of slavery. Even the primary author of the Declaration, Thomas Jefferson, enslaved hundreds of human beings who enriched him and made his life comfortable. He also notoriously had ongoing sexual relations with an enslaved woman, Sally Hemings, who birthed several of his children.[2]

In hindsight, it may seem as if the enslavement of Black people was inevitable, as if nothing could have prevented it from happening. But Black people, who were increasingly victimized by hardening racist ideas and the enshrinement of race-based chattel slavery, did not believe their case for freedom was hopeless. In fact, the same revolutionary ideals promoted by white colonial leaders emboldened Black claims for emancipation. They too appealed to the language of liberty that suffused the era with the aroma of revolution.

Even amid an ossifying racial hierarchy, Black people spoke up and acted to resist their dehumanization. In the American Revolution, they fought both for the colonists and for the British. Leading up to the conflict, Black people filed "freedom suits" in court and consistently referred to their Christian faith as an argument for their liberation. In this chapter, we will see how Christians helped forge a new nation and how the spirit of justice informed Black resistance to enslavement as the revolution approached.

REVOLUTION IN THE AIR

Romans 13:1 says, "Let everyone be subject to the governing author-ities, for there is no authority except that which God has established. The authorities that exist have been established by God." This verse recognizes God-established civil authority, but it was also used by Christians as a way to encourage blind obedience to local, state, and federal government and to discourage attempts at civil disobedience, including the revolutionary overthrow of existing governmental powers. Anglican pastor Jonathan Boucher appealed to this verse in 1774 when he preached a sermon arguing that colonists in North America owed Britain their loyalty as the governing authority. He railed against the ideas of revolution spreading among the people.[3]

Boucher's loyalist stance was in direct conflict with the philosopher John Locke, whose writings did much to influence emerging ideas of the "separation of church and state." Boucher saw Britain's rulers as providentially placed by God in their positions, and believed a rebel-lion against them was a rebellion against God. In this view, the church and the state are inextricably linked. Locke, however, taught that the church and the state had authority in separate domains. He wanted to avoid the creation of a state church that imbued political officials with divine authority. "I affirm that the magistrate's power extends not to the establishing of any articles of faith, or form of worship, by the force of his laws."[4] Locke saw the function of the state primarily as protecting private rights, especially property rights.

It could be argued that the deeper revolution happening in the formation of the American Revolution was not the military conflict that created a new nation but the ideological shift that separated the church from the state. The Declaration of Independence, and later the Constitution of the United States, appealed more to Lockean ideas of natural rights than to religious ideas of morality and truth. The men who led the founding of the nation did not establish an official church attached to their newly formed government. Instead, they saw religion as a private matter decoupled from the exercise of politics for the public.

Influential figures of the American Revolution such as Samuel Adams, Thomas Jefferson, and many others adopted Locke's views on the separation of church and state as well as the "natural rights of man." In fact, the Declaration of Independence's phrase "life, liberty and the pursuit of happiness" closely mirrored the language of John Locke's "Second Treatise on Civil Government." Locke wrote in 1690, "Man being born, as has been proved, with a title to perfect freedom and uncontrouled enjoyment of all the rights and privileges of the law of nature, equally with any other man . . . hath by nature a power not only to preserve his property, that is, his life, liberty, and estate."[5]

As the American Revolution inched closer to outright violence, the colonists who opposed Britain's rule increasingly employed the language of liberty and freedom to bolster their arguments. They even characterized Britain's political and economic power over the colonies as "slavery." In 1773, a document outlining the purpose and principles of the "Sons of Liberty"—the group responsible for the Boston Tea Party—proclaimed that if Britain continued taxing the colonists, then "we shall have no property that we can call our own, and then we may bid adieu to American liberty. Therefore, to prevent a calamity which, of all others, is the most to be dreaded—slavery and its terrible concomitants."[6] The colonists consciously insisted on their liberty, tied to property rights, and explained that the inevitable alternative was "dreaded slavery." In practice, however, these rights only applied to property-owning white men. They did not extend to the people of African descent in their midst. Ironically, European colonists used the language of liberty on their own behalf even as they passed laws that enshrined and protected the bondage of Black people.

Black Christians appealed to these same ideas of natural rights and equality while simultaneously making a religious case for their freedom. The Revolutionary era represents a time in US history when the spirit of justice motivated Black people and their allies to apply the principles of the Revolution as an argument against white supremacy and for emancipation. The Revolutionary era was also a time when some white Christians put forth early arguments opposing slavery and built a moral and legal foundation for the later era of abolition in the early 1800s.

THE POEMS OF LIBERATION

Even when physical chains restrain feet and hands, the mind and heart can find freedom through art. Two early African American poets, Jupiter Hammon and Phillis Wheatley, demonstrated a blend of faith, beauty, and liberty that would come to characterize so much of the Black freedom struggle. Their poetry in the eighteenth century helped express the struggle of the enslaved in a way that swayed emotions while calling awareness to injustice.

Jupiter Hammon was born in 1711 in Long Island, New York, and spent his entire life in slavery. But these hardships did not prevent him from becoming the first published African American author in North America. At an early age he received a basic education and learned to read and write. His sharp mind leveraged his exposure to literature, and he began writing poems. His first published piece in 1761 was a poem, "An Evening Thought: Salvation by Christ with Penitential Cries."

> Dear Jesus, give thy Spirit now,
> Thy Grace to every Nation,
> That han't the Lord to whom we bow,
> The Author of Salvation.[7]

The act of publishing a work in a public setting severely limited what people of African descent could say about slavery. Few publishers at this time wanted to court a controversial antislavery stance. In addition, Hammon's education was filtered entirely through the lens of his European slaveholders. It is highly unlikely they taught him any antislavery views for fear of encouraging him to escape or making themselves look bad in front of other white people. Yet the spirit of justice taught Hammon the inherent dignity he held as bearer of God's image, and he used poetry to express his disgust at the practice of slavery.

In 2011, a graduate student discovered a lost poem of Hammon's that was titled "An Essay on Slavery, with Submission to the Divine Providence, Knowing That God Rules over All Things."[8] In it he wrote,

> Dark and dismal was the Day
> when Slavery began
> All humble thoughts were put away
> then slaves were made by Man.[9]

Here Hammon recognizes the sinfulness and misery of slavery and makes no excuses for it. Amid his deplorable situation as an enslaved person, though, he still trusted that God had not abandoned him and put his faith in God for deliverance.

> We look unto our God
> To help with our hearts to sigh and pray
> And Love his holy word.[10]

THE POETRY OF PHILLIS WHEATLEY

On rare occasions, a Black person's prodigious abilities in some area afforded them a measure of freedom. These skills could literally put a person in the presence of kings and rulers, bringing them fame and entering their name into the annals of history. That is what happened in the life of Phillis Wheatley.

Phillis was not her original name. She was simply a girl from West Africa, kidnapped by slave traders and placed on board a ship named the *Phillis*. Upon making shore in Boston, a rich merchant and tailor named John Wheatley bought her to serve his daughter. He named the girl Phillis Wheatley after the slave ship that had brought her to this new land. While in bondage, Phillis had an opportunity rarely afforded to girls in general and African girls in particular: she received an education. She was taught by her slaveholder's daughter, Mary, and then by another member of the family, Nathan. Phillis learned how to read and write in English and how to read Greek and Latin fluently. Wheatley immersed herself in works of literature, especially Homer, Virgil, Alexander Pope, and the Bible. She produced her first volume of poetry, *Poems on Various Subjects, Religious and Moral*, through the help of benefactors in England in 1773 and is credited as the first enslaved woman to publish a book of poetry in North America. Shortly thereafter, her slaveholder freed her.

Phillis Wheatley

When the book came out, her poetry was so good that racially prejudiced white people refused to believe a Black young woman had written it, and they sued her. By the end of the trial, however, they were convinced she had written it—and were amazed.

At some point in her young life, Phillis became a Christian. Her faith in Christ infused her art, and she did not separate her creative passion from her earnest devotion to Jesus. In this we see someone fully inhabiting her calling as both a creative and a Christian. Wheatley also put her skill with words in service to her fellow enslaved Africans, arguing for their freedom. Probably her most well-known poem is "On Being Brought from Africa to America." It displays ambivalent attitudes toward her homeland of Africa, her enslavement, and her Christian religion.

Wheatley opens with gratitude that the hand of God, as she understands it, brought her from Africa where she had a "benighted soul" to North America "to understand that there's a God, there's a *Saviour* too." Because of her faith in Christ, she entreats her readers not to dismiss Africans as hopelessly lost moral beings. "Some view our sable race with scornful eye, 'Their colour is a diabolic die.'" She references the dark skin color of Africans and how it was often associated with evil or a curse, such as the one God pronounced on Cain after he killed his brother, Abel (Genesis 4:1–16). However, writes Wheatley, salvation is possible for the African. "Remember *Christians*, *Negros*, black as *Cain*, May be refin'd, and join th' angelic train."[11]

ON BEING BROUGHT FROM AFRICA TO AMERICA

'Twas mercy brought me from my *Pagan* land,
Taught my benighted soul to understand
That there's a God, that there's a *Saviour* too:
Once I redemption neither sought nor knew.
Some view our sable race with scornful eye,
"Their colour is a diabolic die."
Remember, *Christians*, *Negros*, black as *Cain*,
May be refin'd, and join th' angelic train.[12]

No matter how Phillis Wheatley made sense of her enslavement and the existence of a benevolent God, she also used her poetry to argue against slavery. In October of 1772, a white British man named Thomas Woolridge asked Wheatley to write a poem for William Legge, who had just been appointed secretary of state for the colonies. The result was a poem called "To the Right Honourable William, Earl of Dartmouth." Wheatley used this opportunity to flatter the earl, perhaps in an effort to make an even more significant point—that he should use his new power and position to free enslaved people.

No longer shalt thou dread the iron chain,
Which wanton Tyranny with lawless hand
Had made, and with it meant t' enslave the land.[13]

Wheatley also revealed hints of her interior life in the poem. Even though she experienced slavery in a different way than most of her peers—gaining an education, publishing a book of poetry, traveling to

London, meeting with the wealthy and the powerful—slavery was still slavery. She wrote,

> Should you, my lord, while you peruse my song,
> Wonder from whence my love of Freedom sprung.[14]

These stanzas reveal that she still longed for freedom, a desire that defied the ignorant fantasy entertained by many white people that Black people were happy in bondage. Then Wheatley describes her kidnapping from Africa. These verses appear in the same book of poetry that expresses gratitude for hearing the gospel of Christ in North America rather than remaining in Africa and perhaps never hearing of it.

> I, young in life, by seeming cruel fate
> Was snatch'd from Afric's fancy'd happy seat.

Despite the horrors of the past, Wheatley knew the future did not have to repeat the same awful pattern. It was in the power of the Earl of Dartmouth, wrote Wheatley, to relieve the suffering of many enslaved people.

> Since in thy pow'r as in thy wil before,
> To sooth the griefs, which thou did'st once deplore.[15]

Wheatley stands as an early voice in a long tradition of Black artists who used their creativity to imagine new worlds, argue for greater rights, and elevate humanity in a way that only true beauty can do. Though she was an enslaved Black person, her exceptional skills afforded her the opportunity to publish and achieve renown. Yet what many white people refused to see were the countless other Black people with exceptional talents. Black people often simply lacked education and opportunity. Even with Wheatley's brilliant mind and gifts, she was never able to secure a stable existence for herself or her family. Her poetic genius was more of a novelty than a reason for people to reevaluate their treatment of Black people, or even to support Wheatley.

When her former slaveholders died, Wheatley married but lived on the brink of destitution. Her first two children died at a very young age. Her husband died. Then she died at the age of thirty-one, and her third son, an infant, died shortly after. Wheatley's hardships throughout life, especially after her emancipation, would seem to suggest that "good" white people who were progressive on slavery and race when compared to their peers still did not see ongoing economic support as necessary for Africans in America, even those as skillful as Phillis Wheatley. Did they, after all, truly believe Black people "may be refin'd"? And were they willing to do anything about it?

One can imagine the kind of Christianity Phillis Wheatley was taught as an enslaved person surrounded by white Christians in the eighteenth century. It typically emphasized spiritual salvation over physical liberation and may have included copious references to slaves obeying their masters, a favorite Bible passage of slaveholders found in Ephesians 6:5. Wheatley may have been taught that slavery was ultimately good because it was the means whereby she heard the gospel instead of living and dying as a pagan in Africa. Yet Phillis Wheatley's art and faith worked against this "slaveholder Christianity."

Wheatley's poetry reflects the spiritual maze Africans in America had to navigate. Even as they heard about the love of God, they learned religion through the filter of white supremacy and race-based chattel slavery. They learned about a Jesus who loved you more if you adopted European customs and culture and a God who cared deeply for their eternal salvation but not for their physical liberation. Such a culturally convoluted Christianity comes through in Wheatley's poetry, yet the spirit of justice spills forth as well. We hear the spirit in her ever-present desire for freedom, in her subversive use of the arts to upend notions of Black inferiority, and in her unwavering faith in a God who remains active in human affairs.

BENJAMIN BANNEKER WRITES
TO THOMAS JEFFERSON

Just as some Africans in America used their art to argue for their rights, others used their scholarly achievements and reputation to do the same. Benjamin Banneker never personally knew the misery of being enslaved. He was born free, but his status did nothing to dispel the prejudice against Black people in eighteenth-century colonial North America. A frequent argument for keeping Black people enslaved was that they were intellectually inferior to Europeans as a matter of biology. White people looked at Black people and scoffed at their illiteracy and seeming lack of appreciation for the arts and sciences.

Benjamin Banneker's achievements defied the stereotypes. He was born in 1731 in Baltimore County, Maryland. His parents were free and owned a tobacco farm. Benjamin received an informal education from his family and his grandmother, a white woman of European descent and former indentured servant. In 1771, a Quaker family from Pennsylvania, the Ellicotts, moved near the Banneker farm in Maryland. Benjamin and the farm owner, George Ellicott, struck up a friendship, and Ellicott allowed Banneker to borrow books and lunar tables for astronomy. Banneker quickly mastered the material and eventually became well-known for his almanacs published from 1792 to 1797. In 1790, he was part of the team that conducted land surveys to plan for the new nation's capital, Washington, DC.

Despite his status as a free Black man and a renowned mathematician and intellectual, Banneker understood he was part of a larger community of Black people, many of whom were enslaved. Instead of ignoring his brothers and sisters of African descent, and rather than admonishing Black people to simply work harder to improve their state in life, he used his status and abilities to advocate on their behalf.

Banneker wrote a series of letters to Thomas Jefferson, who was then Secretary of State, to persuade him to work for Black emancipation. In these letters, Banneker pointed to Christian morality as a basis for his arguments. First, he referenced the unjust state of Africans in America, a people who "have long been considered rather as brutish than human, and Scarcely capable of mental endowments."[16] Banneker went on to point out the universal equality of all people by referencing God: "One universal Father hath given being to us all, and that he hath not only made us all of one flesh." Banneker may have had Acts 17:26 in mind: "From one man he made all the nations."

Banneker didn't stop there. He contended that no matter a person's race or status, "we are all of the Same Family, and Stand in the Same relation to him [God]." He wrote that anyone who professes the "obligations of Christianity" ought to work for the uplift of all people. Banneker then made his argument personal for Jefferson. He reminded the distinguished statesman and slaveholder that the liberty from Britain that allowed Jefferson to attain a prominent station in life, "you have mercifully received, and that it is the peculiar blessing of Heaven." Banneker then used Jefferson's own words in the Declaration of Independence to argue for Black freedom. He bid Jefferson to recall the time "you publickly held forth this true and invaluable doctrine . . . that all men are created equal."[17]

Banneker pointed out the hypocrisy of Jefferson's position—and indeed the betrayal of values that the Declaration of Independence articulated. How could it be, wrote Banneker, "that you should at the Same time counteract his mercies, in detaining by fraud and violence so numerous a part of my brethren under groaning captivity and cruel oppression."[18] Banneker included in his letter a copy of his latest almanac. The intent was to show Jefferson that Black people were not intellectually inferior to white people and were capable of advanced scholarly work. For his part, Jefferson responded warmly and wrote in a follow-up letter that he hoped Banneker's words and reasoning would demonstrate "that nature has given to our black brethren, talents equal to those of the other colours of men."[19]

Banneker's letter to Thomas Jefferson demonstrates how Black people asserted their innate equality with white people by virtue of being fellow human beings, creations of the same God, with gifts, abilities, and talents. Even in the early days of the republic, Black Christians saw in their faith significant resources to protest their captivity and highlight the contradictory arguments of white people who claimed Christ and at the same time claimed ownership over those made in God's image. The spirit of justice motivated them to argue and demonstrate in words and actions that all people are part of the same human family.

PRINCE HALL APPEALS TO "THE MILD RELIGION OF JESUS"

Most of what we know about Prince Hall's early life remains vague. He was born in either 1735 or 1738, likely in New England, but perhaps in

Barbados. Historians know he was enslaved at an early age by William Hall of Boston, a leather worker who trained young Prince in the trade. Eventually he was freed and became one of the most prominent Black leaders of the Revolutionary period.

Prince Hall is best known for forming the first Black Freemason lodge in North America. Right around the time that some Africans were forming their own Black churches and denominations, the African Grand Lodge 1 was perhaps the first secular Black institution formed to advance the cause of Black emancipation and equality. Hall advocated for emancipation and a return to Africa. He was also instrumental in securing one of the earliest and only cases of reparations for a formerly enslaved person, Belinda Royall/Sutton. Hall likely wrote the petition that successfully procured for Belinda an annual pension of fifteen pounds and twelve shillings for her servitude.

While Hall is most often remembered for his political activism and his role in founding the Black Freemasons, what is less known but no less significant is how he incorporated the Christian religion into his efforts to advance Black rights. In 1772, Hall became a member of a Congregational church, frequently drawing on his religious beliefs in his public work on behalf of Black people.[20] He started a school for Black children in his own home and advocated to release free Black people who had been kidnapped into slavery.[21]

In 1777, Hall coauthored a well-known petition to the Massachusetts General Assembly asking for emancipation. In it he wrote that "a great number of Blackes" in a "free & Christian country" understood that "they have in common with all other men a natural and unalienable right to freedom."[22] In this section of the petition, Hall echoed the natural rights arguments and language of the Declaration of Independence. But he rooted his call for freedom in the existential equality of all humankind as granted by God, whom he called the "Great Parent of the Unavers." Hall went on to argue that God had "equalley bestowed" freedom on all people. He appealed to the moral sensibility of white people as fellow Christians as he wrote, "A people professing the mild religion of Jesus . . . need not be informed that a life of slavery . . . is far worse than nonexistance."[23]

In 1783, Prince Hall is believed to have penned one of the first and only successful appeals for reparations on behalf of an enslaved person.[24] He wrote for Belinda Sutton (or Royall), who, according to the appeal sent to the Massachusetts General Court, had been kidnapped from Africa and labored as an enslaved person for fifty years. After her slaveholder, a British loyalist, fled his lands during the Revolutionary War, Belinda, whose face was "marked with the furrows of time" and was now elderly and caring for an infirm daughter, demanded an annual pension of fifteen pounds and twelve shillings.

One part of the argument was economic. Belinda had labored for decades at the behest of her slaveholder and helped to enrich him, yet she was never compensated for her labors. Despite these years of bondage, she was "denied the enjoyment of one morsel of that immense wealth, a part whereof hath been accumulated by her own industry, and the whole augmented by her servitude." In her plea she sought only the "just return of honest industry."[25]

Another part of the appeal was religious. Prince Hall, writing on behalf of Belinda, claimed the divine right of liberty to which all people were entitled. He wrote of "the preservation of that freedom which the Almighty Father intended for all the human Race."[26] As the winds of the Revolutionary War still swirled with cries of liberty, a humble and elderly enslaved woman joined her voice to the chorus. Hall was her ally in demanding reparations for a life spent in bondage, and he pointed to the Almighty in the heavens for justification.

Prince Hall wrote appeals to legislative bodies and helped build Black institutions to advance the cause of Black people in the fledgling United States. Along with many other Black Christians, he saw in his religion the foundation to call for freedom because God had created all people as equals, each one with the universal right to self-determination. Hall deftly drew on Enlightenment and Revolutionary principles of independence as well as Christian claims to the inherent dignity of all people as creations of the Most High God.

THE METHODIST ANTISLAVERY TRADITION

History demonstrates that there would be no Black church if racism had not been present in the white church. The formation of the African

Methodist Episcopal church was initiated by a racist incident at Saint George's Methodist Episcopal Church in Philadelphia in 1787 when white church officials attempted to pull Black worshipers off their knees and into a segregated section during a prayer. The notorious departure of Richard Allen, Absalom Jones, and their fellow Black compatriots due to racism is even more repulsive given Methodism's original antislavery commitments. As far back as 1743, John Wesley, one of the founders of Methodism in England, came out forcefully against slavery. In a document called "General Rules," he outlined the behaviors that he believed characterized a life of holiness.

John Wesley

He wrote, "It is therefore expected of all who continue therein that they should continue to evidence their desire of salvation, *First:* By doing no harm, by avoiding evil of every kind, especially that which is most generally practiced, such as: . . . Slaveholding; buying or selling slaves."[27] In this brief line Wesley upheld the spirit of justice and called out the slave trade as a moral evil to be avoided by Christians. In so doing, he positioned the growing movement of Methodism in opposition to the enslavement of Black people in the United States. Years later, Black minister Richard Allen refused to become the pastor of an Episcopal church on the grounds that his future was with the Methodist movement: "No religious sect or denomination would suit the capacity of colored people as well as the Methodist."[28]

Methodism's antislavery sentiments were reaffirmed in the official actions of a meeting held in 1780. At the annual conference that year, ministers approved a document that asked, "Ought this conference to require those traveling preachers who hold slaves to give promises to set them free? Ans. Yes." Another question asked, "Does this conference acknowledge that slavery is contrary to the laws of God, man and nature and hurtful to society . . . ? Ans. Yes."[29]

Then in 1784 at the "Christmas Conference," where the Methodist denomination in the United States was officially formed, Methodist ministers formally condemned slavery, declaring it "contrary to the golden law of God, on which hang all the law and the prophets, and the inalienable rights of mankind, as well as every principle of the Revolution." The "golden law of God" refers to Jesus' response when someone asked about the greatest commandment. "'Love the Lord your God with all your heart and with all your soul and with all your mind.' This is the first and greatest commandment. And the second is like it: 'Love your neighbor as yourself'" (Matthew 22:37–39).

As concerned as they were with personal piety, many Methodists also kept up with politics. In arguing against slavery, they echoed the language of inalienable rights from the Declaration of Independence. They also pointed to "every principle of the Revolution" to show that slavery violated the spirit of liberty and equality that suffused the rhetoric of the American war for independence.

Again in 1796, the General Conference meeting of Methodists reaffirmed the denomination's antislavery position: "We declare that we are more than ever convinced of the great evil of the African slavery which still exists in these United States." The ministers insisted that slaveholders could not hold official positions in the denomination, that no one could become a member until they had been spoken to "freely and faithfully" on the topic of slavery, and that anyone who had sold a slave was barred from membership in the Methodist church.[30]

However, while a truth can be forcefully stated, rules must be enforced. Few ministers were willing to oppose the wealthiest members of their congregations over the issue of slave trading or slaveholding. The Methodist documents themselves often came with the caveat that the state laws should be respected. This internal tension eventually led to a regional split in the Methodist denomination between northern antislavery and southern proslavery members in the buildup to the Civil War.

THE EARLY QUAKER ANTISLAVERY MOVEMENT

In 1688, a group of four members of the Pennsylvania Society of Friends (Quakers) led by Francis Daniel Pastorius put forth a petition calling for the abolition of slavery. This was more than a century before the height of the abolitionist movement in the United States. Their written protest also predates some of the Enlightenment ideas that animated the American Revolution. Yet the existence of this document shows that antislavery advocates were already making a religious case against slavery even before political and philosophical arguments had gained hold.

In what is now recognized as one of the earliest written antislavery documents in North America, the 1688 "Germantown Friends' Protest against Slavery" argued for the total elimination of the practice based on the Golden Rule (cf. Mark 12:31). "There is a saying, that we shall doe to all men like as we will be done ourselves; making no difference of what generation, descent or colour they are."[31] The simple principle of treating others as one would want to be treated was sufficient rationale to oppose slavery. This group of Quakers also believed that the Golden Rule applied not only to Europeans but to everyone, regardless of skin color or nationality.

A far back as the seventeenth century, some Quakers were able to discern the spirit of justice in what Jesus had said about loving your neighbor as yourself. From this ethical imperative they deduced that slavery was evil. No European would desire to be stolen from their land, enslaved for life, robbed of wages, separated from their family, and subject to the cruelest indignities of body and mind. If they did not desire this for themselves, how could they condone it among other human beings made in the image and likeness of the Creator? While the petition did not gain widespread acceptance, it planted a seed for the Society of Friends' later opposition to slavery.

Decades later, John Woolman would become perhaps the Society of Friends' best-known champion for abolition in the Revolutionary era. Born in 1720 in the New Jersey area of the British colonies, Woolman began his professional life as a clerk and a merchant, but early in his career he had a crisis of conscience.

In his posthumously published autobiography, Woolman recalled an event when he served as clerk to a merchant. At the time, his boss asked him to write a bill of sale for a "Negro Woman" he held in slavery. "The Thing was sudden," Woolman wrote, "and, the Thoughts of writing an Instrument of Slavery for one of my Fellow-creatures felt uneasy." But given his young age and the command of a superior, Woolman wrote the bill of sale. Afterward, he was so troubled by his complicity in slavery that he told his employer and the man who bought the enslaved woman, "I believe Slave-keeping to be a Practice inconsistent with the Christian religion."[32]

A few years later, when he was in business for himself, he was presented with a similar quandary. A man came asking him to write a will for the man's brother, who wanted to leave the people he enslaved to his daughter. Although he didn't relish conflict, Woolman told the man that "the Practice of continuing Slavery to this People was not right; and had a Scruple in my Mind against doing Writings of that Kind."[33] Increasingly over the course of his life, Woolman sensed the growing conviction of the spirit of justice leading him to oppose slavery.

In a 1754 pamphlet titled "Some Considerations on the Keeping of Negroes," Woolman elaborated on his antislavery stance from a biblical perspective. He wrote, "When we remember that all nations are of one blood, (Gen. lii. 20,) . . . it seems to raise an idea of general brotherhood, and a disposition easy to be touched with a feeling of each other's afflictions."[34]

The actions of Woolman and other Quakers, principally directed toward members of their own Christian community, show the critical role white people had in persuading other white people to work for racial justice. As insiders to a predominantly white tradition, antislavery advocates in the Society of Friends were able to argue and reason with their peers for abolition. Even though many Quakers continued to hold human beings in slavery, this group emerged as early opponents of the transatlantic slave trade. And even though an outright abolitionist stance was not immediately adopted by their fellow white Christians, Quakers eventually became well known for their opposition to slavery. While Black people stood at the forefront, the example of Quaker abolitionists illustrates that the labor of convincing other white people of the need for racial justice is a task white people must undertake for themselves.

CONCLUSION

The Revolutionary era could have been a decisive moment when European colonists directed the language of liberty toward themselves as well as the enslaved Africans in their midst. The phrase "all men are created equal" could have been applied to everyone—men, women, African, indigenous, the poor, and others. Instead, wealthy white men with political power and social influence decided on the narrowest interpretation of citizenship and set up rigid boundaries between who counted and who was discounted. The United States continued its tradition of enslaving people of African descent, and in the decades after the Declaration of Independence and the ratification of the Constitution, the despicable practice of slavery grew. But not without opposition.

With the sounds of freedom echoing in the air in these revolutionary years, Christians recognized the contradiction between bondage and liberty at the heart of their fledgling nation. People like Jupiter Hammon, Phillis Wheatley, Benjamin Banneker, Prince Hall, and groups within the Methodist and Quaker traditions protested race-based chattel slavery. They wrote poems and letters, confronted political and religious leaders, and reasoned using the nation's founding documents and the Scriptures. While their efforts to eliminate the trade and practice of slavery were unsuccessful in their day, they constructed the scaffolding on which abolitionists would later build a movement opposing the practice of slavery well into the nineteenth century.

CHAPTER
FOUR

THE ANTISLAVERY MOVEMENT

Frederick Douglass had no patience for slaveholders who called them-selves Christians. In the first of his three autobiographies, he wrote about the inverse relationship between religiosity and kindness toward enslaved Black people. One of his own slaveholders, Thomas Auld, had attended a Methodist camp meeting in 1832 and then converted to Christianity. "I indulged a faint hope that his conversion would lead him to emancipate his slaves, and that, if he did not do this, it would, at any rate, make him kinder and more humane. I was disappointed in both these respects."[1] He went on to describe how Auld, in becoming a Christian, became "more cruel and hateful in all his ways; for I believe him to have been a much worse man after his conversion than before."[2] Throughout his written recollections, Douglass described the deplorable behavior of those who claimed to be disciples of Jesus Christ.

In one of the most repeated descriptions of the hypocrisy of Christian slaveholders, Douglass wrote:

Between the Christianity of this land, and the Christianity of Christ, I recognize the widest possible difference—so wide, that to receive the one as good, pure, and holy, is of necessity to reject the other as bad, corrupt, and wicked. . . . I therefore hate the corrupt, slaveholding, women-whipping, cradle-plundering, partial and hypo-critical Christianity of this land. Indeed, I can see no reason, but the most deceitful one, for calling the religion of this land Christianity.[3]

Douglass, like so many other enslaved Black people, knew the difference between slaveholder Christianity and the Christianity of Christ. Douglass had, in fact, been licensed to preach in an African Methodist Episcopal Zion (AMEZ) church and had preached many times.[4] He was not hostile to religion or Christianity. He simply knew from experience that a mere profession of belief did not automatically result in character or conduct becoming of Christ. He wanted so dearly for his readers to understand that he respected true Christianity that he wrote an entire appendix, in which the above passage appears, to explain his comments. "What I have said respecting and against religion, I mean strictly to apply to the slaveholding religion of this land, and with no possible reference to Christianity proper."[5] Throughout the abolitionist era in US history, Christians argued and acted in opposition to slaveholder Christianity. Their efforts to eradicate race-based chattel slavery arose not in spite of their Christian faith but because of it.

Frederick Douglass

A SEASON OF CHANGE

The opening decades of the 1800s were marked by dramatic developments in the United States and across the world. Technology played a large role in the growth of slavery and, thus, the need for abolition as well. Like many college graduates, when Eli Whitney matriculated from Yale, he had debts to pay. He postponed his plans to go to law school and took a job assisting Catherine Greene, the widow of a Revolutionary War general, on her plantation near Savannah, Georgia. While working there, Greene explained to Whitney the problem of removing the seeds from cotton. It took one enslaved laborer a whole day to remove the seeds from about one pound of cotton.[6] Whitney came up with a mechanism that pulled cotton fibers through mesh that was small enough for the cotton but strained out the seeds. In 1794 he obtained a patent for his invention and called it the cotton gin (short for "engine").

The invention and widespread use of the cotton gin led to the expansion of slavery. Even though the cotton gin reduced the labor needed to separate seeds from cotton, it increased the demand for enslaved people to plant and harvest more cotton. Between 1790 and 1808—the year the importation of enslaved people was outlawed—US slaveholders transported 80,000 Africans through the transatlantic slave trade. The number of slave states grew from six in 1790 to fifteen in 1860. By the start of the Civil War, nearly one in three southerners was an enslaved person.[7] Coupled with advances in manufacturing, the growth of the telegraph and railroads, and massive global demand for cotton, slavery became an economic and cultural cornerstone of the nation.

By the dawn of the nineteenth century, northern states had already moved to abolish slavery in their lands. In 1777, Vermont became the first colony to abolish slavery outright. Its constitution said, "No male person, born in this country, or brought from over sea, ought to be holden by law, to serve any person, as a servant, slave or apprentice." It applied specifically to men over the age of twenty-one and women over the age of eighteen. By 1804 all the northern states had passed laws to abolish slavery, at least gradually, in their territories. It is important to note that these antislavery policies did not result in equality for Black people. Many states still prohibited Black people from owning property, voting, or sharing in full rights as citizens. Nevertheless, opposition to slavery in the northern states built momentum for the abolitionist movement over the next several decades.

The abolitionist movement was international in scope, with the British abolitionist movement having an especially significant impact on abolition efforts in the United States. In late 1781, sailors aboard a British slave ship named *Zong* committed one of the most notorious acts of the slave trade. In what became known as the *Zong* massacre, British sailors threw overboard 132 Africans.[8] The ship's crew had made a serious navigational error and failed to stop in Jamaica for additional drinking water because they mistook it for a different island. It was common practice to insure a ship's cargo in humans. So, short on water, leaders of the vessel decided to jettison some "cargo" in the hopes of obtaining insurance money for the Africans they killed. Upon returning to Britain, the ship's owners made a claim that the insurance company refused to pay. The case went to court and a judge initially ruled in favor of the ship's owners. That ruling was later overturned when new evidence indicated that the water shortage was due to miscalculations by the crew and that, in the midst of these murders, the ship took on heavy rainfall that gave them plenty of water with no need to kill additional Africans.[9]

Despite such a massive loss of life, the *Zong* massacre initially garnered little attention until a formerly enslaved man, Olaudah Equiano, brought it to the attention of a white British abolitionist, Granville T. Sharpe. Sharpe informed the British Society of Friends (Quakers), and they soon drafted a petition to the British Parliament demanding an end to the trade in humans. They wrote, "Your Petitioners regret that a Nation professing the Christian Faith should so far counteract the Principles of Humanity and Justice as by cruel treatment of this oppressed Race, to fill their minds with Prejudices against the mild and beneficent Doctrines of the Gospel."[10] Like some of their counterparts in the United States, many British Quakers became abolitionists who saw the slave trade as incompatible with a Christian profession of faith.

The *Zong* massacre was one of several factors that led to the growth of British abolitionism in the late 1700s and early 1800s. The British movement included notable figures such as Anthony Benezet, William Wilberforce, and John Newton. British abolitionists formed antislavery societies and organized to petition the government and shift public sentiment toward abolition. Still, it was nearly fifty years from the time of the *Zong* massacre to the legal abolition of slavery in Britain and its colonies. In 1807, Parliament outlawed the slave trade. But outlawing the slave *trade* was not the same as outlawing *slavery*. The practice of holding people of African descent in bondage for life and without pay continued for another twenty-six years until Parliament passed the Slavery Abolition Act in 1833.[11] Though change came slowly, the movement to end slavery in Britain cast a vision of resistance for abolitionists in the United States.

In the United States several religious innovations helped fuel the abolitionist movement. From the 1790s to the 1830s, a series of Protestant religious revivals broke out across the country. Itinerant Methodist circuit riders and local Baptist preachers led the way in evangelizing, often hosting multiday outdoor events called "camp meetings." Preachers such as Charles Grandison Finney deviated from the staid and erudite expositions of Scripture that often accompanied more institutional forms of Christianity. They used passion and drama to stir the emotions of listeners and emphasize the need for immediate conversion. New denominations such as the Disciples of Christ, Seventh-Day Adventists, the Church of Jesus Christ of Latter-Day Saints, and the African Methodist Episcopal Church (AME) emerged in this time period.[12] With an emphasis on immediate conversion and sharing the good news, the Second Great Awakening is sometimes marked as an origin point for major segments of US evangelicalism.

The Second Great Awakening also saw large numbers of Black people convert to Christianity. Some revivalists encouraged both Black and white people to attend evangelistic meetings, leading to both enslaved and enslaver being converted under the same preaching. The religious ethos of the day also shifted away from formal academic requirements for preachers to emphasize the direct connection all believers had with God through the Holy Spirit.[13] Even an enslaved person with no formal education could be recognized as a preacher and religious leader. This opened up ways for Black people to develop a distinctively Afro-American form of Christianity that could challenge the system of slavery and the racism of white Christians. Using the truncated and often racist teachings about Christianity they received from white teachers, Black people made the religion their own, recognizing its liberatory potential.

The spiritual story of the era of abolition cannot be told without mention of figures like Richard M. Allen and the leaders and parishioners of the newly established African Methodist Episcopal (AME) Church. Spurred by egregious acts of racism when he was part of the largely white Saint George's Methodist Episcopal Church in Philadelphia, Allen and a group of Black Christians started the Bethel African Church, which later became known as "Mother Bethel," the founding church of the AME.[14] As one of the early efforts to form an independent Black denomination, the AME quickly became a vital institutional model of Black religious self-determination and autonomy. The freedom to worship and govern themselves within the AME was rare at a time when Black religious practices were closely monitored by the white power structure. The rapidly growing AME denomination provided a platform from which Black people could protest slavery and racism as they developed a distinctly Afrocentric Christianity.

Richard Allen was by no means the only major force in the formation of the AME, but as the most recognized minister of the denomination, he was lauded by many. David Walker, whose *Appeal to the Coloured Citizens of the World* became one of the most well-known pieces of abolitionist literature in history, wrote that Allen will "stand on the pages of history among the greatest divines who have lived since the apostolic age."[15] Allen also figures prominently in the story of evangelist and preacher Jarena Lee, whose story appears later in this chapter. Although Allen initially refused her request to preach on the grounds that women were not allowed to fill such a role, he later changed his mind and supported her pioneering ministry.

THE HAITIAN REVOLUTION

No other event in the antebellum era inspired the spirit of justice among enslaved Africans more than the Haitian Revolution. It is the only successful slave rebellion that resulted in an independent, Black-led nation. Even though they emancipated themselves, the people of Haiti suffered massive sanctions by majority-white countries, including Britain and the United States. To this day, the nation is wracked by poverty brought on by the backlash among white people in Europe and the United States. But during the revolution, from 1791 to 1804, Haiti stood as a demonstration that enslaved Africans could rebel against white enslavers and win.

Toussaint Louverture

The leader of the rebellion was a Black man named Pierre Toussaint Louverture. Born in 1743, he obtained some education through the Catholic order of the Jesuits. Toussaint was also baptized Catholic and became a devout adherent to the Catholic faith. A leader noted for his acumen in military strategy, Toussaint trained his troops in guerilla tactics and secured many victories.

While Toussaint is known for his military and political activity, religion played a significant role in his leadership. Though Toussaint was a faithful Catholic, he did not force Catholicism on the people as a national religion after Haiti gained independence. "I would not jeopardize the sacred rights of conscience, so dear to every man, but grant all the privilege of worshipping God according to the dictates of their conscience."[16] In this new nation, forged from the fires of a rebellion against slavery, the idea of religious freedom and tolerance took hold. In Toussaint's view, establishing a state religion and forcing everyone to conform to that religious view was neither democratic nor Christian.

Toussaint himself was a spiritual man who practiced Catholicism sincerely. An early slave record about him described Toussaint as "eager to proselytize."[17] The memoir Toussaint wrote toward the end of his life "clearly placed him within the Euro-Christian cultural framework typical of the black elite of Saint-Domingue."[18] Documentary evidence also shows that he was the godfather of a Senegalese friend's daughter and gave all of his own children Christian names. He consistently portrayed himself as a "devout Catholic during the Haitian Revolution."[19] Yet Toussaint, like many other Christians of African descent, did not merely parrot the religion of his oppressors. He saw no contradiction between his military exploits to overthrow slavery and his Catholic faith. In fact, it was largely because of his religious beliefs that he believed he and all African-descended people deserved freedom.

Toussaint became a legend for helping lead Black people to freedom, but he was eventually captured and imprisoned in 1802. Although Toussaint had agreed to lay down arms, French leaders suspected him of plotting a rebellion and invited him to a meeting to discuss "troop movements," but it was all a ruse.[20] The French arrested him and forced him onto a ship bound for France. This episode evoked one of his most well-known statements: "In overthrowing me, you have cut down in San Domingo only the trunk of the tree of liberty. It will spring up again by the roots for they are numerous and deep."[21] Toussaint was deported to France and put in a prison near the Swiss border. He died in his cell in 1803.

THE JOURNAL OF DAVID INGRAHAM

Historians rely on primary sources for their scholarship. This, in many ways, is what defines the discipline. Most of the time this work takes place in an archive where items have been donated, curated, and carefully cataloged for study. But occasionally, in a rare and exciting moment, historians discover a new primary source. Thankfully, scholars are still uncovering new primary sources, and that is what happened in October 2015 when the archivist at Adrian College in Adrian, Michigan, handed Chris Momany—chaplain, professor, former pastor in the United Methodist Church, and enthusiast of abolitionist history—a journal.[22]

The journal was written by a white Methodist missionary and abolitionist named David Ingraham who had taken note of his observations and thoughts in the journal while on a mission trip to Jamaica between 1839 and 1841. Ingraham died of tuberculosis in 1841 at the age of twenty-nine. But his journal survived.

The journal is over 100 pages. Significantly, it contains the sketch of the interior of a Portuguese slave ship named the *Ulysses*. In 1839, the vessel carried 556 Africans from Dahomey (present-day Benin). Its hold was divided into four compartments, one each for girls (117), boys (93), women (107), and men (216). These human beings were held captive in a space just 1,380 square feet in size. According to Ingraham's precise notes on the dimensions of each room, this worked out to 1.9 sq. ft./girl; 1.9 sq. ft./boy; 3.7 sq. ft./woman; and since there were more of them, 2.88 sq. ft./man.

Image from David Ingraham's unpublished 1839–41 journal
courtesy of the Adrian College Archive, Adrian, MI.

They were held captive in such conditions for fifty days until the ship was intercepted by a British schooner named the *Skipjack* and released in Jamaica.[23]

Reflecting on their conditions, Ingraham wrote in his journal, "When [I was] told that 556 slaves occupied . . . it seemed almost impossible. O where are the sympathies of Christians for the slave, and where are there exertions for liberation? O it seems as if the church were asleep and Satan has the world following him."

Ingraham believed slavery was a sin, and it necessarily followed for him and many other Christian abolitionists that living a sanctified life entailed fighting the evil of slavery. Ingraham wrote in his journal, "Salvrey [sic] must fall + may the time soon come. 'The Lord executeth judgment for all that are oppressed' + blessed be his name. O that the oppressor may see + repent ere it be too late."[24] His oppressed-oppressor language echoes the Bible's calls for justice and the equitable treatment of all people as image bearers of God.

As exceptional as Ingraham is for recognizing the evil of slavery as a white Christian man, he could not have done his work apart from the influence of Black Christians, the recently freed people of Jamaica, and others. Among those who shaped his own views on the matter were Ingraham's wife and daughter; a Black man and former classmate at Oberlin, James Bradley; and a Black woman named Nancy Prince, whom he recruited out of Boston to help in his missionary journeys.

Ingraham was by no means a perfect man, but he represents the rare example of a white Christian abolitionist who also consciously and consistently cultivated interracial cooperation in his pursuit of racial justice. The diary offers an intimate account of a man fervent in faith and devotion to God, who because of that faith chose to resist the proslavery sentiments of his day and work among recently freed Black people.

STATE OF MISSOURI V. CELIA, A SLAVE

Celia was just fourteen years old when the abuse began. A young Black girl, she was bought and enslaved by a white man in Missouri named Robert Newsom. He began sexually assaulting her as soon as they got back to his plantation, and the abuse happened repeatedly over the next five years. Then, on the night of June 23, 1855, Celia had enough. Newsom had told her earlier that day that he would come to her cabin that night to demand sex. When he entered, Celia retreated to a corner and refused him. She then picked up a nearby stick and hit him on the head with it. Newsom stumbled to a chair, and Celia struck him over the head again. The blows killed him.

She sat in her cabin for more than an hour deciding what to do next. Then she gathered up all the wood she could and began a roaring blaze in her fireplace. She dragged Newsom's body into the fire and stoked it until morning. She then distributed his ashes and bits of bones to hide the remains. Throughout the entire ordeal, Celia was pregnant.

To some, Celia's actions constitute murder. That was what the jury decided in her trial, *State of Missouri v. Celia, a Slave*. She was tried and confessed to killing Newsom, but she insisted that she had not intended to take his life, only to defend herself from this rapist. Nevertheless, the jury convicted her. Her court-appointed lawyers appealed the decision and waited months to see whether there would be another trial. While she languished in jail awaiting the outcome of the appeal, she gave birth to a stillborn child. In the end, the appeal was refused. Celia was hanged on December 21, 1855.

Celia's story is a tragic one. She had no allies. Men did not help her. Celia's slaveholder repeatedly assaulted her throughout her teenage years. Toward the end of her life, she had been seeing a Black man named George, who was also enslaved. In an act of jealousy, he demanded that she stop having sex with her slaveholder, as if Celia had a choice in the matter. White women didn't help her either. Celia had begged Newsom's daughters to intervene on her behalf as a fellow woman. They either refused or were ineffective because the assaults continued. The judge in her case made a self-defense acquittal impossible by accepting the prosecution's reasoning that "the defendant had no right to kill [Newsom] because he came into her cabin and was talking to her about having intercourse with her or anything else."[25] In desperation, Celia did what she felt she had to do to protect herself. But both the judge and the prosecutors disregarded her motives and any possible arguments for self-defense. In their view, Celia was, after all, merely a slave woman.

Although her fate was tragic and unjust, in the end, the spirit of justice in Celia empowered her to literally strike a blow against oppression and her oppressor. Resistance for Black people has always been dangerous, and sometimes it proved deadly. In horrifying detail, Celia's ordeal reveals the evils of slavery and sexual assault, as well as the failures of the so-called justice system.

We know about Celia because we have a record of her trial. But so many other enslaved women endured similar abuse and, when they resisted, paid the ultimate price. Celia's life and unjust death at the hands of the state compel deep reflection about whom the legal system was built to protect and punish. It prompts the questions of how much torture Black people must endure before they can retaliate and why so few people join Black women in solidarity and resistance.

PAUL CUFFE AND THE "BACK TO AFRICA MOVEMENT"

Black nationalism is the idea that Black people should have self-determination of their economic, social, and political power, especially by establishing and cultivating their own nations.[26] The concept of Black nationalism became more widespread in the 1900s, but an early pioneer of the movement was a man named Paul Cuffe (or Cuffee). Through his efforts to colonize Sierra Leone with formerly enslaved Black people, Cuffe pioneered an early version of Black nationalism and the "Back to Africa" movement, which suggested Black people return to their ancestral homeland on the continent of Africa to find true freedom and self-empowerment.

Cuffe was born in 1759 in Massachusetts as one of ten children born to a formerly enslaved African father and a Native American mother. His parents were able to save enough money to buy a 116-acre farm in Dartmouth, New Hampshire. But the enterprising Paul Cuffe soon left his life working the land for a life on the sea. He served on whaling ships and during the Revolutionary War was taken captive by the British Navy and jailed for three months in New York.[27]

After his release, Cuffe's protests for justice took many forms. In 1780, he and his brother John petitioned the Massachusetts legislature

for relief from taxation. They appealed to their Native American ances-
try to argue "that [we] are Indian men and by Law not the subjects of
Taxation for any Estate Real or personal."[28] The legislature did not
approve their request, and later the brothers were briefly jailed for
refusing to pay property taxes.

In the 1780s, Paul partnered with a brother-in-law to start a shipping company. Cuffe recognized that the way for Black people to gain
wealth was through business ownership. Instead of renting or sailing
someone else's ships, he acquired a small waterfront property and started
building increasingly larger trading and fishing ships. Ownership
allowed Cuffe and his colleagues to reap the benefits of a growing local
population and economy. In time he became one of the wealthiest Black
people in the country. [29]

But Cuffe was not content simply to have more money. He wanted to
use his prosperity and position to assist other Black people. He partnered
with Quakers in the United States and abolitionists in Britain to encourage formerly enslaved Black people from both nations to move to Sierra
Leone—a colony established by England in 1791 to serve as a home for
Black people who had fled to the British during the Revolutionary War.
Many of the Black people who had sought protection in Sierra Leone had
first been relocated to Nova Scotia and were still uncertain of their future.

Cuffe made several voyages to Sierra Leone to investigate its prospects as a settling place for formerly enslaved Africans. After a multiyear
delay brought about by the War of 1812, Cuffe was able to take a group
of thirty-eight Black people to resettle in the country.[30] Most of the cost
for this journey fell on Cuffe, and this remarkable movement was only
possible because of Cuffe's financial independence and the fact that he
owned his own ships. Sierra Leone became a dynamic mix of indigenous
Africans, formerly enslaved Africans from the northern United States,
and "maroons" from Jamaica who had participated in a failed rebellion
and been deported.

While Cuffe had visionary plans for commerce and relocation for
Black people in Sierra Leone, they largely did not come to fruition.
The country was still a colony of Britain, and many of the British men
involved in the colony feared losing their economic monopoly over the
land. In addition, the colonization movement to bring Black people

back to Africa soon became associated with bad-faith attempts by white people to rid the United States of free Black people and further tighten their political and economic grip on North America.

Nevertheless, Paul Cuffe demonstrated there was power in financially independent Black people who were innovative and courageous enough to imagine a nation for themselves. As a sailor, traveler, and entrepreneur, Cuffe cultivated a Black international and Pan-African mind-set that recognized the unity of all people of African descent. He pictured a day when Black people would be politically and economically self-sufficient, working toward that end until his death in 1817.

Cuffe was a devout Christian and member of the Society of Friends. His faith drove many of his actions, and he was committed to the uplift of his people. In remarks by a good friend of his, Reverend Peter Williams Jr., a pastor of an African Methodist Episcopal Zion (AMEZ) congregation in New York City, Cuffe was called "pious without ostentation, and warmly attached to the principles of Quakerism," and "he manifested, in all his deportment, that he was a true disciple of Jesus."[31]

DAVID WALKER'S APPEAL (1829)

The word *radical* derives from the Latin word *radix*, which means "root." Over time the word *radical* has come to characterize certain social movements or ideas that are designed to get at the root of a problem. Yet while that's the dictionary definition of *radical*, the term can have a broader meaning in practice.

What makes a person or an idea radical? As we consider the fight against racism in the United States, the term *radical* has been selectively used to describe the actions of the oppressed and not the oppressor. When Black people who endured the suffering of slavery called for immediate abolition, reparations, or relief by any means necessary, they were quickly labeled radicals. By contrast, slaveholders, who cracked whips, bought and sold children away from their parents, and waged the Civil War to protect their property in people, were hardly ever called radical.

Nevertheless, it is likely because he was labeled a radical by the white establishment that we remember David Walker today. Born in the 1790s to an enslaved father and a free Black mother, Walker was

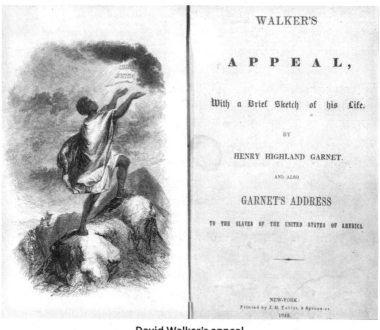

David Walker's appeal

raised as a free person in Wilmington, North Carolina. He learned to read and write and traveled extensively throughout his young adult life. He eventually settled down in Boston where he ran a clothing store.

Walker gets labeled a radical because he wrote a phenomenally controversial pamphlet, *Walker's Appeal in Four Articles; Together with a Preamble, to the Coloured Citizens of the World, but in Particular and Very Expressly to Those of the United States of America.* His words set the hearts of the enslaved, and the hair of slaveholders, on fire. This brief pamphlet was so packed with the potential for revolution that smugglers had to sew its pages into the lining of their clothes to sneak it to enslaved people. The audience for his pamphlet was primarily the enslaved women and men of the United States. In it he called on them to remember their dignity and resist their oppressors.

"Oh! my coloured brethren, all over the world, when shall we arise from this death-like apathy?—And be men!!"[32] Walker urged the masses of enslaved Black people to shake off the idea that they were consigned to servitude without any ability to rise in protest. He pointed out that

Black people far outnumbered white people in slave states, and they had the numbers to quickly throw off their chains and drive out their slaveholders. In fact, Walker would put 450,000 Black people ("let them be well equipped for war") against the entire population of white people in the United States. "Why? why because I know that the Blacks, once they get involved in a war, had rather die than to live, they either kill or be killed."[33]

But, asked Walker, "why is it, that those few weak, good-for-nothing whites, are able to keep so many able men, one of whom, can put to flight a dozen whites, in wretchedness and misery?"[34] Here Walker pointed out one of the most deleterious effects of racism, the internalized sense of inferiority it forced on the oppressed. In Walker's estimation, Black people had all they needed to secure freedom—the numbers, the strength, and the moral high ground. What they lacked was the will to make it happen. To make his point, Walker compared Black people to other groups that had successfully opposed slavery and white efforts to exploit them. "The Indians would not rest day or night, they would be up all times of night, cutting their cruel throats. But my colour, (some, not all,) are willing to stand still and be murdered by the cruel whites."[35]

While his words seem accusatory, Walker was trying to show enslaved Black people their power and potential to fight for justice. His words were necessary for a people who had lived their entire lives under the slave driver's lash. The system of racialized injustice was so complete that enslaved people almost never had an opportunity to hear a word about their intrinsic worth, their toughness, or the righteousness of their longing for freedom. Reading Walker's words or hearing them read aloud expanded the horizons of possibility for a people who had been intentionally forced to keep their spiritual gaze low.

Walker also opposed any program of colonization that would send Black people back to Africa. Although colonization was supported by some prominent Black people, such as Paul Cuffe, Walker saw it as yet another form of oppression perpetuated against Black people by white people. "Will any of us leave our homes and go to Africa? I hope not. America is more our country, than it is the whites—we have enriched it with our blood and tears."[36] To Walker and many other Black people, the idea of sending formerly enslaved people back to the continent of

Africa from which they were stripped was an act not of justice but of outrage. Black people had literally built the wealth of the nation with the sacrifice of their bodies, lives, and loves. Now they were being told they could not remain in the land to which they had contributed so much. Walker argued it would be better for Black people to remain in the United States and insist on equity and fairness rather than to move to a different country.

While most of Walker's *Appeal* was addressed directly to Black people, he did not refrain from speaking to white people as well. What enraged white people was the way Walker, in the spirit of the Black Christian tradition, indicted their supposed Christian faith. "Have not the Americans the Bible in their hands? Do they believe it? Surely they do not."[37] He pointed out the cruelties of race-based chattel slavery. He was especially angered at the pointed effort by white people to keep Black people in ignorance. "They keep us sunk in ignorance, and will not let us learn to read the word of God, nor write—If they find us with a book of any description in our hand, they will beat us nearly to death."[38] If knowledge is power, then white people wanted to keep Black people powerless by preventing them from learning to read, write, or access the Bible for themselves.

In light of their continued support of slavery and the malicious maltreatment of Black people, Walker called down the wrath of God on white people. "O Americans! Americans!! I call God—I call angels—I call men, to witness, that your DESTRUCTION is at hand, and will be speedily consummated unless you REPENT." In the spirit of the prophets of the Old Testament, Walker insisted that white people turn from their wicked ways and seek justice for Black people and forgiveness from God. If they would not, prophesied Walker, then "I am awfully afraid that pride, prejudice, avarice and blood, will, before long prove the final ruin of this happy republic, or land of liberty!!!!"[39] While he could not have known the exact contours of the conflict, Walker effectively predicted the Civil War as the inevitable result of the injustice at the heart of the young republic. A nation could not claim to be the "land of liberty" while holding millions in bondage. The two notions were irreconcilable and would rend the country in pieces.

David Walker's words were just that—words. They were not guns, knives, or bullets. Yet they had the power to kill ideas of Black inferiority or powerlessness. The words of his *Appeal* had power to enliven the hopes, creativity, and courage of a people who had heard very little to contradict the lie that they were subordinate to the white race. These words of affirmation cut a small tear in the fabric of white supremacy that, if tugged upon, might rip the entire lie apart. Oftentimes, the most radical acts do not start with mass movements but with words that powerfully remind people of their worth and their ability to resist injustice.

JARENA LEE PREACHES A "WHOLE SAVIOR"

While David Walker was bold in his pronouncements, he did not have to face the added injustice of sexism. Jarena Lee became the first Black woman authorized as a preacher in the African Methodist Episcopal church. But her pathbreaking achievement did not come without a struggle. Her mission to share God's Word and pursue her calling in

Jarena Lee

Christian ministry illustrates that for Black women, resisting injustice entailed fighting not only racism but also sexism and patriarchy in a male-centered world.

Lee was the first Black woman in America to have her autobiography published.[40] It is a sign of Lee's deeply held faith that her book serves primarily as a diary of her spiritual journey. She was born on February 11, 1783, in New Jersey. At the age of seven she was sold as "servant maid" to a white family. In 1804, she attended a service conducted by a Presbyterian missionary, but far from bringing her comfort, the sermon so convicted Lee that she was "driven of Satan" to throw herself into a river and drown.[41] Although she did not proceed with that act, Lee continued to be troubled by the sinful state of her soul.

Lee soon moved to Philadelphia and went to hear a Methodist preacher named Richard Allen. "During the labors of this man that afternoon," Lee reflected, "I had come to the conclusion, that this is the people to which my heart unites."[42] Three weeks after hearing Allen preach, she converted to Christianity. Still, Lee had not experienced what some Christian traditions call "full sanctification." Not until another Black minister told her about this experience did she begin praying for her total purification from sin. Finally, it happened. "'Lord sanctify my soul for Christ's sake.' That very instant, as if lightning had darted through me, I sprang to my feet, and cried, 'The Lord has sanctified my soul!'"[43]

Four or five years after her experience of full sanctification, Jarena Lee wrote of her call to preach the gospel. She heard a voice telling her, "Preach the Gospel; I will put words in your mouth and will turn your enemies to become your friends."[44] A few days later, she went to see Richard Allen, who had become the first bishop of the African Methodist Episcopal denomination. She told him of her divine call to preach the gospel and her desire to do so within AME churches. Until this time, women had been "exhorters" and could speak publicly in prayer meetings and in other capacities. "But as to women preaching, he said that our Discipline knew nothing at all about it—that it did not call for women preachers."[45] At first, Lee was relieved of the solemn burden of expounding God's word. No doubt she was familiar with the text, "Not many of you should become teachers, my fellow believers, because you know that we who teach will be judged more strictly" (James 3:1). But her relief did not last long.

It was as if being forbidden to preach threatened to extinguish a spiritual spark within her. She wrote, "That holy energy which burned within me, as a fire, began to be smothered."[46] The feeling that she was disobeying God's will and losing the fervor of her faith was enough for Jarena Lee to take action.

At this point in her autobiography, she launched into an eloquent theological defense of a woman's calling to preach the word of God. "And why should it be thought impossible, heterodox, or improper for a woman to preach seeing the Saviour died for the woman as well as for the man?" she wrote.[47] If a man could preach the good news that brought him from death to life, then a woman should be able to preach that same good news of the same salvation. "Is he not a whole Saviour, instead of a half one as those who hold it wrong for a woman to preach, would seem to make it appear?"[48] If only men could preach, Lee explained, then Jesus is half a savior because he only died for the full inclusion of half the people in his plan of salvation. But if Jesus' salvation is for both women and men, then he is a "whole Saviour," and both sexes had an equal right and duty to preach the gospel.

Although he had given her leave to hold prayer meetings in her house and to be an "exhorter," Bishop Allen did not permit Lee to preach when she initially approached him. She still had a sense that God would make a way for her to preach but was unclear about how and when. In the intervening time she got married, had a family, and moved to a town near Philadelphia. Sadly, her husband died and left her struggling to raise and financially support two infant children. Nevertheless, she persisted. She moved back to Philadelphia and started attending Mother Bethel AME church again. But she never relinquished her compulsion to preach.

One day, quite unexpectedly, she got the chance to fulfill her calling. She was at church listening to a Black male preacher, Reverend Richard Williams, begin to preach. The preacher couldn't get through his sermon. "He seemed to have lost the spirit," Lee recalled. In that moment, she sensed her opportunity. "In the same instant, I sprang, as by altogether supernatural impulse, to my feet, when I was aided from above to give an exhortation on the very text which my brother Williams had taken." Bishop Allen was in the congregation that day. So powerful was Lee's preaching that he stood up afterward and explained to those assembled that Lee had come to him eight years prior asking for permission to preach. Although he had refused her that day, "he now as much believed that I was called to that work, as any of the preachers present."[49] Through this spontaneous act of exposition and courage, Jarena Lee followed the leading of the spirit of justice and became the first Black female preacher in the AME.

Lee preached for more than twenty years as far south as Maryland, as far north as Canada, and as far west as Ohio and Michigan. She also joined in the abolitionist cause and spoke at the Philadelphia meeting of the American Anti-Slavery Society that was attended by Sojourner Truth, William Lloyd Garrison, and Lucretia Mott.[50] She did all this as a single mother and while working uphill in a society that favored men in leadership roles and still enslaved Black people. In spite of her labors, she died nearly destitute on February 8, 1864. Lee's passion for Jesus and her desire to share the good news with as many people as possible led her to overcome the obstacles she faced, even those within the Black church. Jarena Lee's life and witness demonstrate that even a prophetic church needs its own prophets to speak from within for the health of the body and the cause of justice.

ANNA MURRAY DOUGLASS

A common pattern in popular historical understandings of the abolitionist movement is to view men as the central characters in the drama against slavery. But such a view is inaccurate. Women fought, died, and sacrificed for freedom as often as the men did. In many cases, the husband in a married couple gets all the attention but, in reality, he could not have succeeded without his spouse. The case of Anna Murray and Frederick Douglass is a clear example of how there would be no great men to remember without the great women who stood beside them.

Anna Murray was born in Maryland around 1813, though the exact date of her birth is unknown. Her parents had been enslaved but were freed just one month before Anna was born, making her the first of their

Anna Murray Douglass

twelve children born into freedom. She left home at seventeen years old to support herself as a seamstress.[51] Anna remained largely illiterate for the rest of her life, but she excelled in management, financial planning, and resourcefulness.

Most of what we now know about Anna Murray comes from accounts by her children. In 1900, her daughter Rosetta Douglass Sprague delivered a speech to the Women's Christian Temperance Union titled "My Mother as I Recall Her." The speech was later made into a book by the same name, which offers an intimate portrait of this lesser-known abolitionist.

In the opening strains of her address, Douglass Sprague acknowledged the fame of her father. "The story of Frederick Douglass' hopes and aspirations and longing desire for freedom has been told—you all know it." She then continued by explaining the significance of her mother, Anna Murray, particularly in comparison with Frederick Douglass's exploits. "It was a story made possible through the unswerving loyalty of Anna Murray, to whose memory this paper is written."[52]

Frederick Bailey, as Douglass was known at the time, and Anna Murray met sometime in 1838 in Baltimore, perhaps while attending the same church. Their affection for each other was hindered by the fact that Anna was free but Frederick was enslaved. Douglass's harrowing escape from slavery is well detailed in his autobiographies, but Anna Murray's role in his emancipation is lesser known. She sewed for him the sailor's uniform he used as a disguise to board a ship bound for the North. She also borrowed a freedman's certificate that Douglass could use as a sort of fake ID during his escape. In addition, she provided the money for them to settle in Massachusetts and begin life together. "The little that they possessed was the outcome of the industrial and economical habits that were characteristic of my mother," wrote Douglass Sprague.[53]

Throughout their forty-four-year marriage, Anna Murray Douglass used her prodigious skills as an organizer and manager to run their household. As her husband's notoriety increased, Anna Murray Douglass "in every possible way that she was capable of aided him by relieving him of all the management of the home as it increased in size and in its appointments."[54] She also risked her life by harboring Douglass as a fugitive slave until English friends raised money to purchase him out of slavery in 1845.[55] She opened her home as a stop on the Underground Railroad to assist others escaping from slavery. She provided for her husband by saving money and raising their five children, including a two-year stint when he was away on a speaking tour in Europe.

In all her efforts, Anna Murray Douglass professed faith in God and aspired to live a life of Christian integrity. Anna was a Methodist, as was her husband. Even though there was no "family altar" in the house, her daughter recounts their regular spiritual practices. "Our custom was to read a chapter in the Bible around the table, each reading a verse in turn until the chapter was completed."[56] This was no mere exercise or hollow ritual for Anna. "She was a person who strived to live a Christian life instead of talking it."[57]

Anna Murray Douglass suffered a stroke in 1842 and died soon thereafter. Frederick got remarried to a white woman named Helen (Pitts) Douglass eighteen months later, a pairing not without controversy and criticism.[58] Even though we rightly remember Frederick Douglass for his daring, his speechifying, his writing, and his activism, he may never have made it out of slavery if not for the tireless efforts of his wife Anna Murray. His career as an abolitionist would not have been successful without her four-decade partnership. Anna Murray Douglass, through her steely strength and humble willingness to work without renown, exemplifies the spirit of justice.

CONCLUSION

The antislavery movement of the early nineteenth century was international, interracial, institutional, and grassroots in nature. From antislavery societies to abolitionist newspapers, from slave narratives to the Underground Railroad, the movement to abolish slavery entailed a multitude of strategies, tactics, and personnel. Women figured prominently in the movement to abolish slavery, even if their contributions have often gone unmentioned in popular discourse. From Jarena Lee to Anna Murray Douglass and many others, emancipation would not have been possible without the vigorous, though often unheralded, work of women on behalf of freedom.

Women and men, often motivated by their Christian religion and their belief in the equality of all people, risked their lives and fortunes to help set captives free. Frederick Douglass, the most well-known spokesperson for the abolition of slavery, wrote, "If there is no struggle, there is no progress. . . . This struggle may be a moral one; or it may be a physical one; or it may be both moral and physical; but it must be a struggle. Power concedes nothing without a demand. It never did and it never will."[59]

No single event catalyzed the abolition movement. It required decades of on-the-ground work by myriad groups and individuals to shift public opinion toward abolition and instigate action, which indicates how long it takes to achieve society-wide change. Yet the spirit of justice instilled in antislavery advocates the will to resist slavery and the dehumanizing ideologies that attended it. Their efforts forced a confrontation that would sever the tenuous unity of the young United States.

FIGHTING FOR FREEDOM

For generations, Black Christians both enslaved and free had watched for, prayed for, and sought God's judgment on a nation that held its darker-hued people in bondage. Through the Civil War, Black people not only fled slavery but fought to end it. Yet this was more than a mere political or military struggle; it was a spiritual battle against the evil of slavery. They understood themselves to be contending against pharaohs in the form of plantation owners and slave drivers. They crossed to a land of safety behind Union lines like the Hebrews crossing the Red Sea. Black people by the tens of thousands gathered as refugees like the huddling masses of the tribes of Israel in the wilderness. Black Christians had longed for a promised land of freedom. Now, with the Civil War, they could finally gaze over the mountaintop and catch a glimpse of liberty.

THE ONSET OF WAR

When Confederate forces started shelling Fort Sumter in Charleston, South Carolina, the military dimension of the Civil War officially began. But the dynamics leading to this division had been in place several decades prior. Two of the nation's three largest white Christian denominations had already split over the issue of slavery. The Methodists had split in 1844 over an argument about whether a bishop could conduct his clerical duties in good standing while also enslaving human beings. Methodists in the North voted to censure him, and Methodists in the South broke off to form the Methodist Episcopal Church, South (MECS). In 1845, Baptists saw a similar split in their ranks. The key issue for them concerned whether a white missionary could carry out his evangelistic duties while enslaving Black people at his plantation in Georgia. The Home Mission Society of the Baptist convention eventually declared, "If, however, anyone should offer himself as a Missionary, having slaves, and should insist on retaining them as his property, we could not appoint him."[1] Baptists in the South took this as their cue to exit and formed the Southern Baptist Convention. The ever-deliberative Presbyterians followed suit in 1861 after the Civil War began and formed the Presbyterian Church of the Confederate States of America (PCCSA) to preserve the supposed right of white Christians to enslave Black people.[2]

Other factors leading up to the Civil War included the passage of the Fugitive Slave Act in 1850. This act stated that when an enslaved person "in any State or Territory of the United States, has heretofore or shall hereafter escape into another State or Territory of the United States, the person or persons to whom such service or labor may be due . . . may pursue and reclaim such fugitive person."[3] The law effectively nationalized slavery since it required enslaved people who had run away from plantations in the South to be apprehended "with such reasonable force and restraint as may be necessary" and returned to their slaveholders. This law also stated that anyone helping an enslaved person escape, such as the network of people who formed the Underground Railroad, could be fined up to $1,000 and imprisoned.[4] The law incensed Black people and abolitionists. It created a police state to surveil Black bodies and threatened any Black person in the United States with capture and bondage, regardless of their legal status as enslaved or free. This was the case with Solomon Northup, whose story was adapted into the film *12 Years a Slave*.

The final straw leading to sectional division for many southerners was the election of Abraham Lincoln in November 1860. Lincoln was no advocate for Black equality. Although he personally thought all people should be free, his priority as president of the United States was to preserve the Union. In an 1862 letter to Horace Greeley, editor of the *New York Tribune*, Lincoln wrote, "My paramount object in this struggle is to save the Union, and is not either to save or to destroy slavery. If I could save the Union without freeing any slave I would do it, and if I could save it by freeing all the slaves I would do it."[5] Despite his comments in the letter, Lincoln ultimately thought the nation would have to move on from enslaving people if it was to thrive in the future.

This stance was radical enough for southerners, who saw in Lincoln's election the imminent demise of legalized human bondage. Less than a week after Lincoln's presidential victory, South Carolina Senator James Chestnut resigned from the Senate and helped draft the state's articles of secession. That document declared that northern states "have united in the election of a man to the high office of President of the United States, whose opinions and purposes are hostile to slavery."[6] The state's white politicians, "appealing to the Supreme Judge of the world for the rectitude of our intentions," saw no other recourse than to separate from the Union. Other southern states soon followed their lead and formed the Confederate States of America (CSA).

WHITE AMBIVALENCE ABOUT THE ROLE OF BLACK PEOPLE IN THE CIVIL WAR

Even though Black people had fought in every major US war from the Revolutionary War to the War of 1812, their participation as soldiers in the Civil War was debated by both the Union and the Confederates. At least since the Militia Act of 1792, Black people had been explicitly excluded from military service as the law applied only to "each and every free able-bodied white male citizen."[7] At the beginning of the war, Lincoln's primary focus was the restoration of the union between northern and southern states. He did not want to enlist Black soldiers for fear of alienating slaveholding border states such as Kentucky, Maryland, Delaware, and Missouri.

Several attempts to form Black regiments met with limited success. These included gathering volunteers in Boston and New Orleans. The First South Carolina Volunteers are often referred to as the first all-Black regiment in the Union. Although an initial effort to form this unit was disbanded, the Black troops were eventually called back into service under the command of Thomas Wentworth Higginson, a white abolitionist from Massachusetts. Higginson had gained a reputation as a militant abolitionist. He was an ordained minister, and parishioners at the first church he pastored disagreed with his antislavery views so strongly that he had to depart. In 1854, he participated in the attempted rescue of a Black man named Anthony Burns who was captured under the Fugitive Slave Act. Higginson was at the head of the battering ram used to smash the doors of the courthouse where Burns was being detained.[8] When Higginson took command of the South Carolina regiment, it was unique at this point in the war because it "contained scarcely a freeman, and had not one mulatto in ten."[9] This unit was comprised almost entirely of men who had been formerly enslaved just months prior. They were ready to fight and even die for their freedom.

Higginson kept a journal of his time with the First South Carolina soldiers. In it he recounts their fervent piety, especially when faced with the possibility of death in battle. "The most reckless and daring fellows in the regiment were perfect fatalists in their confidence that God would watch over them, and that if they died, it would be because their time had come."[10] This "almost excessive faith" made the former slaves into enthusiastic soldiers who viewed their fight not simply as North against South or a white man's war but as a divine battle for existential freedom, dignity, and a future.

Early in the war, the Union had no standard policy on what to do with Black people who escaped from slavery and sought refuge across Union lines. Some military commanders even returned escapees to their former slaveholders. But there were also leaders who recognized the humanity of Black people or at least acknowledged the military advantages of depriving the South of their unpaid laborers. Political considerations over the allegiance of slaveholding border states meant that Union leaders were reluctant to free or provide refuge to escaped slaves. But military considerations compelled commanders to find ways to keep the escaped people on their side and thus weaken their Confederate opponents.

In May of 1861, General Benjamin Butler used the exigencies of war to enact a new policy regarding enslaved Black people. Three Black men escaped their plantation and made their way to Butler's ranks at Fort

Monroe in Virginia. Soon thereafter, their slaveholder sent a representative to demand the return of the men under the Fugitive Slave Act of 1850. This southern plantation owner had joined in seceding from the United States but still appealed to a US law as a rationale for having the people he enslaved sent back to him. Butler did not find such reasoning persuasive. Instead, he used the southern rationale that enslaved people were property against them. In war, an army that captures a town or territory may seize the property thereof. These properties are called "contraband of war." If an enslaved person was indeed property, then they could be "confiscated" under the same principle. General Butler called the three men who had escaped to his lines "contraband" and put them to work at the fort. For the first time in the Civil War, enslaved people had some assurance that if they could make it to the Union, they would at least not be returned to the plantation.

To be clear, the term *contraband* is dehumanizing, and it revealed the timidity of white people in the North. Many of them did not want to free enslaved people and believed the war was about restoring the Union. Words like *emancipation* aroused their resistance. But a word like *contraband* seemed more palatable. A newspaper article in 1861 described the effect of the terminology: "The venerable gentleman, who wears gold spectacles and reads a conservative daily, prefers confiscation to emancipation. He is reluctant to have slaves declared freemen but has no objection to their being declared contrabands."[11] While a physical battle for emancipation played out in the South, another battle for the hearts and minds of white people regarding emancipation raged in the North.

It would take further official action to determine a standard policy for treating enslaved people who escaped across Union lines. Congress passed the first Confiscation Act in August 1861, specifying that any property, including property in people, could be confiscated by the Union. This effectively made General Butler's policy legal. The second Confiscation Act, passed in July of 1862, went even further in declaring "all slaves [in rebellious states occupied by the Union Army] . . . shall be deemed captives of war, and shall be forever free of their servitude, and not again held as slaves."[12] These acts weakened the South militarily and began to clarify that the heart of the Civil War was the slavery question, paving the way for emancipation.

For all their eagerness and willingness to fight with the Union during the Civil War, Black soldiers did not receive equal treatment compared to their white counterparts. They typically received less pay than white soldiers. Their duties consisted of such tasks as digging ditches, building fortifications, and cooking. White leaders seldom commissioned Black soldiers as officers or put them in command of troops, especially white troops. Prejudice ran deep, and many white people believed Black soldiers were cowardly, disorganized, and unintelligent. Time and again, Black soldiers and their supporters would prove these prejudices wrong.

The political and technical distinctions that determined the status of enslaved people during the Civil War were largely argued and discussed by white people. Many of them were ambivalent about or outright opposed to the emancipation of enslaved Black people. They saw restoration of the Union as a worthy goal but did not want Black people competing for jobs or sharing social or political equality with white people. For Black people, however, the purpose of the Civil War was clear from the outset. It was a war to abolish slavery and to redeem the soul of the nation. Thousands of Black people tapped into the spirit of justice during the Civil War era to finally secure their freedom from race-based chattel slavery.

ROBERT SMALLS STEALS AWAY

Robert Smalls knew the risks. As he loaded his family onto a Confederate supply ship named the *Planter*, he knew that he would face a severe punishment, perhaps even death, if they were caught. More than that, his young family—a wife, son, and daughter—surely also would suffer repercussions if his plan failed. But on the morning of May 13, 1862, he had a few things going for him. He wore a captain's hat with a wide brim to help conceal his identity. The darkness of 3:00 a.m. would make further identification difficult. Most of all, Smalls was a good pilot. He knew that if he could just make his way out of the harbor, he would be able to pilot the ship with precision and skill—and without arousing any suspicion. Thus began one of the most daring escapes from slavery during the Civil War.

Robert Smalls

Smalls was just twenty-three years old that fateful night when he commandeered the *Planter*. He had been born enslaved in 1839 in Beaufort, South Carolina. In contrast to most other enslaved Black people, Smalls lived and labored in a relatively urban setting. His mother, Lydia Polite, served in the home of her slaveholder. At twelve years old, Smalls's slaveholder hired him out to work in the city of Charleston as a waiter in a hotel and then as a dockworker. During this time, Smalls met and married his wife, Hannah, and they had two children.[13]

Smalls eventually moved up from laboring on the docks to laboring on ships as a crewman on the *Planter*, which was hired out by its owners to transport supplies for the Confederacy. In a short time, Smalls became a "wheelman" trained to pilot the ship. During his duties, Smalls noticed that the white captain and crew members often left for the entire night while at port, leaving the Black crew members alone. He saw a chance to escape. That night in May, he stole the Confederate ship and navigated through Confederate waters. Once clear, he had to hope that Union forces would not immediately fire on the enemy ship he was piloting. As soon as a Union vessel spotted them and got within hailing distance, Smalls raised the white flag of surrender. Smalls surrendered the ship and its cargo of artillery canons. Altogether, Smalls brought with him sixteen other enslaved men, women, and children.[14]

As word of Robert Smalls's audacious escape spread across the country, he became an instant celebrity. He could have ridden the wave of popularity to a life of comfort and relative privilege, but he continued to fight for freedom by joining the Union Navy. He so distinguished himself in service that he was quickly promoted to captain and commanded his own vessels. Eventually, the Navy put him in command of the *Planter*, the very ship he had stolen from the Confederates during his escape to freedom. And after some time, Smalls and his family saved enough to go back to Charleston and purchase the mansion that his former enslaver owned. He now owned the house of the man who had once owned him.[15]

It is not clear when or how Smalls became a Christian, but throughout his storied life he often intersected with Christians and churches. After his escape, a white Methodist minister with the American Missionary Association named Mansfield French arrived in Charleston from New York. He took note of Smalls's story and recruited him to help raise funds for the Port Royal Experiment—a comprehensive federal program to support formerly enslaved people. Their first fundraising trip was a speech in front of 1,200 people at Israel Bethel African Methodist Episcopal Church in Washington, DC. It was Smalls's first public speech, but he apparently did well because it soon led to many additional opportunities.[16]

Smalls's faith likely played a role in his work after the Civil War ended. He helped draft South Carolina's new state constitution and served as an elected official, first as a state representative and senator, and then as a US Congressman. He also served in the state militia of South Carolina and rose to the rank of brigadier general. But as far-right forces became ascendant, they sabotaged his political career with lies and accusations. In the face of this slander, Smalls wrote in 1909, "But notwithstanding all this, the same God still lives, in whom we place our hope."[17]

When he died in 1915, a service was held at First African Baptist Church in Charleston where he had been a member for ten years. The funeral service was said to have been "the largest ever held in the city."[18]

Throughout his life, Smalls displayed a bravery and willingness to battle racism and white supremacy in a way that has cemented him in the annals of national history. From slavery to Civil War hero, statesman, and celebrity, Smalls embodied the spirit of justice. He lived by his own words: "My race needs no special defense, for the past history of them in this country proves them to be equal of anyone. All they need is an equal chance in the battle of life."[19]

H. FORD DOUGLAS PASSES AS WHITE TO FIGHT

Prior to the Civil War, Hezekiah Ford Douglas kept a keen eye out, looking for a nation or location where Black people could emigrate and truly be free. At first, he set his sights on Canada.[20] He lived there for two years and extolled it as a place where Black people could enjoy their full humanity. Eventually, he looked in Central America for sites where Black people could form communities and live with full dignity. Although he lived most of his life in the United States, he never wavered from insisting that Black people owed nothing to a nation that protected slavery. Yet at the onset of the Civil War, Douglas chose to fight for Black freedom with the Union.

Douglas was born in Virginia in 1831. His mother was enslaved, and his father was her slaveholder. The young Douglas escaped slavery at the age of fifteen and settled in Cleveland, Ohio. His experience of enslavement left an indelible impression on him, and he later devoted his life to passionate, and sometimes iconoclastic, efforts to abolish slavery and uplift his race. He condemned the United States as an inherently racist nation that had written bondage into its founding documents. In a speech delivered in July 1860, Douglas said, "Every department of our national life—the President's chair, the Senate of the United States, the Supreme Court, and the American pulpit—is occupied and controlled by the dark spirit of American slavery."[21] He opposed Abraham Lincoln's run for Illinois senator on the grounds that Lincoln was not sufficiently antislavery. Douglas also spoke extensively about the impossibility of Black people gaining equality in a land so committed to their oppression.[22]

Douglas defied official US military policy at the time and volunteered himself to serve in the Union Army. He joined up with Company G of the Ninety-Fifth Regiment Illinois Infantry Volunteers on July 26, 1862. Evidently his light skin and overall appearance made his presence acceptable. Historian Robert L. Harris surmised that "because of his light complexion, Douglas was probably not questioned about his race."[23] A newspaper article at the time described him as possessing "a physique so noble and a presence so attractive as to charm and interest the listener at once."[24] In the war to determine the slavery or freedom of Black people, a lighter-skinned Black soldier enjoyed certain advantages over his darker-hued brethren.

Douglas's light skin gave him the opportunity to creatively navigate racial boundaries. He did not attempt to "pass" as white to gain comfort or privilege but to fight for the freedom of Black people. Evidently, soldiers in his own troop knew that he was Black, but they still treated him with courtesy. Their tolerance, however, did not insulate him from the prejudice of others. "Although I am respected by my own regiment and treated kindly by those who know me, still there are those in other regiments . . . who have no regard for my feelings simply because I have the hated blood coursing in my veins."[25] He was even offered a commission as an officer if he would claim that he was white. Douglas refused and instead entered military service as a private.[26] As soon as the Emancipation Proclamation legally allowed Black soldiers to enter the military, he requested a transfer from his majority white unit in Illinois to one of the all-Black regiments in Louisiana or South Carolina. Leaders assigned him to the Tenth Louisiana Regiment of African Descent in June 1863.

Ultimately, Douglas gained permission from Union military leaders to recruit his own regiment, and if he proved successful, they assured him he would be commissioned as an officer. In the period between his service to different units, Douglas channeled his zeal for Black emancipation into the pulpit and became a preacher.[27] After months of recruiting, as well as a serious bout with malaria, Douglas formed his own unit. In February 1865, Douglas was commissioned at the rank of captain in the Independent Battery, US Colored Light Artillery. They joined with the garrison at Fort Leavenworth and were specifically assigned to Fort Sully. But the threat of imminent attack had passed. The soldiers Douglas commanded mostly busied themselves with endless drills and dreary maintenance work.

Despite their lack of action, Douglas's unit is the only all-Black unit in the Union that never had a white commanding officer.[28] Douglas also had the distinction of being part of a small group of less than thirty Black commissioned officers during the Civil War. Records indicate that every other Black commissioned officer had a noncombat role, such as chaplain, quartermaster, or surgeon. This would mean that H. Ford Douglas may have been the only Black combat captain in the Civil War.[29] Unfortunately, Douglas died shortly after his service in 1865 at the age of thirty-four due to complications from the malaria he had contracted earlier.

Douglas rooted his antislavery activity and military service in a deep understanding of the image of God in Black people. He had no patience for those, even Black people, who did not recognize Black dignity and who did not use every means available, including fighting in the Civil War, to throw off the chains of slavery. "He exclaimed that a people who understood their divine origin, yet submitted to bondage, committed a serious crime against God."[30] Douglas also criticized the hypocrisy of white Christians who professed to follow Christ and at the same time supported slavery. It was absurd to him that America, "with her cant of liberty, democracy and Christianity on her lips," could condone the continued enslavement of Black people and still claim to be a free country.[31] For this reason, he advocated Black emigration to other countries where freedom might be a more realistic possibility. Yet when the Civil War started, Douglas did not hesitate to put his life in service to the cause of freedom by fighting for the Union. Douglas's short life evidenced the rare commitment and fervor that forced the nation to reckon with slavery and work toward its end.

THE EMANCIPATION PROCLAMATION

The Emancipation Proclamation was a moral and spiritual document as much as it was a political and military one. The announcement of freedom from the president, limited though it was, acknowledged a self-evident but often-denied reality: Black people were fully human and deserved liberty. For Black Christians, the Proclamation indicated that they embodied the image of God just as much as any person of European descent. It came as a glad tiding that, like the Hebrews delivered from Pharaoh in the book of Exodus, Black Americans would be delivered from the plantation pharaohs and make their way to the promised land of freedom.

Although the Emancipation Proclamation went into effect on January 1, 1863, gestures toward the immediate and complete freedom of enslaved Black people had already begun during the first year of the war. In August of 1861, Major General John C. Frémont, commander of the Department of the West, declared martial law in Missouri and issued a proclamation that said if a slaveholder was in rebellion to the United States, "their slaves, if any they have, are hereby declared free."[32] The order was quickly rescinded by President Abraham Lincoln, and Frémont was soon relieved of duty. In December 1861, Lincoln sent an annual address to Congress in the form of a letter that outlined a controversial plan for gradual emancipation and colonization of Black people to other nations.[33] Then in May 1862, Major General David Hunter, commander of the Department of the South, declared the 900,000 enslaved men, women, and children in his jurisdiction free. Ten days later, Lincoln revoked Hunter's order.[34] A month earlier, in April 1862, one year after the Civil War began, Washington, DC, approved the Compensated Emancipation Act, freeing enslaved people in the district and compensating slaveholders up to $300 per freedperson.[35] Despite the aborted and limited attempts thus far, it was only a matter of time before Lincoln had to take a public and decisive stance on the true issue of the war: slavery or freedom.

By summer 1862, Lincoln was ready to address the most important military and political issue of the Civil War and the Union—emancipation. His sentiments shifted on the matter mainly because of the exigencies of war and the constant pressure coming from Black people both enslaved and free. He composed a draft of the Emancipation Proclamation in July, but his Secretary of State, William Seward, advised the president not to issue it immediately. Given the dismal state of the Union's military exploits at the time, the proclamation would seem like an act of desperation from a failing army and president. But if Lincoln announced the proclamation after a significant military victory, it would seem like a statement from a military that was on the ascendancy. Lincoln took this advice and waited until after the Battle of Antietam in September to make the announcement—hardly a decisive victory, but it would have to do.

In September 1862, Lincoln issued the Preliminary Emancipation Proclamation, which indicated that the full proclamation would go into effect on January 1, 1863, if Confederate forces had not yet surrendered. The proclamation did not "free the slaves." It only applied to enslaved people in Confederate territory that had not been taken over by the Union. It left slavery in the border states untouched. It would take the Thirteenth Amendment to legally abolish slavery nationwide. Nevertheless, the Emancipation Proclamation officially expanded the war from simply restoring the Union to eliminating slavery in the process. It also allowed Black people to formally enlist as Union soldiers. After the announcement, Lincoln made this statement: "I can only trust in God I have made no mistake. . . . It is now for the country and the world to pass judgment on it."[36] Lincoln understood the gravity of the proclamation both for the war effort and for the nation. As he considered his decision and its import, he looked to God for guidance and an eternal perspective on a temporal matter.

For Black Christians, the time between the announcement of the Emancipation Proclamation in 1862 and when it went into effect in January 1863 was one of hope and anxiety. Would Lincoln follow through? Would there be a last-minute compromise? Would Black people finally be free? On December 31, 1862, New Year's Eve, thousands of Black people gathered in churches and other locations for a "Watch Night" service. They counted down the hours until the Emancipation Proclamation would officially go into effect. They prayed, sang, and read Bible stories about the exodus and God's judgment on the oppressor. In Boston, Frederick Douglass gathered with a massive crowd at Tremont Temple, as David Blight relates in his biography of the abolitionist: "Every moment of waiting chilled our hopes. . . . Eight, nine, ten o'clock came and went, and still no word."[37]

Reading the Emancipation Proclamation

At last a man elbowed his way through the crowd and said that word had come over the telegraph. Black people were free. Jubilee.

The elation was unparalleled. Black people "got into such a state of enthusiasm that almost everything seemed to be witty and appropriate to the occasion."[38] In the early morning of January 1, 1863, an aged preacher named Rue led Black people in his church in singing "Blow Ye the Trumpet, Blow" with lyrics that intoned, "Sound the loud timbrel o'er Egypt's dark sea, Jehovah hath triumphed. His people are free."[39] Ever since that night more than 160 years ago, Black people have gathered in houses of worship to celebrate Watch Night or Freedom's Eve. They have placed legalized emancipation in the context of a divine struggle between God's kingdom and the kingdoms of this world, understanding the struggle for liberation as a cosmic conflict that would in time allow them to emerge from slavery to freedom. Through tireless agitation, decades of abolitionist organizing, and an enduring hope in God's divine judgment, Black people had participated in bringing about their own freedom. This generation had finally seen the spiritual moaning of millions fulfilled.

HARRIET TUBMAN, CIVIL WAR HERO

Upon her death in 1913, Harriet Tubman, known as "the Moses of her people," was given a full military burial. How could a woman self-liberated from slavery, who went back time and again to free others, earn this honorable send-off from a government that had condoned her enslavement and at one time considered her a fugitive from the law? Tubman's military service and renowned bravery during the Civil War cemented her legacy as both a hero and a patriot.

Harriet Tubman

Born as Araminta Ross around 1821 to enslaved parents, she grew up and married a man named John Tubman and took her mother's first name, Harriet.[40] According to Tubman, she sustained a permanent head injury as a young woman when she refused her slaveholder's order to tie up another enslaved person for whipping. The slaveholder threw a heavy item—perhaps a rock or piece of metal—at the other enslaved person. The object hit Tubman instead and fractured her skull. Since that time she would often spontaneously fall into a deep, coma-like sleep for brief periods. She credited these instances as moments of divine clarity in which she saw visions from the Lord about dangers to avoid and missions God had for her.[41]

In 1849, Tubman decided she would be free. She self-liberated by escaping from her plantation at night and making her way to the North. Such a venture was perilous for anyone, but it was especially difficult for Black women who also had parents and children to take care of on top of their duties on the plantation. Tubman left her husband, who did not want to endure the danger, and the rest of her family behind. But as soon as she had made it to freedom, she resolved that if she was free, the rest of her family ought to be free as well. Over the course of the next decade, Tubman made thirteen round trips from North to South and back again. She always gathered a group to come with her, and historians estimate she guided over seventy enslaved people to freedom. Her daring trips earned her the nickname "the Moses of her people."

Tubman viewed her mission in spiritual terms. She certainly had the book of Exodus and the story of the Hebrews escaping from slavery under Pharaoh's rule in mind. On her many treacherous voyages she believed she was "always conscious of an invisible pillar of cloud by day, and of fire by night, under the guidance of which she journeyed or rested."[42] Tubman likely displayed such boldness in her emancipation efforts because she believed she was divinely guided and protected.

While Tubman is rightly remembered as a "conductor" on the Underground Railroad, her tenure with the Union Army is no less worthy of renown. Tubman had already attained something of mythical status for her efforts by the time the Civil War had begun. In 1862, the governor of Massachusetts, John Andrew, arranged for Tubman to travel to South Carolina and help the Union military efforts there. After a brief detour in New York, Tubman became one of the first northern Black people to assist the war effort in the South. She lent her talents to the Port Royal Experiment—a government-sponsored program to support newly freed Black people and demonstrate their ability to thrive in freedom.

Tubman helped out wherever she could, exhibiting an entrepreneurial spirit as she addressed the endless needs of a people recently held in bondage. She initially worked at the Christian Commission, a house providing food, clothing, and other necessities to soldiers stationed in Beaufort. She also started a wash house where she trained women to wash clothes, bake, and provide other services so that they could support themselves with wages. She worked as a nurse too, tending to soldiers and freed people afflicted by the numerous diseases that characterized camp life during the war. Tubman also helped recruit Black soldiers, which took up more of her time and was far more effective after the Emancipation Proclamation went into effect.[43]

According to biographer Kate Clifford Larson, Tubman wanted to be closer to the front lines to aid more directly in the army's efforts. With her knowledge of slavery and her status as a Black woman, she was able to gain information from freed Black people about the terrain and the position of the Confederate forces in the area. She also utilized her extensive navigation abilities, honed through many clandestine trips on the Underground Railroad, to serve as a scout for the Union. On July 2, 1863, Tubman achieved yet another historic feat, becoming the first woman to plan and lead an armed mission during the Civil War.[44]

Under cover of night Tubman guided 300 Union soldiers aboard steamships on the Combahee River. They went ashore and ferreted out Confederate soldiers before the Union Army commenced flooding fields, burning plantations, and grabbing any supplies they could carry. During the early morning hours, the soldiers blew whistles to signal to Black people in the area that they could join up with Union forces and gain their freedom. At first tentatively, then in a rush, enslaved Black people descended on the river and the waiting Union steamships. So many people arrived in such a frantic state that the boats threatened to capsize due to overcrowding. Desperate for order, a white Union leader looked to Tubman for help. After standing silently for several minutes, Tubman began singing. The tune caught on and soon the escaping Black people joined in. The effect was calming and the evacuation continued in a swift and orderly manner. By the expedition's end more than 700 Black people had been liberated from slavery. Tubman was able to free more Black people in one night than she did in over a decade of trips to the South. Her heroism and shrewdness during the war were simply an extension of her life's mission of liberation.[45]

Perhaps more than any other single person of this era, Harriet Tubman embodied the spirit of justice. She defied convention, law, and social expectations to become the Moses of her people, and her courageous adventures cannot be understood apart from her religious beliefs. "Tubman's spiritual transformation story is inextricably woven with a story of external liberation."[46] She did not wait for liberation in the hereafter but sought freedom in the here and now. With her abiding faith in God and her selfless dedication to Black freedom, Tubman mined spiritual resources to relieve physical oppression.

ELIZABETH KECKLEY THREADS HER WAY TO FREEDOM

Harriet Tubman and Elizabeth Keckley could hardly have been more different. Although they were both Black women, Tubman stood at five feet tall, had dark skin, and never obtained a formal education. Elizabeth Keckley was light skinned and literate and regularly hobnobbed with the elite of society, both white and Black. Her work mostly entailed the duties of a domestic servant in the household of white slaveholders. Because of her responsibilities, she learned to sew and soon found that she excelled at it. Through her highly skilled and stylish work, she elevated herself to the position of dressmaker for Mary Todd Lincoln and service in the Lincoln White House. While she navigated a complex racial and social location, Keckley also used her position of relative privilege to strive for the uplift of Black people.

There is a common myth that enslaved people who worked in a house had an easier life than those who worked in the field. While enslaved people who worked in a household did not have to do the same kind of manual labor or face the elements of the outdoors like field workers, they faced hazards of a different sort. We should not minimize their labor, which was still very difficult. Washing clothes, cooking multiple meals a day, bringing in firewood, emptying trash, and providing childcare entailed a constant stream of physically demanding tasks. In addition, all of this work was done under the watchful eye of the slaveholder and his family. Unlike those working in the fields, household workers could not escape the slaveholder's gaze.

Elizabeth Keckley
Virginia Museum of History & Culture / Alamy Stock Photo

Every mistake was in plain sight. Women also had to deal with the jealousy and demands of the plantation mistress, many of whom were resentful of an enslaved woman's presence in the household—especially because enslaved women in the house were often raped and had the slaveholder's children, stoking jealousy and anger among the white women of the household.[47] Elizabeth Keckley did not work the fields like the majority of enslaved people, but she nevertheless grew up in a perilous situation.

Much of what we know today about Elizabeth Keckley comes from her autobiography. She was born into slavery in 1818 in Dinwiddie, Virginia. For her entire life, she believed her father was an enslaved Black man with whom her mother had a relationship. Then, one day as she neared death, her mother told her the truth. Elizabeth's father was their slaveholder, a white man named Armistead Burwell.[48] When Elizabeth was a teenager, her father sent her to work for his son, Keckley's half brother by the name of Robert Burwell, in North Carolina. Despite their familial relationship, Robert treated

Keckley harshly. At his wife's insistence, Burwell let another man, Mr. Bingham, severely flog Keckley for imagined infractions. She received a severe whipping with a rawhide strap, but as she recalls, "I did not scream; I was too proud to let my tormentor know what I was suffering."[49] This happened two more times, but each time Keckley resisted. Eventually, she wore him down. "As I stood bleeding before him, nearly exhausted with his efforts, he burst into tears, and declared that it would be a sin to beat me anymore."[50] Her half brother also attempted to beat her into submission, but Keckley again resisted. When it was clear that Keckley would not submit to torture, he finally told her, "with an air of penitence, that he should never strike me another blow; and faithfully he kept his word."[51] Keckley noted in her writings that her half brother Robert Burwell was a Presbyterian minister who had moved to North Carolina to take charge of his first congregation. Mr. Bingham, the man who had first beaten her, was a parishioner at the church.

Keckley's sufferings did not end after leaving her half brother's household. He sent her to another man who was even less scrupulous, and for the four years that Keckley labored in his household, the man repeatedly raped her. "I was regarded as fair for one of my race. . . . I do not care to dwell upon this subject, for it is one that is fraught with pain. Suffice it to say, that he persecuted me for four years, and I—I—became a mother."[52] Her only son, George, would later die during the Battle of Wilson's Creek in 1861 after joining the Union Army and passing as white.

Today, Keckley is best known as the dressmaker for Mary Todd Lincoln. She was able to save enough money to buy her freedom in 1855 and made her way to Washington, DC. Her dressmaking business prospered, and soon she was making garments for the social elites of the district. For a time, her best customer was Varina Davis, the wife of Jefferson Davis, who would later become the president of the Confederacy. She also sewed for Mary Custis Lee, wife of Robert E. Lee, before he joined the Confederacy and became its most celebrated general. A customer also introduced Keckley to Mary Todd Lincoln, and the two began a long and intimate relationship.

But Keckley's interests extended far beyond sewing fabric and making dresses. Having been enslaved, she saw the Civil War and her connections in the Union's capital as assets she could leverage to help her people. "As a 'colored woman' close to power, she used her position not only to advance herself, but to influence the Lincolns' attitudes toward the recently freed slaves."[53] As a free Black person and an entrepreneur with a successful business, Keckley was well-connected among Washington's Black middle and upper class. As a Christian woman, she also immersed herself in the life of the church.

One warm August evening, she and her friend were taking a stroll when she heard music. Following the sound, she found it was coming from a party to benefit hospitals. She thought to herself, "If the white people can give festivals to raise funds for the relief of suffering soldiers, why should not the well-to-do colored people get to work to do something for the benefit of the suffering blacks?"[54] The next Sunday at her church, Union Bethel, she made a suggestion to the congregation that they form a relief society. Within a couple of weeks, she was president of the Contraband Relief Association overseeing forty volunteers. Keckley used her considerable connections, which included Frederick Douglass and Henry Highland Garnet, as well as her association with the Lincoln household, to raise money for the relief of recently freed Black people. After the Emancipation Proclamation permitted Black people to join the army, the association changed its name to the Ladies' Freedmen and Soldiers' Relief Association.

The Black church proved essential to creating the infrastructure necessary to serve the burgeoning population of free Black people throughout the Civil War. Had it not been for the centralization of people and resources that the Black church provided, many more recently freed Black people would have suffered the privations of poverty. Women like Elizabeth Keckley, who had secured their own freedom and economic stability through years of hard labor, regarded it as their duty to assist others of their race. Keckley skillfully navigated Black and white social circles to raise funds and other forms of support for the Ladies' Freedmen and Soldiers' Relief Association. In creating this organization she responded to an acute need, effectively marshaling the resources of her social standing and reputation as a highly accomplished entrepreneur.

BLACK MINISTERS DEMAND LAND

While many today may have heard of Special Field Order No. 15, better known as "forty acres and a mule," few know that Black ministers played a critical role in its creation. Toward the end of the war, the thousands of newly freed Black people needed support of all kinds. Along the Atlantic coast, military leaders had to attend not only to the battlefront but to the droves of recently emancipated Black people, who now sought refuge and provision within the Union. Given the demands of the moment, as well as the desire to weaken Confederate forces, unprecedented measures were employed.

General William T. Sherman was not a radical abolitionist. While he tolerated the presence of Black people in the midst of his army, he relegated them to menial roles. In his memoirs, Sherman wrote, "In our army we had no negro soldiers, and, as a rule, we preferred white soldiers, but that we employed a large force of them as servants, teamsters, and pioneers, who had rendered admirable service."[55] Though he was not an abolitionist, he was a practical soldier, and he sought solutions to problems brought on by the war over slavery.

In January 1865, Secretary of War Edwin M. Stanton visited General Sherman at his camp in Georgia. As Sherman related in his memoirs, "He talked to me a great deal about the negroes, the former slaves."[56] In particular, Stanton inquired about an event that had transpired at Ebenezer Creek in Georgia a few weeks earlier in December 1864. According to reports, Union General Jefferson C. Davis (no relation to the president of the Confederacy) was leading his troops across the creek. They were followed by hundreds of Black refugees seeking escape from slavery and safety with the Union Army. They were also pursued by a small contingent of Confederate soldiers, who harassed them with shelling and skirmishes. On the night in question, Davis's troops built a pontoon bridge for the soldiers to cross the creek. Davis, in a hurry to catch up to other Union battalions ahead of them, ordered his men to cut the ropes and chop up the wood of the pontoon bridge as soon as his troops had finished crossing. The Black people, who had been left behind, realized they would soon be overtaken by the Confederates and left without any way to cross the river. In a desperate attempt to save themselves, "some plunged screaming into the creek and were reported as having drowned." Others may have been killed by the Confederate forces coming up behind them. The remaining Black refugees were captured and returned to their original slaveholders. Davis had abandoned them to face the consequences of their escape attempt on their own.

In the eyes of many, Davis had committed an unpardonable sin. A private wrote in his diary, "Where can one find in all the annals of plantation cruelty anything more inhuman and fiendish as this?" A chaplain named John J. Hight described Davis as a tyrant "without one spark of humanity in his makeup." Another commentator wished that Davis would be immediately hanged for his crime. When Black people heard of what happened to their kinsmen at Ebenezer Creek, they raised an uproar. The incident made it into the newspapers, and it was largely in response to the Ebenezer Creek debacle that Stanton spoke to Sherman and "inquired particularly about Jeff C. Davis," wanting to know more about the plans for Black refugees among the Union ranks.[57]

In addition to inspecting the general operations of the military there, "Mr. Stanton seemed desirous of coming into contact with the negroes to confer with them, and he asked me to arrange an interview for him."[58] In response, Sherman "sent out and invited the most intelligent of the negroes, mostly Baptist and Methodist preachers."[59] The vast majority of Black people at that time did not have a formal education. Black communities looked to their male clergy not only as the most knowledgeable community members but as leaders in ecclesiastical, economic, and political matters. Thus, it made sense that Sherman would send for Black ministers to represent the concerns of the people when meeting with high-level military officials.

Twenty Black ministers assembled on the evening of January 12, 1865. According to a recap of the meeting in a contemporary newspaper, they ranged in age from twenty-six to seventy-two years old. Some led congregations of more than 1,000 Black people. Many of them had been born into slavery and either had been emancipated by their slaveholders, had bought their freedom, or had become free men when the Union took over Confederate territory.[60] The assembly selected sixty-seven-year-old minister Garrison Frazier as their spokesperson. On behalf of the group, Frazier provided answers to a series of questions asked by the military commanders. Most of the questions related to the potential enactment of Special Field Order No. 15 and concerned how Black refugees might best provide for themselves. Frazier responded, "The way we can best take care of ourselves is to have land and turn it and till it by our own labor . . . and we can soon maintain ourselves and have something to spare."[61] The Black ministers made it clear they did not want to live on government-sponsored support forever. They were eager to make their own way in the world and take care of themselves. Even though Black people had a legitimate claim to reparations in recompense for generations of unremunerated labor, they were willing to work the land "until we are able to buy it and make it our own."[62]

Frazier and the ministers also addressed another question about their feelings regarding integration with white people. A contemporary newspaper recounted the question: "State in what manner you would rather live—whether scattered among the whites or in colonies by yourselves." In response Frazier told Stanton and Sherman, "I would prefer to live by ourselves, for there is a prejudice against us in the South that will take years to get over."[63] All but one of the other nineteen ministers agreed, with a single dissent from a free-born Black person from Maryland, the youngest member of the group. He believed white and Black people should live together.

Four days after meeting with the Black ministers, Sherman, with Stanton's approval, issued Special Field Order No. 15, which stipulated that "each family shall have a plot of not more than forty acres of tillable ground." Sherman later permitted the lending of mules to the farmers as well. The order also honored the will of the ministers to form their farms and communities separate from white people. It stated that "no white person whatever, unless military officers and soldiers detailed for duty, will be permitted to reside; and the sole and exclusive management of affairs will be left to the freed people themselves." Within months, 40,000 Black people had taken up residence on farmland formerly run by slaveholders and had begun cultivating crops.

The Black families that had claimed their forty acres did not even have time to complete a full harvest cycle. Months later, after the surrender of General Robert E. Lee and the assassination of Abraham Lincoln, Andrew Johnson became president of the United States. In the fall of 1865, Johnson overturned Special Field Order No. 15, and much of the land given to the Black community reverted to the white men who had previously been slaveholders.[64] This novel wartime measure to put recently freed Black people in a position to provide for themselves and build generational wealth was over almost as soon as it had begun. Had it not been for Black ministers demanding land and autonomy, however, it might never have happened at all.

CONCLUSION

When Robert E. Lee surrendered his Army of Northern Virginia in April 1965 to Union general Ulysses S. Grant, the Civil War all but ended. Skirmishes continued for several more months, but the rebel yell had diminished to a whimper. The war had morphed from an endeavor to restore the Union to one that would determine the fate of slavery in the nation. Black people always knew the Civil War was about slavery. They used the conflict as their opportunity to self-liberate and take up arms against their own dehumanization. When the last battle cries had faded, Black people finally awakened to a world where race-based chattel slavery had been defeated. Black Christians viewed the war as a battle against Pharaoh himself. They escaped, enlisted, rallied, and prayed in support of the Union. One minister remarked, "If the prayers that have gone up for the Union army could be read out, you would not get through them these two weeks."[65] Yet even after their literal fight for freedom, Black people would still face many more challenges, some as violent as the Civil War itself.

CHAPTER
SIX

BUILDING BLACK INSTITUTIONS

In the decades immediately following emancipation, Black people engaged in their most vigorous community-building efforts to date. Prior to the Civil War and the end of legalized slavery, Black people simply had not had the opportunity to undertake widespread initiatives in the pursuit of life, liberty, and happiness. Now that freedom had come, Black people eagerly took advantage of their liberty to build new worlds of which they had only been able to dream in the past. They built primary schools, colleges, hospitals, and, critically, churches to advance their people. William J. Simmons, whom we will meet later in this chapter, put it this way: "Untrammeled, we have, out of our ignorance and penury, built thousands of churches, started thousands of schools, educated millions of children, supported thousands of ministers of the Gospel, organized societies for the care of the sick and the burying of the dead."[1]

What is historically significant about the strivings of Black people in the decades following the Civil War and emancipation is their freedom and ability to start Black institutions. From new churches to historically Black colleges and universities (HBCUs) and Black-owned businesses, millions of people finally had the opportunity to channel their entrepreneurial energy into new ventures never before available to them under the system of race-based chattel slavery.

Although Black people met resistance in the form of white supremacy, and the gains of the Reconstruction era quickly eroded under new forms of oppression such as the racial terrorism of lynching, Black people modeled to themselves and the world that they were ready for freedom. In all of these efforts, Black churches and Christians provided several key contributions.

FINALLY FREE

Slavery—the central economic, political, and social issue of the Civil War and all of US society up to that point—was finally resolved on December 6, 1865. That is the day when the required three-fourths of states ratified the Thirteenth Amendment, which legally abolished slavery. This constitutional amendment, not the Emancipation Proclamation, legally dismantled race-based chattel slavery. The Thirteenth Amendment states, "Neither slavery nor involuntary servitude, except as a punishment for crime whereof the party shall have been duly convicted, shall exist within the United States, or any place subject to their jurisdiction."[2] It was the first of three amendments passed after the Civil War that are collectively called the Reconstruction Amendments.

Reconstruction was the multifaceted endeavor to rebuild the nation after the Civil War. First, Reconstruction entailed the literal reconstruction of buildings and towns, especially in the South. Most of the major battles of the Civil War took place below the Mason-Dixon Line, and the devastation was extensive. Entire towns had been decimated. Roads, railways, farms, houses, government buildings and more all had to be rebuilt. Another aspect of Reconstruction involved reunifying the nation both socially and politically. A pressing question after Union victory in the Civil War was, "What should be done with the Confederates?" How do you deal with the defeated people who broke off from the rest of the country to defend slavery? How do you create a *United* States of America after this catastrophic attempt at disunion? Yet another aspect of Reconstruction concerned the nearly four million Black freed people who now sought their full incorporation into the nation's citizenship.

The House joint resolution proposing the Thirteenth Amendment to the Constitution, January 31, 1865.

Reconstruction immediately faced opposition from the highest elected official in the land. Andrew Johnson took over as president after the assassination of Abraham Lincoln at Ford's Theatre in Washington, DC, on April 14, 1865. Johnson was an avowed racist who had no desire to promote Black equality during his administration. Arrayed against him were the so-called "Radical Republicans." This group of US representatives and senators advocated for equal protection of the law for all people and were deemed "radical" because they believed a thorough restructuring of the political landscape was required to ensure Black civil rights. Led by white men such as Congressman Thaddeus Stevens of Pennsylvania and Senator Charles Sumner of Massachusetts, the Radical Republicans pushed for progressive laws and policies that would ensure the full equality of Black people.

Legislation at the federal level marked a dramatic shift in the way that the US government treated Black people. Congress established the Bureau of Refugees, Freedmen, and Abandoned Lands on March 3, 1865. Commonly called the Freedmen's Bureau, it was charged with providing relief to the formerly enslaved and establishing the systems and infrastructure for Black people to succeed in their new status as free people. In January 1866, a month after the Thirteenth Amendment went into effect, Senator Lyman Trumbull introduced the first civil rights legislation in the form of the Civil Rights Act of 1866. It was designed to help enforce the Thirteenth Amendment by defining citizenship and equal protection of laws.[3] The act served as a precursor to the Fourteenth Amendment, ratified on July 9, 1868, which defined "birthright citizenship" by stating that citizens were "all persons born or naturalized in the United States."[4] The Fourteenth Amendment also ensured the right to due process. The Fifteenth Amendment, ratified on February 3, 1870, guaranteed Black male suffrage. At long last, the most sought-after marker of Black civil rights, the right to vote, had been secured by law for Black men. The Reconstruction amendments and other legislation had gone further than the US government ever had to include Black people as full members of society.

The long history of injustice in this country demonstrates that racism never goes away—it just adapts. From the earliest attempts at Reconstruction, white supremacists engaged in whitelash to counter Reconstruction and reestablish white rule. The Ku Klux Klan first organized in Tennessee in 1865. They donned white robes and hoods to keep their identities hidden and were often called "nightriders" because they conducted their racial terrorist programs under cover of darkness. The Klan and similar groups "aimed to destroy the Republican party's infrastructure, undermine the Reconstruction state, reestablish control of the black labor force, and restore racial subordination in every aspect of southern life."[5] In this era, known as "Redemption," lynching emerged as a tool of racial terrorism. Thousands of Black people fell victim to the bodily mutilations, hangings, and burnings that were expressions of white rage. Southern states passed "Black Codes," policies that curtailed Black freedom and caught many Black people up in the system of incarceration. With the *Plessy v. Ferguson* Supreme Court Ruling in 1896, the doctrine of "separate but equal" came to define the Jim Crow era. But Black people and their allies tapped into the spirit of justice to do something that had been nearly impossible under slavery—build Black institutions.

ELIAS CAMP MORRIS AND THE FOUNDING OF THE NATIONAL BAPTIST CONVENTION

After the Civil War, Black people rushed to build churches, form congregations, and organize denominations. Under slavery, many Black Christians had endured second-class citizenship in the household of God. They were relegated to sitting at the back or in the balcony of churches (usually the hottest and most uncomfortable section). They were often barred from preaching to white or mixed-race audiences. They were forced to have white preachers, who emphasized obedience to masters instead of liberation. And Black Christians were barred from holding their own worship gatherings for fear that such groups might lead to slave rebellions. After slavery, however, Black people used their newfound freedom to live fully as beings made in the image of God. They did this by forming new networks of Black Christians that eventually coalesced into Black denominations.

Elias Camp Morris was born enslaved in Georgia in 1855. In contrast to many other Black people at the time, he attained a college education at Nashville Normal and Theological Institute (now Roger Williams University). Morris felt the call to ministry early in his life and was licensed to preach as a Baptist minister at the age of nineteen while working as a shoemaker. Like many other Black people in the last quarter of the nineteenth century, Morris headed west for greater opportunity.[6] His original destination was Kansas, but he stopped before he arrived in a small town called Helena, Arkansas, in the Delta region of the state.[7] In his memoirs, Samuel Clemens (Mark Twain) wrote that Helena "occupies one of the prettiest situations on the Mississippi."[8] Morris may have agreed, because he settled down in Helena and spent the rest of his life there.

Elias Camp Morris
Heritage Image Partnership Ltd / Alamy Stock Photo

Morris's education, speaking abilities, and organizational skills quickly propelled him to leadership in Helena, and in 1879, the congregation of Centennial Baptist Church ordained him as their pastor. The church itself was a feat of ingenuity, the product of a disadvantaged people, and a sign of the centrality of the Black church in the Black community. The church building began as a small structure, but Morris led a building campaign to construct a new and remarkable edifice. The permanent church for Centennial Baptist was designed by a Black man named Henry James Price in the Gothic Revival style, and it opened in 1905. The redbrick building with two towers, stunning stained-glass windows, and gracefully curved wooden beams inside seated 1,000 people. It boasted a full pipe organ and served as a primary meeting and organizing site for the Black community in Helena for over a century.[9]

Centennial Baptist Church, so named because the congregation started near the dawn of a new century, had just twenty-three members when Morris became pastor. Under Morris's tenure the congregation grew to more than 1,000 members. Morris gained standing with the state Baptist convention in Arkansas, and his fellow ministers elected him first as secretary of the convention in 1880 and then as president in 1882.

Centennial Baptist Church
Arkansas Historic Preservation Program

These positions helped raise Morris's status as a leader far beyond Helena. One of Morris's first statewide initiatives was to create the *Baptist Vanguard*, a periodical and Sunday school curriculum designed to free Black Baptists from dependence on the white-led Baptist publication they had been using. Morris also helped found the Arkansas Baptist College in Little Rock for the Christian education of Black people in the state, started a chapter of the Negro Business League in Helena, and was a prominent presence in the state Republican party (the party of Lincoln and emancipation at the time).[10] He even served as a delegate to the Republican National Convention on several occasions and cultivated positive relationships with white leaders. He served on several boards and committees of predominantly white Baptist institutions.[11]

The National Baptist Convention had been founded in 1890, but it was one of several networks and associations of Black Baptists. These networks were typically scattered, disorganized, and underresourced and had overlapping or redundant functions. The need for consolidation became pronounced, but the question of who would lead a newly unified denomination was complex. They needed someone with clear leadership and administrative skills, a person who had visionary dreams and a rootedness in the Black community, and someone who could navigate the treacherous white power structure with savvy and a delicate touch. Elias C. Morris emerged as the preferred leader. He was elected president of the NBC in 1895. He held that position for more than a quarter of a century until his death in 1922.

Morris's sense of justice was severely tested in the late summer of 1919, today remembered as Red Summer. On September 30, 1919, Black sharecroppers in Phillips County, Arkansas, near the town of Elaine, gathered in a clapboard church to strategize about negotiating fair prices for the cotton they picked. The people assembled were part of the Progressive Farmers and Household Union. Long exploited for their labor, they were finally organizing to gain the just due for their efforts. This group of Black farmers knew such meetings would be under scrutiny by the white establishment, so they set armed guards outside to keep watch.

As is often the case in these circumstances, the precise sequence of events that night is lost to history. What we do know is that a group of white men showed up. A shootout ensued. One of the white men was wounded. Another was killed. Word of the incident quickly spread throughout the white community. Early the next day, the news hit the wire: "Negro insurrection!" Over the next two days, hundreds of white people from Arkansas, Tennessee, and Mississippi formed posses and sought to suppress the supposed uprising. They indiscriminately hunted down and targeted almost any Black person they could find. The riot of white violence was quelled only when the governor of Arkansas received permission to deploy 500 US troops from Camp Pike. Reports indicate that even some of the soldiers engaged in the indiscriminate killing of the Black people they had been deployed to protect. Although the total number of people killed may never be precisely known, estimates range up to nearly 200 people murdered among the rural Black population of Elaine.[12]

White leaders in the county then coordinated the arrest of hundreds of Black people on spurious charges. In the court cases that ensued, none of the juries spent more than eight minutes deliberating. They ended up convicting twelve men, later known as the Elaine Twelve, and sentenced them to death. In her reporting on the massacre and the subsequent mockery of justice in the courts, investigative journalist Ida B. Wells wrote, "The bare statement of these facts is so shocking to the sense of justice that it almost defies belief."[13] Over a series of years-long trials, all the men survived and were eventually released, but not until after many of them had served several years in prison on false charges.

Amid national scrutiny concerning the Elaine massacre and with a country still reeling from Red Summer, Arkansas governor Charles Brough assembled an interracial committee to advise him on how to proceed. One of the members of that committee was Elias Camp Morris. Since he pastored the largest Black church in the county and led the National Baptist Convention, his participation would send a strong message that the Black community was well-represented on this committee. Initially, Morris accepted the version of events promoted by white elites, that a group of radical Black famers had been plotting to overthrow plantation owners and take over the area. However, Morris soon heard firsthand accounts of what had happened, and he changed his mind. Ultimately, he sided with the Black community and the poor tenant farmers in calling for justice.[14]

The events of that summer and his long years of ministry may have taken their toll on his health. After the Elaine race riot, hundreds of residents fled the area.[15] Race relations remained tense as propaganda about the riots persisted and tenant farmers continued to experience economic exploitation from plantation owners. While still at the helm of Centennial and the NBC, Morris died after an extended illness in 1922. His legacy stands as one of the clearest examples of how a member of the Black clergy employed a holistic spirit of justice. Morris employed his prodigious skills to uplift his people across a spectrum of fields—from business to education to the church and organizational leadership. While he contended with white supremacy in the form of Jim Crow externally, he also helped build Black-centered institutions that could speak to the needs of the people.

THE INTERRACIAL ORIGINS OF THE PENTECOSTAL MOVEMENT

While every Black church was concerned with broader justice issues in its community, some Black Christian traditions became well-known in the early twentieth century for breaking down racial barriers within their congregations. The Pentecostal movement, with roots in the

Wesleyan holiness tradition, emerged as a powerful, if brief, example of interracial worship among Christians at a time when strict racial separation was the norm.

The birth of the modern Pentecostal movement can be traced to 1906 in Los Angeles where a Black minister named William Joseph Seymour led a revival that focused on the baptism of the Holy Spirit, especially speaking in tongues. When Seymour first moved to Los Angeles at the invitation of a church, some of the congregation rejected his teachings on the "baptism of the Spirit" and speaking in tongues. But Seymour fasted and prayed for a month and then began preaching at the home of Richard Asberry on Bonnie Brae Street. The crowds who came to hear him soon overwhelmed the small home, so they moved the services to an abandoned African Methodist Episcopal Church on Azusa Street.[16] For three years from 1906 to 1909, Seymour and his team led thousands of visitors and worshipers in services three times a day, seven days a week. Some came to gawk at the spectacle. Others came as pilgrims to experience a new moment in church history and a true move of the Spirit in action. The services had no order of worship since the Spirit was leading. At any moment, a person could begin speaking in tongues or start shouting or dancing in ecstasy. Hundreds of people packed into the small forty-by-sixty-feet edifice, fervently praying for the gifts of the Spirit.[17]

Los Angeles proved to be a perfect setting for a multiracial revival. "The city's vibrant social and political environment was comprised of not just black-white interactions, but a range of multiethnic relations involving Anglo and African Americans, Native and Mexican Americans, and European and Asian immigrants."[18] Reports at the time indicated that people of many races and ethnicities gathered to witness or experience the revival. At certain points, white people even outnumbered Black participants. Not only was the gathering racially diverse, but it attracted people across the strata of society, especially poor and working-class people. A journalist at the time wrote, "The color line was washed away in the blood."[19]

The Azusa Street Revival may not have happened if not for the interracial collaboration between two of the men credited with founding Pentecostalism—William J. Seymour and his mentor, Charles Parham, who was white. Seymour knew he had a divine calling early in life and aggressively pursued both a knowledge of God and experiences of God.

William J. Seymour

He moved to Houston in 1903 and encountered a Black woman named Lucy Farrow, the pastor of a small church and a governess for the Parham family. Farrow told Seymour about Parham's school and encouraged him to attend. Seymour, eager to learn about Pentecostalism, decided to go to the school even though racial segregation meant he had to sit at a desk in the hallway while his white classmates received lessons inside the classroom. "Early in their relationship, [Parham] was nothing but kind to Seymour."[20] When Seymour received the invitation to minister in Los Angeles, the journey that would spark the revival, Parham raised money to pay his train fare west. Largely due to Parham's teachings, Seymour developed his theological outlook on the gifts of the Spirit.

Parham, however, did not support Seymour after learning of what was happening at the revival. He visited Los Angeles in October 1906 and came away with scathing words about the burgeoning movement. Parham had already incorporated several idiosyncratic and racist ideas into his theology, believing that God had created dominant and subordinate races of people and that intermarriage between the groups caused the flood of Genesis 4 and all sorts of diseases and plagues throughout history.[21] He frequently referred to Black people as "darkies" and exhibited support of the Ku Klux Klan, and the publication he edited, *Apostolic Faith*, often published overtly racist articles.[22] So, while jealousy at the success of Seymour's revival was likely a factor, Parham needed little excuse to revile his former pupil. From the moment of his visit and throughout the rest of his life, Parham denigrated the Azusa Street Revival with racist tropes. He called the revival "a cross between the old fashioned Negro worship of the South and Holy-Rollerism."[23] Parham also dismissed evidences of the Holy Spirit at Azusa as "spiritualistic and hypnotic forces with a lot of the old fashioned Negro performance which were dubbed Pentecostal manifestations."[24]

Seymour and other Pentecostals, however, continued to espouse the principles of interracial unity in their teachings. In "Doctrines and Disciplines of the Azusa Street Mission of Los Angeles, California," Seymour wrote, "We want all of our white brethren and white sisters to feel free in our churches and missions."[25] He viewed this movement toward inclusivity as an outworking of the Bible's teachings and the theology he was developing. "Jesus Christ takes in all people in his salvation. Christ is all and for all. He is neither black nor white man, nor Chinaman, nor Hind[u], nor Japanese, but God. God is a Spirit, because without his spirit we cannot be saved. St. John 3:3–5; Rom 8:9."[26]

Other Pentecostals followed Seymour's example. Elizabeth J. Dabney, a Pentecostal evangelist and revivalist, said she had received a commission from the Lord to share the gospel and assurance from God that all people would give her a hearing. When she conducted revivals, "all nations met me. . . . There was no discrimination, no denomination, no class, color nor creed."[27] Although the Pentecostal denominations that formed after Azusa endured split after split along racial lines, a few valiantly attempted to maintain the interracial character of the 1906 revival. The Pentecostal Assemblies of the World, for example, intentionally maintained a biracial leadership structure that often recognized a presiding bishop of one race and an assistant presiding bishop of another race.[28]

Herbert Daughtry, a Pentecostal pastor and activist, reflected on the revival and said that participants experienced dramatic personal changes, "but perhaps the greatest miracle was that color and class lines were broken down. Everybody was the same. There was a democratization of the gifts."[29] The example of the Azusa Street Revival and the early Pentecostal movement demonstrates that a focus on the Holy Spirit creates space for interracial interaction. By focusing on the shared experience of an encounter with God, Pentecostals briefly experienced the reality of Galatians 3:28: "There is neither Jew nor Gentile, neither slave nor free, nor is there male and female, for you are all one in Christ Jesus." While the diversity and harmony of Pentecostalism did not persist in its denominational forms, this past spirit of inclusivity serves as a historical touchpoint for the possibility of future racial unity.

THE BLACK CATHOLIC
STRUGGLE FOR EQUALITY

While most other Black Christian groups had to create new institutions in the late eighteenth and early nineteenth centuries, Black Catholics already had a millennium-long infrastructure spanning the globe. Despite the international character of the Roman Catholic Church, many white Catholic leaders in the United States succumbed to the same white-supremacist ideas held by white Protestants. White Catholics owned and sold slaves, relied on slave labor, barred Black people from ordination to the priesthood and other leadership roles and, in the days following emancipation, segregated the Catholic Church according to race. Despite these obstacles, Black Catholics continued to claim the tradition as part of their spiritual inheritance and demanded dignity.

One way Black Catholics circumvented the racial discrimination that restricted their role within the Catholic hierarchy was by passing as white. Regardless of how much certain white people decried "race mixing," there were always many interracial pairings in the United States—many of which were sexual assaults perpetrated by slaveholders against enslaved women. There were Black people whose skin was so light they could "pass" as white. This is exactly what one prominent Catholic family did in order to participate more fully in Catholic life. The Healy family consisted of ten children. James A. Healy, the eldest son, became known as the first Black American Catholic priest. He was born enslaved as the son of a biracial mother, Eliza, and a white slaveholder. Patrick Healy's father sent him and his siblings north as soon as they reached school age so they could enjoy some measure of freedom.

In the North, Healy passed and identified as white. This allowed him to go through holy orders and become a priest in 1854 and later bishop of the Diocese of Portland, Maine.[30] James's younger brother Patrick also passed as white and became a Jesuit priest, pursuing a career in academia that culminated with him as president of Georgetown University. Several of their sisters pursued a religious life in Catholicism as well. One sister, Eliza, became a nun and the superior of several convents.[31] The Healys carefully hid their African heritage, even though it was known or suspected by some. Of course, passing raises questions of identity, racial boundaries, and solidarity with oppressed communities. The Healy children chose to exploit ambiguous racial classifications to follow a calling they felt to serve God in the Roman Catholic Church. While their decisions deserve examination, the system that forced them to obfuscate the African part of their identity also deserves scrutiny.

In contrast to the Healys, Augustus Tolton was darker-skinned and sought to more directly confront the racism that prevented his ordination into the Catholic priesthood. After Tolton was born enslaved in Missouri in 1854, his mother carried her family to the free state of Illinois where they settled in Quincy. A pious boy from a young age, Augustus declared his intention to become a Catholic priest, but no seminary in the United States would admit a Black person. Through the efforts of white allies in the church hierarchy, he was able to enroll at a seminary in Rome, Italy, and in 1886, he was ordained as a priest. Originally assigned to the Diocese of Alton in Illinois, Tolton faced sharp opposition because of his race. He was soon reassigned to the Chicago archdiocese at Saint Monica's Parish in 1889. "He was for the Black Catholic people a sign of what the Church could be."[32] Tolton consciously identified as Black and labored for increased opportunity and equality for Black people in the Catholic Church.

Historian Shannen Dee Williams has emphasized the importance of Black Catholic women in the movement for racial justice. The Handmaids of the Most Pure Heart of Mary formed in response to a racist law proposed in Georgia in 1915 that would "prohibit white teachers from teaching in colored schools and colored teachers from teaching in white schools."[33] Since the white sisterhoods did not admit Black women, the Catholic school system in the area that served Black students would completely collapse. Father Ignatius Lissner, a white priest assigned to "African Missions" in Savannah, asked Eliza Barbara Williams to help. Williams was a Black Catholic laywoman in Washington, DC, at the time. When she heard of the need, she agreed to lead a new community of Black religious women who could teach Black children in Black Catholic schools.

By 1917, the Handmaids of the Most Pure Heart of Mary had enough women to staff the local Black Catholic school in Savannah. Their order did not survive long in the Jim Crow South, however. Father Lissner, constantly opposed for proposing an integrated seminary, relocated to New Jersey. The Black sisters were left without an ally in the hierarchy of the church, and the local bishop soon expelled the sisters from their teaching roles. Over the course of several years, the sisters moved to New Jersey and then to Harlem, where they took over a nursery and a school. In 1930, the order merged with another to become the Franciscan Handmaids of the Most Pure Heart of Mary.[34] Racism forced the creation of an entirely new Black Catholic sisterhood, and ongoing opposition compelled them to leave the South. But through the resilience of these Black Catholic nuns, they established an enduring legacy in education and Black community uplift.

WILLIAM J. SIMMONS AND THE KENTUCKY NORMAL AND THEOLOGICAL INSTITUTE

Historically Black colleges and universities (HBCUs) have become one of the most enduring and impactful Black institutions in the country. To be considered an HBCU, a school must have been founded before 1964 and have had an explicit mission to educate people of African descent. Today there are just over 100 HBCUs, a number that is shrinking due to decreased enrollment and a history of underfunding and disinvestment.[35] Despite these disadvantages, and while HBCUs make up just 3 percent of all colleges and universities, they produce nearly 20 percent of all Black college graduates.[36]

The positive academic outcomes for Black people at these schools is undeniable. "HBCUs have graduated 40 percent of all Black engineers; 40 percent of all Black US Congress members; 50 percent of all Black lawyers; and 80 percent of all Black judges."[37] HBCUs have even demonstrated positive health effects in students. A report published in the National Library of Medicine indicated that "HBCU enrollment was associated with a 35% reduction in the odds of metabolic syndrome"—a constellation of conditions affecting one's risk of developing many chronic diseases.[38] The people who led these institutions tapped into the spirit of justice to forge educational enterprises that have changed the trajectory of countless lives. One such leader is William J. Simmons.

William J. Simmons

Bishop Henry McNeal Turner wrote of his friend William J. Simmons, "As an educator, he has likely no superiors. . . . As a [college] president, his executive ability is excellent. . . . A man of forcible character and deep convictions."[39] Simmons earned such effusive praise by one of the most eminent political and religious leaders of the late nineteenth century through his energetic and innovative efforts on behalf of Black people as a preacher, editor, and higher education administrator in a season of both great opportunity and great obstacles.

Simmons became the second president of Kentucky Normal and Theological Institute in 1880. He served there for ten years until he died from heart failure at the age of just forty-one years old. He so distinguished himself as an academic and administrative leader of the school that they later renamed it Simmons University in his honor. Simmons also became editor of the *American Baptist* newspaper, which allowed him to share his "racy, versatile, and logical" opinions in editorial articles.[40] He served as the first president of the American National Baptist Convention starting in 1886, one of the networks that merged to form the National Baptist Convention headed by Reverend E. C. Morris. Wilberforce University recognized Simmons in 1885 with an honorary Doctor of Divinity (DD) degree to acknowledge his achievements and leadership in education and justice. Throughout all his activities, his wife, Josephine (née Silence), raised their seven children and served as a partner in his ministry.

Simmons was an unlikely candidate to become a college president. He was born enslaved in Charleston, South Carolina, to Esther and Edward Simmons in 1849. His mother escaped with William and his two siblings to freedom in Philadelphia while they were still children. "While in Philadelphia, they were harassed by poverty, anxieties, and, most cruel of all, slave traders, who seemed never to tire searching for and haunting that little band of runaways."[41] As fugitives, the family frequently had to relocate until they finally settled down in Bordentown, New Jersey. They lived in financial destitution, working day and night for barely enough to eat. Simmons never received a formal education as a child, but the uncle who helped care for the family after their escape tutored Simmons, who was an apt pupil.[42] Simmons ended up graduating from Howard University in 1873.

In his few decades of life, Simmons accumulated a breadth of experiences. He apprenticed as a dentist for a couple of years. He joined the Union Army and served in Company B of the Forty-First US Colored Infantry. As a member of that force, he was present at Appomattox when Robert E. Lee surrendered his army to General Ulysses S. Grant in

April 1865. He was elected president of the Colored Press Association, and he served as chairman of the State Convention of Colored Men for Kentucky for several years. Simmons also wrote the book *Men of Mark*, which contained biographies of over 170 prominent Black men. He intended later to "accompany it with a companion illustrating what our women have done" before his death at an early age.[43] He even played a pivotal role in the work of famed investigative journalist Ida B. Wells. He gave Wells her first paying job as a journalist, and in gratitude she wrote in her autobiography, "In every way he could, Dr. Simmons encouraged me to be a newspaper woman, and whatever fame I achieved in that line I owe in large measure to his influence and encouragement."[44]

Simmons became well-known as a "race man" who exerted every effort on behalf of Black people, but his education and ministry were amply supported by white benefactors. He became a Christian in 1867 at a white Baptist church pastored by J. W. Custis. This congregation not only accepted Simmons as a member but affirmed his calling as a minister. They paid his tuition for several years as he attended Madison University (now Colgate University) in New York. But Simmons truly made his mark as an educator of Black people. After his graduation from Howard University, he began a career in teaching that culminated in his role as a higher education administrator.

The Kentucky Normal and Theological Institute (KNTI) began as a vision among Black Baptist ministers in 1865. Twelve men assembled at Fifth Street Baptist Church in Louisville, Kentucky, all members of the State Convention of Colored Baptists.[45] They sought to address the critical need for education among the millions of recently freed Black people after the Civil War. It took fourteen years for that vision to become concrete when the Kentucky Normal and Theological Institute opened in 1879 with eighteen students. But the endeavor was difficult. Many HBCUs were started by white missionaries with access to denominational funds. Or the schools were public and could gain some funding, even if unequal, from the state. KNTI was a private, faith-based school started by Black people and had only fundraising to support it. As the school's founders looked for new leadership, the young pastor of a Baptist church in nearby Lexington rose to the top of their list. "Few men of Professor Simmons' ability and standing would have been willing to risk their future in . . . an enterprise without capital and but a few friends."[46] Yet Simmons accepted the position in 1880, and under his leadership the school thrived.

Simmons added departments, and by the start of the 1883 academic year, enrollment had ballooned to more than 200 students. In 1884, the school was renamed the State University of Kentucky. Black Baptist women, encouraged by Simmons, formed the "Baptist Women's Educational Committee," which provided indispensable fundraising for the school. Its cornerstone role in graduating Black professionals and its role in forming the Black middle class of Louisville garnered its nickname as the "Black Harvard of the South."[47] Simmons actually left KNTI to found the Eckstein Norton Institute in Bullitt County, Kentucky, but he died a few months into the endeavor. A subsequent president of KNTI, Charles H. Parrish, successfully led the effort to change the name of the college to Simmons in honor of its second president.

The school fell on hard times financially during the Great Depression and was bought by the University of Louisville in 1930. But the core of the school persisted as a theological institute and has operated continually ever since. The school has enjoyed a renaissance in the twenty-first century. In 1997, Rev. Dr. Kevin W. Cosby led the effort by his church, Saint Stephen Baptist, to purchase the original property and buildings that Simmons held. Cosby became the thirteenth president of the school in 2005. He also led the effort to regain accreditation for the school, and it was officially designated as the 107th HBCU by the US Department of Education in 2015.[48]

The survival of Simmons College of Kentucky may not have been possible apart from the efforts and expertise of William J. Simmons. In leading an educational institution specifically designed to uplift the Black community, he exhibited an unfailing commitment to the good of his people. Upon his death, the *Baptist Home Mission Monthly* remembered him by saying, "Whatever else may be said of him, he was an unconditional and uncompromising negro. Whatever interested the negro, interested him; nothing concerning the negro was foreign to him."[49] All of his work on behalf of Black people arose from his deeply held faith. The *Baptist Home Mission Monthly* article also said, "His fervent, hopeful Christian spirit was ever an inspiration to all with whom he was associated."[50] Dozens of HBCUs owe their existence and longevity to Black Christians who devoted themselves to educating the community and instilling in their students a dedication to faith, scholarship, and justice.

MARCUS GARVEY AND RELIGION IN UNIA

At its height, the Universal Negro Improvement Association (UNIA) was the largest Black nationalist organization in the United States. One historian wrote that it was "the largest black mass movement in Afro-American history."[51] By 1923, the organization claimed as many as six million members and 900 branches in the United States and other predominantly Black nations in the Caribbean, Africa, and elsewhere.[52] UNIA struck like black lightning on the racial landscape of the 1920s, an era characterized by exclusion, segregation, and lynching. The organization and its principles gave Black people the words and institutional structure to assert a positive self-identity and the vehicle to consolidate and allocate resources for Black uplift.

Marcus Garvey

UNIA is most remembered for its bold and visionary leader Marcus Garvey and for its ability to inspire pride and self-determination among Black people. Another important aspect of UNIA's influence is the strong religious strain that undergirded its philosophy and actions.

Marcus Garvey immigrated to the United States from Jamaica in 1916 and, with his first wife, Amy Ashwood, formed the Universal Negro Improvement Association (UNIA) to voice his ideas of Black nationalism to a Pan-African audience. In just a few short years, Garvey and the UNIA became worldwide phenomena. From starting a Black-owned shipping company to designating international ambassadors, Marcus Garvey tapped into the nascent feeling among people of the African Diaspora that they were meant for more than exploitation and subjugation.

Born in 1887 in Saint Ann's Bay, Jamaica, Garvey had an exceptional upbringing under his father, who was a skilled stonemason and kept a small library in the house. Access to books developed in Garvey an early love for reading and learning. As a quick learner and someone with an adventurous spirit, he traveled and worked in a variety of countries in his teens and twenties, formative experiences that helped him see instances all over the world where Black people were being tyrannized. Whether by colonial European forces in South Africa or Jim Crow in the United States, Garvey realized that Black people around the globe needed uplift. "For Garvey, the black man was universally oppressed on racial grounds, and any program of emancipation would have to be built around the question of race first."[53] Garvey's bold and vocal focus on Black people as the center of his institution-building made him a renowned figure of the era.[54]

Although UNIA had no official religion, Garvey had close ties to the African Orthodox Church (AOC), which functionally served as the spiritual arm of the movement. The denomination spiritualized the racial pride that Garvey espoused and that had attracted so many Black people to the UNIA. A key figure in the AOC was George Alexander McGuire. Born in Antigua, McGuire was originally ordained as an Anglican but later became the first bishop of the AOC in 1921. Garvey appointed McGuire as the chaplain-general of UNIA, and together they worked to promote a Black-centered expression of Christianity.

McGuire and Garvey commemorated Christian holidays such as Christmas and Easter but depicted Christ as Black, referring to him as the "Black Man of Sorrows." At a UNIA meeting in August 1924, McGuire told the audience that there should be an "international day when all the negroes of the world should tear the pictures of a white Madonna and a white Christ out of their homes and make a bonfire of them." Then he went on to urge Black painters to "supply a black Madonna and a black Christ for the training of our children."[55]

Later that year, at the close of their thirty-day convention in New York City, Garvey led a ceremony with oil paintings of a Black Madonna and a Black Jesus as the background. Arrayed in robes of "vivid cardinal," Garvey, along with Bishop McGuire, "canonized" the Black Madonna and Christ.[56] McGuire also helped develop an early form of what could be considered Black liberation theology. He wrote the "Universal Negro Catechism" for the education of the African Orthodox Church's followers. His catechism is formatted as questions and answers and designed for instruction and memorization. One section asks, "What is the color of God?" The response to be recited is, "A spirit has neither color, nor other natural parts, nor qualities." The catechism then asks, "If, then, you had to speak of the color of God, how would you describe it?" And the answer is, "As black, since we are created in His image and likeness."[57] The catechism also contains information on history and even a revised Declaration of Independence designed to recenter religion on Black experience.

The AOC is an early example of how Christianity would be reimagined during the twentieth century, serving as a forerunner of Black liberation theology and other religious elements utilized during the Black power era. It expressed Christianity in a way that emphasized Afrocentric expressions of spirituality. McGuire summarized his beliefs in a single statement: "I believe in God; I believe in the Negro race."[58] The African Orthodox Church gave Black people an example of a Christian denomination that fully embraced both their religious and racial identity. Alongside the UNIA, the AOC became one of the most forthright and confident forms of race-conscious Christianity in the early twentieth century.

ANNA JULIA COOPER AND UPLIFT
THROUGH EDUCATION

If you have a US passport today, you can flip to a particular page and read this quote: "The cause of freedom is not the cause of a race or a sect, a party or a class—it is the cause of humankind, the very birthright of humanity."[59] This quote comes from Anna Julia Cooper, and it is one of several ways people have commemorated the legacy of this Black educator and scholar. Cooper also has a project at Wake Forest University named after her—that is, the Anna Julia Cooper Center—as well as a school in Richmond, Virginia, called the Anna Julia Cooper Episcopal School. She has been recognized as an early proponent of Black feminist (or womanist) theory.[60] Cooper spent her life and prodigious intellectual skills devoted to Black education, especially for Black women.

Anna Julia Cooper

Cooper lived an astonishing 105 years. She was born into slavery in 1858 in Raleigh, North Carolina. Cooper's mother was loaned out to her slaveholder's brother and worked in his house. This brother was likely Anna's father, but her mother would never confirm the identity of her father.[61] Anna had the opportunity to attain a formal education at an early age and took full advantage of this intellectual foundation. She excelled as a student at Saint Augustine's Normal and Collegiate Institute in Raleigh. Upon graduation at age eighteen, she married a classmate, George Cooper, who had trained to be a minister. Their marriage lasted only two years because George died. For the rest of her life, Anna remained single and committed her time and energy to education.

She enrolled in Oberlin College, well-known for its ties to abolitionism prior to the Civil War and for being one of the few colleges open to Black students at the time. Her extraordinary academic accomplishments allowed her to enter college as a sophomore, and she trained in classical studies. After she graduated, Cooper went on to earn her master's degree from Oberlin in 1887. Thereafter, she moved to Washington, DC, where she would spend the majority of her professional career.

Cooper's role in building Black institutions focused on pioneering educational theory and practice. She accepted a teaching position at the prestigious M Street High School (later Paul Laurence Dunbar High School), the same school Charles Hamilton Houston (the topic of our next section) attended. She later became principal of the school. At that time, Booker T. Washington's philosophy of education, that Black people should gain skill in various trades, had become popular with many people, both Black and white. In contrast, W. E. B. Du Bois highlighted the ability of Black people to learn the liberal arts as something both helpful to the community and for counteracting white-supremacist beliefs about Black intellectual inferiority. Like Du Bois, Cooper promoted the idea that Black people can and should learn subjects like Latin, Greek, French, and philosophy just as she had.[62] She was successful in forging M Street High School into a feeder school to universities such as Harvard and Yale. But the prospect of Black intellectualism often intimidated white people. The white superintendent of colored schools in Washington, DC, wanted the high school to focus more on industries and trade. So in 1906, Cooper's contract was not renewed, and she left the school.[63]

This professional setback, however, set her up to pursue a long-held aspiration to earn a PhD. For more than a decade she engaged in doctoral research and finally graduated with a PhD from the Sorbonne in Paris in 1925 at the age of sixty-six years old. She became just the fourth Black woman to earn a PhD. In 1931, Cooper became the president of Frelinghuysen University in Washington, DC, a nontraditional school educating Black working-class adult learners that served as a forerunner of the modern community college model.[64]

Cooper is best known for a series of essays she wrote that were collected into the volume *A Voice from the South*. In this volume she expounds on topics ranging from women's education to racial conflicts to the Episcopal Church, all with the incisiveness of disciplined thinking honed through years of meticulous study. The book, originally published in 1892, cemented Cooper as a forerunner of Black feminism (or womanism), whose work is still studied to this day. *A Voice from the South* centers the educational and moral uplift of Black women as central to the Black community and the overall well-being of society. While most of Cooper's commentary focuses on education and women's rights, the role of religion in society and in her personal life appears throughout the volume.

Cooper defined faith as "treating the truth as true."[65] And for her, no one embodied this principle of faith more than Jesus Christ. "His faith was . . . an optimistic vision of the human aptitude for endless expansion and perfectibility."[66] Cooper derived her approach to Black social improvement through education from the lived example of Jesus as the person who modeled the infinite possibility of humankind's moral, social, and intellectual capacities. Her conception of Christianity was not as a set of theological propositions meant for discussion. Rather, hers was a lived faith. "Religion must be *life made true*," she wrote. "And life is action, growth, development—begun now and ending never."[67] She thought Christians should apply their faith to the pressing issues of the day such as racism. "Don't spend your time discussing the 'Negro Problem' amid the clouds of your fine Havana [cigar]. . . . Let go your purse strings and begin to *live* your creed."[68]

Cooper also applied her Christian beliefs to social issues in a 1902 speech she gave called "The Ethics of the Negro Question." In it she argued that prioritizing the education of Black people would lead to the best outcomes for the community. "What is the best means of the Negro's uplift and amelioration? In a word I answer: Christian Education."[69] By education, Cooper meant both intellectual and moral education that spilled beyond the confines of the classroom. To Cooper, Christianity encouraged both mental progress and the ethical edifice for virtuous living. She asked for the nation to live up to the religion many professed and to apply the teachings of Jesus to racial conflict. "Does anyone question that Jesus' vision would have pierced to the heart and marrow of our national problem? And what would be His teaching in America today as to who is my neighbor?"[70] Cooper observed that instead of following the example of the Savior, however, many white people had twisted his teachings to justify racism. In her estimation, it was as if Jesus taught, "Love the Lord thy God with all thy heart, soul, and strength and thy white neighbor as thyself!"[71] She cautioned that "Anglo Saxon America is in danger of forgetting how to deal justly, to love mercy, to walk humbly with its God."[72] Anna Julia Cooper, like many other Black Christians, detected the hypocrisy of white Christians who promoted and defended segregation, as well as the unequal educational prospects of Black and white people. True faith meant treating Black people as neighbors and loving them as oneself, not only in word but also in deed.

Anna Julia Cooper's long life and her unfailing efforts helped establish enduring educational institutions such as M Street High School. The Frelinghuysen University closed in the early 1960s, but Cooper's leadership of the school helped lay the foundation for continuing education and the community college model. Some criticized Cooper's emphasis on elite education and moral purity as a manifestation of white Victorian ideals, but Cooper's life was cast in the mold of the classic "race woman."[73] As a Black person who had achieved a level of professional success and education, she saw it as her duty, her Christian duty, to help others of her race who had not gained such advantages. In applying her undeniable intellectual aptitude to the work of educating Black people, Cooper fulfilled a desire: "Better to light a candle than curse the darkness. It has been my aim and hope to light candles that may carry on lighting others in God's own way of goodwill and helpful living."[74]

CHARLES HAMILTON HOUSTON
AND THE NAACP

Charles Hamilton Houston may not be a well-known name today, but he was instrumental in establishing the National Association for the Advancement of Colored People's (NAACP) legal strategy that secured historic advances in jurisprudence related to race. While *Brown v. The Board of Education* (1954) rightfully garners much attention, the legal architecture for that case had been built decades prior, mainly under the leadership and influence of Charles H. Houston.

Charles Hamilton Houston
Everett Collection Historical / Alamy Stock Photo

Historian Genna Rae McNeil connects Houston's work as a lawyer on behalf of his people to the more public, national movement for Black empowerment that came in the 1950s and 1960s. She helpfully retrieves the life and legacy of an exceptional but overlooked stalwart in American justice movements. Although connected by history to the common struggle of people of African descent in the United States, Charles Houston enjoyed a privileged upbringing compared to many others of his race. As the only child of a successful Black lawyer and an attentive mother in Washington, DC, he grew up in a family whose social and economic background helped instill a sense of security in him and enabled him to envision a future as a professional. Houston graduated Amherst College as a valedictorian. He joined the US Army where he was commissioned as a second lieutenant and served in France and Germany during World War I. His service in the army during World War I gave him a personal and bracing experience with racism. African Americans like Houston faced obstacles to becoming officers and constantly bore humiliations among white soldiers. The young Houston reflected, "I made up my mind that I would never get caught again without knowing something about my rights, and . . . I would study law and use my time fighting for men who couldn't strike back."[75] Thus began an illustrious career as a law student.

After his discharge from the army, the academically skilled Houston enrolled in Harvard Law School where he became the first Black person to serve on the editorial board of the *Harvard Law Review*. After graduation he taught at Howard Law School, a historically Black college, and transformed it from a part-time, unaccredited night program into a highly respected school accredited by the American Bar Association. Houston's leadership helped position Howard as the destination school for Black lawyers. At one point, Howard Law trained up to 25 percent of all Black lawyers in the nation.[76] The high standards he set for his students made him unpopular with some, but Houston crafted his classroom on the basis that lawyers should be "social engineers."[77] They must use the law to shape a better society for the marginalized, not just for personal gain. Nothing less than the best-prepared Black lawyers could engage in this struggle.

Houston's success at Howard Law gained the attention of the NAACP. He served as special counsel for the organization and was the primary architect of a strategy that attacked segregation in various public venues as unconstitutional. In a US Supreme Court case, he argued that the state of Missouri could not bar Black students from entering the state university law school because no "separate but equal" institution existed for Black students. The goal of the tactic was to use the logic of the oppressor against them. If the white establishment wanted to maintain separate facilities, then they must make them equal, as the *Plessy v. Ferguson* ruling stated. This, of course, would be far too expensive and impractical to execute. Thus, in Houston's reasoning, segregation would collapse under the weight of its own requirements.

He brought his strategy to the NAACP leadership. They agreed to pursue it as the main plank of their legal platform. And it worked. Lawyers such as Thurgood Marshall, one of Houston's most famous students, would employ it to overturn legalized segregation with the *Brown v. Board of Education* decision in 1954. While Houston and his team won many cases and opened new avenues for pursuing rights in the courts, the countless hours of labor took their toll. He and his first wife divorced, and when he remarried, he had little time for his second wife and son. Houston had long struggled with illness, and his obsession with work only exacerbated that condition. He died of heart failure at the age of fifty-four.

Throughout his career, Houston held on to a strong Christian faith. His father, William, was the son of a pastor and instilled in him a strong sense of duty, and his mother had a deep and devout faith that helped as she led her son Charles to develop a "keen religious-moral sense."[78] Yet Houston, like many Black people, had little confidence that the professed faith of white Christians would make a difference in the battle against racism. In an address titled "An Approach to Better Race Relations" given at the National Young Women's Christian Association (YWCA) conference in 1934, Hamilton told his audience, "Christianity has always seemed to fight a losing battle against race prejudice. . . . The trouble is that most of our churches are social clubs masquerading under the guise of religious institutions."[79] Despite the recalcitrance of most white people, Houston devoted all his prodigious talents to laying the groundwork for legal challenges to segregation and racial inequality.

Houston's vision that law could be used "as an organism for social justice through social engineering" serves as a juridical application of the command to "love your neighbor as yourself."[80] He sought to use "the instrumentality of law to disrobe and destroy the perceived encumbrances and trappings of birth, origin, color, creed or religion."[81] Houston's boundless dedication to Black progress helped him build both Howard Law School and the NAACP into enduring institutions dedicated to Black advancement.

CONCLUSION

After the Civil War and emancipation, Black people emerged from the depths of financial destitution, widespread illiteracy, and cruel exploitation to build enduring Black institutions. Through denominations, colleges, businesses, and more, they secured for themselves and their posterity all the advantages that had been denied them for so long under slavery. This occurred amid vigorous white-supremacist efforts to deny Black people full liberty. The racial terrorist violence of lynching punctuated the daily indignities of racial segregation. Black people knew that partial freedom was not true freedom. And as a people who had endured the oppression of race-based chattel slavery, they would not settle for the truncated liberty that a Jim Crow society offered. Decades of disenfranchisement and inequality eventually came to a public and decisive confrontation in a massive movement for Black civil rights.

CHAPTER SEVEN

BEYOND THE QUOTABLE KING

More than half a century after his murder, Martin Luther King Jr. stands as the most well-known figure of the civil rights movement. His governance of the Southern Christian Leadership Conference (SCLC) and his principled adherence to the philosophy of nonviolence established him as a remarkable leader for social change. Yet perhaps more than any of King's other skills or accomplishments, his words have made him an enduring voice in the national memory. King's speeches, books, and sermons are an exercise in poetic prose that inspire through their content and their construction. His mellifluous statements are posted on monuments, T-shirts, mugs, and posters. Phrases like "I have a dream" have become a ubiquitous part of the linguistic landscape.

But King's facility with words has been a double-edged sword. While his statements preserve his legacy in the present, they also truncate it. Reducing King's life and mission to a few short phrases and oft-repeated excerpts diminishes the expansiveness of his labor and thinking. The selective use of King's words can also serve to sanitize his more radical calls for justice. Words from the "I Have a Dream" speech delivered in 1963 have been misapplied as a cover for colorblind approaches to dealing with racism that King himself never advocated. Reducing King's sentiments to phrases that can fit on a postcard conveniently leaves out his views, considered controversial by some, on such topics as economics, war, and Black empowerment.

This chapter goes beyond the "quotable King." It captures a more detailed portrait of a major historical figure in the Black freedom struggle by focusing on lesser-known stories from his life and by highlighting some of his more contested beliefs about racial justice. This extended treatment of King runs the risk of reinforcing the trope that history is made mainly by towering male figures with all others playing minor roles in their stories. This is called the "Great Man" approach to history—the idea that most of history has been made and can mostly be understood by examining the actions of a few prominent and exceptional men throughout time. From the so-called Founding Fathers to the framing of the civil rights movement mainly in terms of people like King, the Great Man method of viewing history leaves out women, the poor, members of other oppressed communities, and the masses that made grassroots movements happen.

That is not the intent here. The impetus for this treatment is acknowledging that MLK has become, for many, the personification of the Black Christian pursuit of racial justice and ensuring that we have a more accurate understanding of the man beyond the myth. In the chapter that follows this one, we will look more closely at the women who made the civil rights movement possible and dispel any notion that only famous men like MLK deserve attention. But since King attracts outsized attention in our collective historical memory, we should at least get that memory right. As much as any single individual in the civil rights era, he represents the essence of the spirit of justice in pursuit of racial equality.

THE CHRISTIAN AND THE PREACHER

In a 1965 article he wrote for *Ebony* magazine, King reflected, "In the quiet recesses of my heart, I am fundamentally a clergyman, a Baptist preacher."[1] Despite King's self-assessment, many remember him almost solely for his political activism and direct-action nonviolent protests. They examine the laws and policies he and his colleagues attempted to change. They assess his legacy mainly in terms of the social and cultural changes he promoted or provoked. They acknowledge, of course, that he was a Christian and a minister, but those aspects of his life sit in the back of the bus behind his activism.[2] Yet we cannot understand King the activist if we do not understand King the Christian and the preacher first. What we now know and admire about King's bold stances for racial justice arose from his convictions as a follower of Jesus and a churchman.

Martin Luther King Jr.

King's father, Martin Luther King Sr., was the prominent pastor of Ebenezer Baptist Church in Atlanta, Georgia, for more than forty years. When King Sr. first started ministering at Ebenezer, he was an assistant pastor under Reverend A. D. Williams. King Sr. fell in love with and married the pastor's daughter, Alberta Williams, who was a devout Christian and became a leader in the church when her husband took over the pastorate in 1931. She started the choir at the church, earned a bachelor's degree, and served in the women's auxiliary of the National Baptist Convention.[3] Martin Luther King Jr. was the middle of three children, sandwiched between his older sister, Willie Christine, and his younger brother, Alfred Daniel. King wrote of his family life: "Our parents themselves were very intimate, and they always maintained an intimate relationship with us."[4] Even in adulthood he and his siblings maintained "that intimate relationship which existed between us in childhood."[5]

Although King joined the church at five years old, he reflected in a paper for seminary titled "An Autobiography of Religious Development" that "conversion for me has been the gradual intaking of the noble [ideals] set forth in my family and my environment, and I must admit that this intaking has been largely unconscious."[6] He spoke of the church as a "second home" for him and credits Sunday school with instilling in him the fundamentals of the Christian religion. Even though King would undergo a liberalizing of his theological views in seminary, he never lost his faith in Jesus Christ or his belief in the ethical demands of Christianity. "At present I still feel the affects [sic] of the noble moral and ethical ideals that I grew up under. They have been real and precious to me. . . . Religion for me is life."[7] Thus, from the earliest of ages, King was imprinted with Christianity at the core of his thought and actions.

King's journey with Christianity continued with the calling he felt to ministry. By the age of eighteen, young King felt a desire to serve as a minister. He preached his trial sermon—designed as a test of a potential preacher's ability to expound on Scripture—at his father's church. Shortly thereafter on February 25, 1948, King Sr. ordained his son to the ministry of the gospel.[8] King Jr. would continue to hone his biblical interpretation skills and views on social activism under the mentorship of men such as Benjamin E. Mays, president of Morehouse College, where King attended as an undergraduate student. Mays set an example of how a preacher could be a scholar and intellectual as well as a powerful expositor of God's Word. King continued his education at Crozer Theological Seminary in Pennsylvania, where he graduated as the class valedictorian.[9] Not yet finished with education, King earned his PhD in systematic theology at Boston University in 1955.

The same year King completed his doctoral degree, he accepted a call to be the senior pastor of Dexter Avenue Baptist Church in

Montgomery, Alabama. At just twenty-five years old, King had his first pastorate and his first opportunity to put into practice his thinking about Christianity and justice. He did not embark on this new journey alone. In 1953, he married Coretta Scott, an accomplished musician who attended the New England Conservatory of Music. Together they had four children, and she served as an important civil rights leader both during and after her husband's life.[10]

Martin Luther and Coretta Scott King

Even though King called his conversion to Christianity gradual, he did have a striking moment when his faith became more personal to him. Just over a month into the Montgomery bus boycott, King and his family were experiencing the acute effects of white supremacy in the face of Black resistance. Death threats had already been coming in, but this was different. After returning home from an organizing meeting late one January night in 1956, the phone rang. The caller said, "Nigger, we're tired of you and your mess. And if you're not out of town in three days, we're going to blow your brains out, and blow up your house."[11] King thought about his newborn daughter. He thought about his loving and supportive wife, Coretta. He thought about how his involvement in the boycott put each of them in mortal danger.

"And I got to the point that I couldn't take it any longer. I was weak," he later reflected. "I discovered then that religion had to become real to me, and I had to know God for myself. And I bowed down over that cup of coffee. I never will forget it. . . . I prayed a prayer, and I prayed out loud that night." King cried out to God for strength, guidance, and reassurance. "Then it happened: And it seemed at that moment that I could hear an inner voice saying to me, 'Martin Luther, stand up for righteousness. Stand up for justice. Stand up for truth. And lo I will be with you, even until the end of the world.' . . . I heard the voice of Jesus saying still to fight on."[12]

Martin Luther King Jr. had grown up surrounded by the church. He was the son of a pastor and the grandson of a pastor. He spent countless hours in the church building. He knew the songs, prayed the prayers. He even had a PhD in theology. Now he was pastoring his first church. Yet with all his exposure to religion, he had not truly made Christianity his own. It was only in the crucible of oppression that King felt a deep, transformative experience of God. He heard the voice of Jesus, and it strengthened him not only for the boycott in Montgomery but for more than a decade as the most prominent leader of the civil rights movement. King had encountered the spirit of justice.

NONVIOLENCE AND DIRECT-ACTION PROTEST

While the Christian faith animated King, his most visible witness took the form of direct-action nonviolent protest. Throughout his years as a leader of the civil rights movement, his philosophy of nonviolence crystallized and, for King, became more than a tactic. It evolved into a way of life.

In his book *Stride toward Freedom*, King recollected that his first "intellectual contact with the theory of nonviolent resistance" came from reading Henry David Thoreau's 1849 essay "Civil Disobedience" while he was a student at Morehouse College.[13] King "became fascinated with the idea of refusing to cooperate with an evil system."[14] King's convictions were not merely theoretical. Although he grew up relatively privileged compared to other Black people, he still felt the sting of segregation and racism. He was raised in the land of lynching. He witnessed acts of police brutality. He saw routine miscarriages of justice as they pertained to Black individuals, and he observed the claustrophobic effects of poverty in his community. King's conscience and Christianity could not allow him to ignore such oppression, and nonviolent civil disobedience gave him a way to express his desire for justice.

While King was a student at Crozer Seminary, he listened to a sermon by Mordecai Johnson, the president of Howard University, and first heard about Mohandas Gandhi's nonviolent social resistance in India. King especially resonated with the concept of "satyagraha," which translated from Hindi means "truth force" or, in King's reasoning, "love force."[15] As he explored the ethic of love through the lens of nonviolent noncooperation with evil, King began formulating an approach to opposing racism in the United States. Throughout his formal studies, King interacted with ideas from Marx, Nietzsche, Niebuhr, and Hegel, among others. He synthesized his learnings and combined them with personal insights to formulate his own philosophical approach to social change. He grew in the "conviction that nonviolent resistance was one of the most potent weapons available to oppressed people in their quest for social justice."[16]

While many other civil rights activists understood nonviolence as a tactic, it became much more than just a tactic for King. One's convictions are proved in their application. The first test of King's philosophy of nonviolent protest arrived in the form of the Montgomery bus boycott. Although King did not conceive of the plan, he agreed to serve as spokesperson of the Montgomery Improvement Association (MIA) that led it. With violent threats against his life and the daily hardship of abstaining from public transportation, King's commitment to nonviolence was tested. "Living through the actual experience of the protest, nonviolence became more than a method to which I gave intellectual assent; it became a commitment to a way of life."[17] In the chaos of conflict, King became persuaded that nonviolence had to be at the core of his leadership and example.

Not all Black people agreed with King's approach to nonviolence. Many Black people throughout US history have advocated and practiced armed self-defense. Most Black people lived in the South where owning guns was a way of life. They used guns for hunting and for protection, and weapons were passed down from one generation to the next. Black people were fully aware of the ways white people had used violence as a tactic to support white supremacy. Harriet Tubman carried a pistol to fend off would-be slave catchers as well as to "encourage" enslaved Black people if they ever lost their nerve during an escape attempt.[18] In her book detailing the horrors of lynching, Ida B. Wells famously wrote, "The only times an Afro-American who was assaulted got away has been when he had a gun and used it in self-defense."[19] She went on to write that "a Winchester rifle should have a place of honor in every black home."[20] Activist Robert F. Williams wrote a book called *Negroes with Guns*, and Charles Cobb of the Student Nonviolent Coordinating Committee wrote a book titled *This Nonviolent Stuff'll Get You Killed*. Fannie Lou Hamer is quoted as saying, "I keep a shotgun in every corner of my bedroom and the first cracker even look like he wants to throw some dynamite on my porch won't write his mama again."[21]

Numerous other examples—the Deacons for Defense, the Black Panther Party for Self-Defense, and the many wars in which Black people fought for their nation and their freedom—attest to the widespread use of guns and violence in the history of the Black freedom struggle. In nearly every instance, however, Black people advocated for the use of guns strictly as armed self-defense against white racist violence. Only the most extreme groups proposed violence as an offensive tactic. Black people did see the usefulness of nonviolent protest during the civil rights movement, but they mainly saw it as a tactic to deploy in certain circumstances. Nonviolence was not a whole-of-life philosophy that could not be violated under any circumstances. Despite famous images from the civil rights movement depicting Black people absorbing beatings during protests, Black people in general did not have qualms about meeting force with force in defense of Black life.

Martin Luther King Jr., though, applied nonviolence not simply as a tool of protest but as an expression of the love ethic. Nonviolence moved King toward pacifism as a manifestation of love. "True pacifism is not unrealistic submission to evil power. . . . It is rather a courageous confrontation with evil by the power of love."[22] King was convinced that violence only leads to more violence. Whether in wars such as

Vietnam, going up against police brutality, or facing individual death threats, King refused to meet such circumstances with physical force. For his leadership and commitment to nonviolent social struggle, King was awarded the Nobel Peace Prize in 1964.

King's pacifist stance went beyond public protest. In September 1963, while King was giving a speech, a white supremacist, incensed at King's views and presence, rushed onto the stage and landed two punches to King's face. Instead of fighting back, "Dr. King dropped his hands like that of a newborn baby."[23] As others ran to King's aid and pulled the man away, King yelled, "Don't touch him. Don't touch him. We have to pray for him."[24] The man turned out to be a member of the American Nazi Party. King refused to press charges and even offered to let the man return to his seat to hear the rest of King's speech. Anyone who felt unsure about King's commitment to nonviolence could not deny that he was willing to be bloodied and bruised, and even killed, before he resorted to violence.

THE SPEECH

Martin Luther King Jr., the man now recognized as one of the greatest orators of the twentieth century, only earned Cs in his preaching classes. His average grades in a subject that was clearly one of his strengths may have been given because King's white professors did not appreciate the Black Baptist preaching tradition.[25] But King eventually mastered a synthesis of academic erudition and folk communication. His sophisticated analysis of philosophy, politics, and theology never impeded his ability to communicate with everyday people in the pews. He had been born into a preaching tradition passed down from his father and grandfather. He had heard countless sermons. He had disciplined his delivery through formal education and time in the pulpit. All of his skill, instinct, and experience as a preacher coalesced in a generation-defining moment on August 28, 1963.

King's "I Have a Dream" speech is the best-known oration of the civil rights era, and one of the most famous of the past century. But there is much more to know about the speech and its message than the handful of quotes and phrases people use today. First, it was not an entirely original speech. The themes in the speech were a blend from numerous addresses he had given over at least the past six years prior to the March on Washington for Jobs and Freedom in 1963. Many elements of the speech had been given before. In 1957, for instance, he ended a speech with excerpts from the song "My Country 'Tis of Thee." In that same speech he repeated the refrain "Let freedom ring." In September of 1960, he spoke about a "dream yet unfulfilled."[26]

What may have been foremost in King's mind during his preparation for the March on Washington speech was an event just two months earlier in Detroit, Michigan. He spoke at the Cobo Hall arena to a crowd of about 150,000 assembled for a civil rights march. His words at the March on Washington two months later were almost a verbatim repetition of what he said in Detroit. He used the refrain "I have a dream" and the vision of his children being judged "not by the color of their skin but the content of their character."[27] As with any frequent speaker, King had little time to develop completely original speeches for every new speaking engagement. Moreover, like the best speakers, King tested ideas in front of different crowds to see what resonated. He kept the best and left the rest. Although King had prepared written remarks, and they had been distributed to the press beforehand, he went off-script toward the end of the speech. Like an accomplished musical artist, he played his greatest hits on his biggest stage yet. "All of a sudden

Inscription of Martin Luther King Jr.'s "I Have a Dream"
speech on the steps of the Lincoln Memorial.
akslam/Stock.Adobe.com

this thing came to me that I have used—I'd used it many times before, that thing about 'I have a dream,'" King later remarked in an interview.[28]

Although the words "I have a dream" have become emblazoned in national memory, the speech contains thousands more words. King brought up many themes relevant to the historic Black freedom struggle and the pursuit of human rights for all. He called the nation to live up to its ideals stated so eloquently in the Declaration of Independence and the Constitution. "This note was a promise that all men, yes, black men as well as white men, would be guaranteed the unalienable rights of life, liberty, and the pursuit of happiness." He gave a dire warning to those who thought that the movement for civil rights would simply blow over with time. "The whirlwinds of revolt will continue to shake the foundations of our nation until the bright day of justice emerges." He sounded the familiar notes of nonviolence. "We must not allow our creative protest to degenerate into physical violence. Again and again, we must rise to the majestic heights of meeting physical force with soul force." He spoke of the "unspeakable horrors of police brutality" inflicted on Black people by those charged to "serve and protect."[29]

Though not technically a "sermon," King consistently referenced biblical passages throughout his speech. In a favorite verse of faith-based justice leaders, he excerpted the words of the prophet Amos in the Bible: "No, no, we are not satisfied and we will not be satisfied until justice rolls down like waters and righteousness like a mighty stream" (see Amos 5:24). He quoted from Isaiah 40:4, declaring his dream that "every hill and mountain shall be made low, the rough places made plain." King frequently used the phrase "all God's children" to remind his listeners of their shared humanity and ontological equality derived from their status as creations of the same Creator. The phrase also alluded to the doctrine of the image of God. In Genesis 1:26, God declares, "Let us make mankind in our image, in our likeness." From a religious perspective, all human beings share certain attributes with God and all have equal dignity and worth. The defiant tone at the beginning of King's speech is interwoven with the call to move toward the "sunlit path of racial justice." A righteous anger and a holy impatience lace his words. It is a speech that could have been fittingly delivered from a podium at the culmination of a mass march or from a pulpit in the sacred halls of a church. Yet for all its religious elements and Black Baptist undertones, the speech was broadly applicable. It applied to "Jews and Gentiles, Protestants and Catholics." It was truly a speech for universal human dignity.

In classic sermonic fashion, Martin Luther King Jr. ended his "I Have a Dream" speech on a note of hope. He did not merely critique the status quo; he offered up a vision of a new reality in the form a dream. And while he went on to highlight specific elements of the dream, one part of that dream has been grossly ripped out of context. "I have a dream that my four little children will one day live in a nation where they will not be judged by the color of their skin but by the content of their character. I have a dream today."[30] Partly as a result of the gains of the civil rights movement, it became less socially acceptable to express ideas of racism openly. No longer could most people use the "*n*-word" with impunity. With the passage of the 1964 Civil Rights Act, it became harder to legally discriminate on the basis of race. But racism had not been eradicated. Racism never goes away entirely. It adapts.

After the civil rights movement, racism shifted to a "colorblind" ideal. "Under color-blind ideology, to acknowledge racial difference was to perpetuate the 'race problem,' as if racism could be out of sight, out of mind."[31] King's phrase referring to children being judged by the content of their character but not the color of their skin has been misinterpreted to mean that King wanted to deemphasize race as a significant factor in the quality of life for Black people. Yet this parsing of King's words ignores the context of the speech and the entirety of the work that would eventually cost him his life.

In the very next line of the speech, King explicitly referred to the state of Alabama and its "vicious racists." King did not believe the best way to ensure Black progress was to ignore the racial realities that made Black people the targets of injustice. When King stated that America had given Black people a "bad check" regarding freedom, he simultaneously demanded "the riches of freedom and the security of justice."[32] This could not be accomplished apart from direct-action protest, as the March on Washington itself modeled, nor could it be achieved by paying less attention to the inequalities caused by racism and hoping that would make them go away.

Beyond the speech, King made explicit the need to pay particular attention to race as a way to bring about equality between Black and white people. In a time before "affirmative action" was a popular phrase, King spoke of the need for special considerations for Black people. In his book *Why We Can't Wait*, King wrote that the nation "must incorporate in its planning some compensatory consideration for the handicaps he has inherited from his past."[33] This "compensatory consideration" required paying attention to race, not cultivating a blindness to it. King went on to state: "Our society has been doing something special *against* the Negro for hundreds of years. How then can he be absorbed into the mainstream of American life if we do not do something special *for* him now."[34] For King, racial progress did not consist of ignoring race altogether but in flipping the tables of discrimination. Rather than using race to exclude people of color, racial considerations could be used to expand opportunities for Black people. Colorblindness as a convenient escape from the difficult and necessary work of racial repair had no place in King's "I Have a Dream" speech nor in his long career of racial justice activism.

KINGIAN ECONOMICS

Martin Luther King Jr.'s vision of the beloved community was not colorblind, nor was it blind to the economic factors that hindered Black progress. It is telling that the occasion of King's most famous speech was called the March on Washington for *Jobs* and Freedom. In the "I Have a Dream" speech itself, King lamented that "the Negro lives on a lonely island of poverty in the midst of a vast ocean of material prosperity."[35] King, the organizers of the March, and civil rights activists in general understood that the true goals of the civil rights movement entailed not only social and political change but also a remedy to the material hardships created by racial oppression.

In examining King's broader economic agenda, we should recognize that his focus on the financial conditions of Black people was nothing new. While his solidarity with striking sanitation workers in 1968 just before his death is often cited as the main evidence of his economic views, such issues had been part of his thinking for many years. As early as 1951, when he was in seminary at Crozer, King critiqued the prevailing economic order. "I am convinced capitalism has seen its best days in America. . . . It has failed to meet the needs of the masses."[36] Although King grew up solidly middle class and financially secure, he had seen the way other Black people had been forced into low-wage jobs and generational poverty. In a 1952 letter to Coretta, whom he was dating at the time, King wrote, "I am much more socialistic in my economic theory than capitalistic." He also articulated the beginnings of a holistic ministry philosophy attuned to both the spiritual and material needs of the people. "Let us continue to hope, work, and pray that in the future we will live to see a warless world, a better distribution of wealth, and a brotherhood that transcends race or color. This is the gospel that I will preach to the world." Even in his early twenties, King had seen the triple threat of war, poverty, and racism. As a young pastor in training, he vowed to address all of them in his ministry.

Beginning with his public spokesmanship for the Montgomery bus boycott of 1955 and 1956, King became well-known for his militant, nonviolent confrontation with segregation in the Deep South. These demonstrations made good political theater as unarmed Black protesters met physical force with soul force. But King never abandoned his conviction that economic changes were needed. Against the backdrop of the Civil Rights Act of 1964 and the Voting Rights Act of 1965, King pressed the need for a new phase of the civil rights movement, one that would be even harder to realize. "Negroes have benefited from a limited change that was emotionally satisfying but materially deficient," he wrote in a 1966 article for *The Nation* titled "Jobs Are Harder to Create Than Voting Rolls."[37] King anticipated more opposition in the effort to change the financial situation of Black people because even white people of goodwill—those who had stood with Black people in their struggle for desegregation—would resist efforts that required material sacrifices on their part. Regarding the chronic problem of Black underemployment, King conjectured a variety of ways to redress it. "Whether the solution be in a guaranteed annual wage, negative Income tax or any other economic device, the direction of Negro demands has to be toward substantive security."[38] The taste of expanded civil rights that Black people began to experience in the 1960s, according to King, only fed their hunger for material progress. The poor would not be satisfied with token social acceptance without a concurrent share in the nation's financial prosperity.

King prepared his team for the heightened focus on economics at a SCLC staff retreat in Frogmore, South Carolina, in 1967, just a few months before his murder. First, he decried the loss of support from white people who had come alongside Black people in the battle for desegregation but who now shrank back in the next phase of the struggle. "The short era of widespread goodwill evaporated rapidly," he told them.[39] He also pointed out the precarious financial status of Black people: "Even as the Negro manages to grasp a foothold on the economic ladder, discrimination threatens to push him off after he has only ascended a few rungs."[40] Then King proposed several measures that the SCLC might support to help alleviate the economic straits of Black people. He said they needed some form of guaranteed employment for the jobless or, alternatively, a "guaranteed annual income" to keep people out of poverty. King called for the "demolition of slums" to give people a fresh start in livable conditions. Finally, he made clear that electing more Black people to political office would be crucial to "retire all the white racists who are in Congress."[41]

In January 1968, King formally presented the Poor People's Campaign to his SCLC staff. "He said sixty staff members would recruit and train some three thousand demonstrators from fifteen poverty-stricken rural areas and from northern cities," writes Michael K. Honey in *To the Promised Land*.[42] These poor people would join thousands of other protesters for sustained demonstrations until Congress acceded to their request for guaranteed jobs or income. The plan also called for a multiyear appropriation of at least $30 billion to fund programs directed toward the poor. Some of this money, King suggested, could be reallocated by ending the war in Vietnam and focusing on antipoverty initiatives.

Mobilizing people for a multiracial, nonviolent, sustained campaign against poverty proved much harder than drawing crowds for marches and boycotts against segregation. King maintained an unrelenting speaking schedule to drum up support, but momentum was slow. Yet King had always adapted to the changing circumstances of the movement. As an internationally known symbol of freedom, he may have been singularly positioned to bring together the necessary coalition for such a significant effort. But an assassin's bullet on April 4, 1968, killed King and all possibility of him leading the next phase of the movement.

The Poor People's Campaign continued after King's murder to honor his martyrdom for the movement. Thousands of people gathered in Washington, DC, and camped on the National Mall for six weeks to demand action from Congress.[43] Demonstrations began on May 12, 1968, Mother's Day, led by Coretta Scott King and a crowd composed predominantly of women. On May 21, campers began setting up a tent city known as "Resurrection City" on the National Mall. The organizers had only obtained a permit for six weeks, and at the end of that time a thousand police officers descended on the camp and removed any remaining demonstrators or arrested those who refused to leave. While limited in its results and subject to mixed and negative reviews in the press, the Poor People's Campaign represented a dramatic attempt by King to press the need for a radical redistribution of the nation's economic resources.[44]

THE UNPOPULAR KING

People who follow the spirit of justice are hardly ever popular or celebrated in their own lifetimes. Martin Luther King Jr., though honored with a national holiday today, did not receive such widespread acclamation during his years of activism. In 1964, the same year Congress passed the Civil Rights Act, Americans were asked in a poll which three people they had the least respect for. MLK Jr. came in second place as the person whom respondents had the least respect for, right after the bombastic segregationist George Wallace.[45] His overall favorability at that time was just 44 percent. In 1966, a Harris poll indicated that 50 percent of white Americans thought King was hurting the cause of Black civil rights. His unfavorability rating had jumped to 63 percent. Right after his assassination, 31 percent of people polled said that King had brought his death on himself. Less than half of respondents (43 percent) said that they were sad or angry at his murder. Even when legislators approved of a federal holiday honoring King, public opinion was split: 48 percent said they didn't want a national holiday honoring MLK, while 47 percent said they did.[46]

But King's unpopularity went far beyond poll numbers and opinions. He faced constant verbal threats and physical assaults. On September 20, 1958, King sat at a table in a Harlem department store signing copies of his book *Stride toward Freedom*. A Black woman who had severe mental health illnesses including delusions and schizophrenia, Izola Curry, stabbed King near the heart with a letter opener. King had to be carefully extricated from the crowd by police without disturbing the blade. The surgeon who removed the blade later told King, "If you had sneezed during all those hours of waiting, your aorta would have been punctured and you would have drowned in your own blood."[47] The American Nazi Party member who punched King onstage at an event, Roy James, has already been mentioned. But that incident wasn't the end of James's targeting of King. After his first assault on King, James was interviewed in the *Rockwell Report* for an article entitled "How I Bashed Nigger King." In it he said he was proud of "administering justice to a vile communist race-mixing nigger agitator."[48] James later stalked King on his campaign in Chicago.

The FBI, under the longtime guidance of J. Edgar Hoover, targeted King to impugn his character and undermine his leadership.[49] In the societal ripple effects of the March on Washington in 1963, Hoover called King "the most dangerous Negro of the future in this Nation from the standpoint of communism, the Negro, and national security."[50] Hoover used all his considerable tools as the head of the FBI to entrap King. Hoover had King's phones at home and in hotels wiretapped. He relied on informants for secret information. In January 1965, an anonymous letter and audio tape arrived at King's home in a mailed package. The tape allegedly contained a recording of King in a hotel room and sounds that indicated he was having an extramarital affair. The letter that came with it said, "It is all there on the record, your sexual orgies. Listen to yourself you filthy, abnormal animal."[51] Then it stated, "You are done. There is but one way out for you. You better take it."[52] For this reason it is called the "suicide letter" because it implied that King should kill himself before the tapes were released publicly. Nothing more came of the tapes, but King's immediate suspicion, that the letter had come from the FBI, was later confirmed. For the remaining years of his life, King was at odds with Hoover and lived with the specter of federal surveillance hovering over his every move. King became the proverbial "man of sorrows" who faced constant suffering. In the autopsy after his murder, the doctor said that although he was just thirty-nine years of age, he had the heart of a sixty-year-old.[53]

During the SCLC campaign in Chicago during the summer of 1966, King faced riots and violence as he turned his attention to racial conditions and poverty in the North. Some civil rights leaders in the city invited King and the SCLC to join in their efforts at school desegregation. But they also recognized, and King agreed, that true victory depended on "removing future generations from dilapidated tenements, opening the doors of job opportunities to all regardless of their color, and making the resources of all social institutions available for uplifting them into the mainstream of American life."[54]

In August 1966, King and a biracial group of about 800 marchers made their way to Gage Park in Chicago. As they were walking, a "screaming" mob of white people surrounded them. One of them—"a burly white man"—threw a rock that struck King in the head just below his right ear.[55] It knocked King down to one knee, but he got up and kept marching. In his posthumously published autobiography, King explained, "I've been in many demonstrations all across the South, but I can say that I had never seen, even in Mississippi, mobs as hostile and as hate-filled as in Chicago."[56] This violent episode put on bloody display that civil rights hostility and racism resided as much in the North as they did in the South.

Near the time of his assassination, anti-King sentiment had risen to a fever pitch. Not only did people oppose his stances on Black civil rights, but King had also become increasingly vocal in opposition to the Vietnam War and in calls for economic redistribution. King characterized this combination of social maladies as the three evils: poverty, racism, and militarism. All of this incensed far-right white supremacists. In Grosse Pointe, Michigan, in March 1968, just weeks before his murder, King gave a speech to approximately 2,000 people. At the same time, hundreds of far-right protesters gathered outside. Protesters inside constantly interrupted his speech with shouts of "Commie" and "Traitor."[57] King reflected that it was "the worst heckling I have ever encountered in all my travels."[58] The accumulation of all these life-threatening and disturbing confrontations left an impact on King.

In his last public address, the day before his assassination, King delivered his "I've Been to the Mountaintop" speech. On April 3, a weary King took the podium at Memphis's Mason Temple. He almost didn't come. He had a sore throat and a fever. But his right-hand man, Ralph Abernathy, called from the venue and told King that the hundreds of people there wanted to see him. So King went to Mason Temple and offered not only a note of hope but also something of a self-eulogy. "Like anybody, I would like to live a long life. Longevity has its place. But I'm not concerned about that now. I just want to do God's will." He said that God had allowed him, like Moses, to ascend to the top of the mountain and look over into the promised land. But also like Moses, King knew that he probably wouldn't live long enough to lead the people into the next stage of the journey of justice. It was as if King could sense the end was near. Perhaps his mind drifted back to that night in 1956 at his kitchen table when he cried out to God for strength to lead the movement. King continued, "And so I'm happy, tonight. I'm not worried about anything. I'm not fearing any man! Mine eyes have seen the glory of the coming of the Lord!"[59]

CONCLUSION

King's lifetime of sacrifice, his bold leadership, and his moral courage have earned him a place as the clear representation of the spirit of justice during the civil rights movement. Over time, however, the man has been obscured by the myth. The specific contours, events, and beliefs of King's life have been overshadowed by his legend. And while it is important to remember that no single person started the movement or led it, it is also critical to develop a more accurate understanding of a person who is so often referenced in popular culture today. The lack of proper perspective about King has made him a tool in the hands of those who would weaponize his legacy to work against the very principles for which he lived and died. In our own efforts to understand how the spirit of justice animated his life and work, we must move beyond the quotable King.

CHAPTER
EIGHT

WOMEN OF THE MOVEMENT

Over the course of half a century in the struggle for Black freedom, civil rights activist Ella Baker served in thirty-six different organizations. She grew up in a very religious Christian household. The influence of her mother and the other Black women in her life taught her an "activist, women-centered faith . . . that urged women to act as positive agents for change in the world."[1] Equipped with this outlook, she spent time working with the NAACP and the Southern Christian Leadership Conference, as well as serving as the main architect of the organizing philosophy of the Student Nonviolent Coordinating Committee (SNCC).[2] Even so, her brilliant intellect and passionate commitment did not thrust her into the forefront of the civil rights movement. Ella Baker was a woman, and even among those most committed to racial equality, only men could lead from the pulpit or the podium.

Baker was cognizant of the sexism she faced, even among Black men, and she was realistic about it. In reflecting on her role in the SCLC alongside Martin Luther King Jr., she said, "I had known, number one, that there would never be any role for me in the leadership capacity with SCLC. Why? First, I'm a woman. Also, I'm not a minister."[3] She traced the reluctance of Black men to put women in prominent leadership roles to the way that they viewed women in the church. Many denominations permitted only men to preach and pastor. That same type of thinking was present in groups like the SCLC, which was largely populated by male ministers. Baker said that men viewed women in the role of "taking orders, not providing leadership." But lead she did. As women in every patriarchal society and male-dominated sector have had to do, she made pathways for her brilliance to manifest and serve the greater good.

This chapter focuses exclusively on women in the civil rights movement by offering profiles of several leaders. Throughout each era of US history, women exemplified the spirit of justice in various ways. This is true as well during the 1950s and 1960s when Black activism toppled the Jim Crow system of segregation. Jim Crow would not have ended without the support, labor, and leadership of women. Although men typically had the most public-facing roles in the movement, women had a much more integral part than popular memory affords. But in correcting the historical memory, there is more work to do than simply adding women to the narrative. Historian Danielle McGuire contends that most histories of the civil rights movement present it as a "struggle between black and white men." By considering Black women's struggles for bodily autonomy and equality, "we have to reinterpret, if not rewrite, the history of the civil rights movement."[4] Martha S. Jones notes that Black women "were the nation's original feminists and antiracists," who worked not only for their own rights but for "political power that was redemptive, transformative, and a means toward realizing the equality and dignity of all persons."[5] Women formed the majority of participants in the civil rights movement. They populated the mass meetings at churches. They turned out by hundreds or thousands for protest marches, they joined in boycotts, they forged formal and informal communication networks, and more.[6] During the 1950s and 1960s, women "helped create, sustain, and direct one of the most important social protest movements in American history."[7] No account of the long struggle against racism is complete without a thorough accounting of women as both participants and leaders. They drew on the spirit of justice to resist both racism and sexism in the movement for Black freedom.

CORETTA SCOTT KING

Coretta Scott King begins her autobiography with the words, "There is a Mrs. King. There is also Coretta. How one became detached from the other remains a mystery to me."[8] Coretta Scott King should be remembered not simply as the spouse and widow of Martin Luther King Jr. but as an independent human being with an identity related to but not dependent on the man she married. Long before she married the most prominent civil rights leader of the movement and long after he had been killed, Scott King formed her own thoughts, pursued her own priorities, and made her own name.

Coretta Scott King

Scott was born on April 27, 1927, in Heiberger, Alabama. She was one of three children and grew up in a rural area. Her family owned a farm, an unusual feat for Black people in those days. Her grandparents had been able to purchase 300 acres of land that her family still farmed when she was a little girl.[9] She milked cows, raised crops, and tended to the livestock. In the late 1930s, while the Great Depression was decimating Black families and communities, Scott began picking cotton, usually for pennies a day. Her family endured other hardships as well. When she was fifteen years old, white people in the community burned down her family's house. When her father took the audacious step of saving his money and starting his own sawmill, they burned that down too. The realities of Jim Crow and white supremacy in the South threatened to destroy what little her family had.

But both Scott and her parents had deep faith in God. Even after arsonists burned down his family's home, her father led them in prayer and told them to forgive the culprits. Scott grew up attending Tabor AME Zion Church, and she would join with her family in walking the four miles to and from church each week. At the age of ten years old, she made a profession of faith and joined the church. There she developed the prodigious singing and musical abilities that she would employ in various settings throughout her years as a civil rights activist. She described herself as a "deeply religious child," and as an adult she believed that "you have to be connected with God, to that divine force in your life, and that you have to continue to pray for direction."[10] During Scott's many tribulations in pursuit of the Beloved Community, she actively drew on her faith in God to sustain her.

Scott's mother instilled in her daughter the dream of an education. For a Black woman in the South, obtaining a quality education was one of the only pathways beyond agricultural work, domestic duties, and a life of poverty. During her high school years, Scott attended Lincoln Normal School, an institution founded by the American Missionary Association with a biracial faculty who had a mission to serve Black students. She flourished at the school. "Inside the protective walls of Lincoln, my horizons were expanded. I began to understand more about being connected to a larger society and to people outside my community."[11] Instructors at Lincoln introduced Scott to classical music and the work of legendary Black musical talents such as Paul Robeson and Marian Anderson. This is when she first began to dream of being a famous concert singer. Scott also learned at this time about pacifism and first encountered Bayard Rustin, one of the architects of nonviolent protest and a key organizer of the March on Washington for Jobs and Freedom in 1963. Scott recalled being "fascinated by Rustin's lecture on how conflict could be resolved without war or bloodshed."[12] Long before meeting Martin, Coretta Scott had already begun pondering nonviolent protest and its potential as a philosophy in the movement for Black freedom.

A stellar student with a sharp mind, Coretta Scott graduated as valedictorian of her class at Lincoln. Her academic achievement afforded her a full scholarship to Antioch College in Ohio, following in the footsteps of her older sister. Scott said that Antioch was a "pioneer in multicultural living and education." She had two white roommates there and, for the first time, began understanding white people beyond the racism she had experienced. She also gained exposure to other religions such as Islam and Buddhism. This relatively diverse culture coupled with the emphasis on peace activism gave Scott a vision of what would later be termed the "Beloved Community." Scott even dated a white Jewish man for two years before the complexities and pressures of a long-term interracial relationship forced them to part ways.

Antioch is also where Scott's activism began blossoming. She wrote a letter to the school administration protesting that she was not allowed to do her student teaching hours at the local white school. She also became involved with the local chapter of the NAACP, delving more deeply into the philosophy of nonviolence. "I began to consider myself a pacifist. Pacifism felt right to me; it accorded with what I had been taught as a Christian: to love thy neighbor as thyself."[13] After her time at Antioch College, the talented Scott applied to some of the nation's best musical schools. She gained an invitation to study at the New England Conservatory of Music in Boston, and it was during her time there she met a man named Martin Luther King Jr.

A friend of Scott's set her up with King. At first, she was not too impressed. She thought he was short. But as they became better acquainted, King mentioned that she had many of the qualities he was looking for in a wife and very quickly brought up marriage. Scott could see King's intelligence, his drive, and his passion for justice. She knew he was a man on a mission and that his calling to pursue equality for all people closely mirrored her own. Despite an initially cold reception by his parents, Scott consented to marry King, and they shared marriage vows on June 18, 1953. In those days, it was very difficult for a woman to have a flourishing professional career and fulfill the expectations of a wife and mother. Scott made the tough decision to shift her focus from becoming a concert performer to music education so she could have the margin to be a wife and mother. But she never lost her love of music or her vision to incorporate arts and activism.

As MLK Jr. finished his dissertation and Scott King graduated from the New England Conservatory, her husband took his first pastorate at Dexter Avenue Baptist Church in Montgomery, Alabama. Almost immediately, the couple was thrust into the vanguard of the burgeoning civil rights movement. In December 1955, the Montgomery bus boycott began and MLK Jr. accepted an invitation to be the spokesperson for the Montgomery Improvement Association, a group that Rosa Parks had long been part of before she refused to give up her seat on the bus. The death threats started mere days later.

On the evening of January 30, 1956, Scott King was chatting with a friend in the living room of their house when she heard a thump. Just weeks into the boycott, she was already conditioned to maintain constant vigilance and knew instantly they should seek safety. She and her friend had barely made it out of the living room when the bomb exploded. It rocked the entire house, blasted a hole in the front wall, and woke Yolanda, their infant child. The attack was Scott King's first life-or-death test in the fiery furnace of civil rights activism and leadership. Her parents came to Montgomery as soon as they heard about the bombing and insisted that she leave town with them. But she refused. "In Montgomery, when tragedy hit, when I was tested, I found that the fear had left. It had been overcome by faith."[14] In the aftermath of that violent disruption, anyone would have understood if she had left town with her infant child. They would have thought it the wise and prudent measure to take. But in that moment, Scott King decided to stay, and in so doing she strengthened the resolve of her husband to continue leading the boycott and her own courage to maintain the strength of her convictions. The spirit of justice arose within Scott King to overcome fear with faith and enabled her to decide to stay. Her choice to remain may have altered the course of the young civil rights movement.

Scott King's courageous commitment to partnering with her husband in leadership of the movement led her to India to study non-violence, to Europe to accompany Martin in receiving the Nobel Peace

Prize, to the March on Washington, and finally to that dreaded moment when she became a widow. Amid the heartbreak and the relentless demands of being a newly single parent, Scott King focused her considerable determination on institutionalizing Martin Luther King Jr.'s memory and legacy. She often called the King Center for Nonviolent Social Change in Atlanta her "fifth child" and envisioned it as the "West Point of nonviolence."[15] She founded the center on June 26, 1968, just over two months after her husband's assassination. As its leader she dedicated the center to continuing the tradition of nonviolent social change and love in action. The center allowed Scott King not only to commemorate her husband's life but to refine her own ideas about the work ahead.

Scott King defined the Beloved Community as "a realistic vision of an achievable society . . . [where caring] and compassion drive political polices and support the worldwide elimination of poverty and hunger and all forms of bigotry and violence."[16] Equipped with this philosophy of the Beloved Community, Scott King set about a decades-long career of advocating for care and compassion for all kinds of people. She continued her opposition to the Vietnam War and frequently gave speeches calling for an end to the conflict. She published a memoir, *My Life with Martin Luther King, Jr.*, in 1969.

Scott King led the effort to make Martin Luther King Jr. Day a national holiday. Representative John Conyers introduced legislation to create the holiday on April 8, 1968, less than a week after MLK Jr.'s assassination. But political conflicts and racism prevented its passage. Conyers, alongside the Congressional Black Caucus, persisted in reintroducing the bill every year until it finally came to a vote in 1979. Scott King gave a powerful testimony about her husband's significance to all people in the United States and the appropriateness of making a holiday in his honor. The vote failed. But the next year, musical artist Stevie Wonder aided the effort by recording the song "Happy Birthday" in 1980 to support efforts to create a holiday for MLK Jr. In it Wonder sang, "There ought to be a law against anyone who takes offense at a day in your celebration."[17] Scott King and Wonder often appeared together at events rallying support for the creation of a new national holiday. It took another three years, but the measure came to another vote in

Congress. This time it passed. Ronald Reagan, hardly an enthusiastic proponent of the holiday, relented and signed the Martin Luther King Jr. national holiday into law. Coretta Scott King stood near Reagan looking on as he signed.

Scott King expanded her focus on racial justice to include the global struggle for equality. In particular, she became an outspoken activist against apartheid in South Africa. In 1985, she and others were arrested at the South African embassy in Washington, DC, during an anti-apartheid protest. In 1986, she orchestrated an important trip to South Africa where she met with prominent African leaders and promoted the end of apartheid.[18] In the tradition of nonviolence, Scott King decried any violent efforts to end the racist practice. Instead, she encouraged economic sanctions to pressure South African leaders to change their policies. She painfully recounted how her visit and general interest in working with existing South African leaders to end apartheid were opposed by Black American leaders such as Randall Robinson and Jesse Jackson.[19] Upon Nelson Mandela's release, Scott King hosted him at the King Center and helped raise funds for his political party, the African National Congress (ANC).

Coretta Scott King was an activist before she met MLK Jr., and she was an activist after his murder. She poured her life out serving others, first her family and then all kinds of marginalized groups of people around the world. In many ways she was ahead of her peers in advocating for women's rights, the end of apartheid, nuclear disarmament, and LGBTQ rights. Throughout her many campaigns and initiatives to bring about the Beloved Community and promote nonviolence, her faith always guided her. In times of fear, grief, and uncertainty, Coretta Scott King consistently relied on her belief in God and hope for progress to guide her.

RUBY DEE, ACTING, AND ACTIVISM

Throughout the Black freedom struggle, arts and activism have journeyed with fingers intertwined. From the spirituals that enslaved men and women sang while laboring in sweltering southern fields to the poetry that poured from the pens of Black people who were sick and tired of being sick and tired, art in its various forms captures the human experience at a level that transcends mere thought. In the grand tradition of artists who are also activists stands Ruby Dee.

Ruby Dee
Glasshouse Images / Alamy Stock Photo

Born in 1922 in Ohio, Ruby Ann Wallace Davis grew up in Harlem, New York. Her biological mother left the family, but her father remarried a schoolteacher named Emma Amelia Benson.[20] She traced her love of the performing arts to elementary school. She described herself as a "painfully shy" child. But in class one day, she was called upon to read a selection from a play, and she did so well that her classmates applauded her performance. She began then to think seriously about becoming an actress.[21] In 1941, Wallace married blues singer Frankie Dee Brown. She started using his middle name as her stage name and kept it even when they divorced a few years later. She attended Hunter College and joined the American Negro Theater, one of the few places where Black actors were free to explore themes of race and the complexities of life as people of African descent in the United States. Other actors in the group included Sidney Poitier and Harry Belafonte. During this time, she met a man named Ossie Davis. They developed a relationship and got married in 1948. They remained married for more than half a century until Davis's death in 2005.

Ruby Dee held a strong belief in God from an early age. She credited her stepmother for ensuring that she and her siblings all attended Mother Zion AME Church. Like many who end up in activism of some form, young Ruby developed a sensitive conscience. When she was a young girl, her brother taught her how to "shop without money"—that is, to steal. She and her brother would steal small items from Woolworth's and either give them away as gifts or keep them for themselves. One night after Ruby had gone to the bathroom, she recalled that "long bony fingers gripped my arms and pinned me to the cold tile wall between the tub and the toilet." She was terrified, but even with her mouth wide open, she couldn't scream, couldn't make a sound. She took this to be a spirit and vowed never to steal again. Even as an adult, she called a hotel to confess that she had accidentally taken a clothes hanger with her in her luggage. The hotel worker to whom she spoke told her not to worry about it, but she said, "It is written, Thou shalt not steal!"[22]

Her religious upbringing instilled in Dee the belief that God had put her on earth for a purpose, and she was determined to follow that purpose as it grew and evolved throughout her lifetime. "I believe that God puts every creature on earth for a particular reason, and looking back, even a blind person can see and have impressions, can connect the dots of recognition and make a picture."[23] Ruby Dee lived a storied life and achieved remarkable success in the performing arts. Some of her most notable performances include roles in *A Raisin in the Sun* and the 1950 film *The Jackie Robinson Story*. Dee became the first Black woman to take on leading roles in plays for the American Shakespeare Festival. She appeared in the blockbuster television mini-series *Roots: The Next Generations* as well as the Spike Lee films *Do the Right Thing* and *Jungle Fever*. Dee was active in the industry into the twenty-first century and received an Oscar nomination for her part as the mother of Frank Lucas, played by Denzel Washington, in *American Gangster*.

For all of her professional accomplishments, Ruby Dee understood the malignant impact of racism on the nation and dedicated herself to fighting against it. She became good friends with activists such as Malcolm X and Martin Luther King Jr. After Malcolm X's assassination, her husband, Ossie Davis, delivered the eulogy.[24] Ruby Dee spoke at Martin Luther King's first address to a national crowd of 25,000 in Washington, DC, in 1957—the largest live audience he had spoken to at that point. Fittingly, it was a religiously focused event called the "Prayer Pilgrimage for Freedom." It was a demonstration to promote voting rights and lodge a protest against Eisenhower's silence in the face of white racist recalcitrance to implement *Brown v. Board*. Dee was among the Black celebrities who were outspoken about civil rights, and she gave an address to the crowd assembled there.[25] In 1963, she and her husband returned to Washington, DC, to take part in a much larger demonstration, serving as masters of ceremonies for the March on Washington for Jobs and Freedom. Their longtime activism in support of Black rights had earned them a place on the national stage. Ruby Dee was also active in groups such as the Congress of Racial Equality (CORE), the NAACP, and the Southern Christian Leadership Conference (SCLC). When it came time for Coretta Scott King to form the Cultural Affairs Department at the King Center to incorporate the arts into their broader message of nonviolent social transformation, she invited Ruby Dee to be on the advisory board.[26]

With her tireless work ethic, Ruby Dee earned the respect of her fellow actors and artists. At her funeral in 2014, Harry Belafonte submitted a letter he wanted read publicly. He wrote that Ruby Dee was "an artist, the likes of which I have never seen. As a matter of fact, because of Ruby Dee, I always tried to stretch myself beyond my capacities and reach for my own untapped expressions of the work."[27] Much like for Coretta Scott King, art and activism danced in harmony in Ruby Dee's life. Her work as a performer reinforced her work as an activist, and vice versa. Her faith honed a sharp sense of justice that compelled her to get involved in the plight of her people despite achieving success and acclaim as an artist. She could have chosen a more comfortable path, one in which she simply enjoyed the golden light of film, stage, and television fame, but she decided to commit herself to the cause of freedom. At a time when many people shied away from taking public stances against racism, Ruby Dee prayed, "God, make me so uncomfortable that I will do the very thing I fear."[28]

ANNA ARNOLD HEDGEMAN AND THE COMMISSION ON RELIGION AND RACE

Even in her teenage years, Anna Arnold Hedgeman believed in Jesus as the "tough courageous Son of God who studied, worked, dreamed, planned, and lived to produce change in his turbulent world."[29] That is to say, she did not believe in a "by and by" faith that was only concerned about the afterlife, but in a "here and now" faith that got involved in the real lives of people as they lived in the present. Hedgeman's active faith took her many places over her more than six decades of public service. According to her biographer Jennifer Scanlon, Hedgeman worked as a teacher in the Deep South, an administrator in the YWCA in the Northeast, a relief worker in New York City during the Great Depression, and a staff member in the New York City mayor's office, and she was the only woman member of the powerful administrative committee for the March on Washington for Jobs and Freedom.[30]

Anna Arnold Hedgeman
Hamline University

Hedgeman was born on July 5, 1899, the day after Independence Day and a few months before the dawn of a new century. She grew up in the northern Midwest in Anoka, Minnesota, and her family constituted the only Black people in that small town. Nevertheless, they found a sense of community there, especially through their membership in the local Methodist church and school. Her father had been born in South Carolina but migrated to North and South Dakota in search of more opportunities. On a trip to Chicago, he met Marie Ellen Parker, who was studying theater at the time. The two married and moved back to the area around Saint Paul, Minnesota, where Marie had grown up. They settled in Anoka, about thirty miles south of Saint Paul. Although he never attempted to "pass" as white, locals often assumed her father was white because of his light skin.

Anna's religious world was narrow but pervasive. "One lived to work, plan, study, discipline one's self, search for truth, and pray God's guidance."[31] Her stern and rigid father led the family in prayer twice a day, and they attended church on Sundays. They would have Sunday "program" each week in which Anna and her siblings were expected to review that day's sermon and Sunday school lesson. Given this upbringing, other children may have run from religion without a second glance, but Anna resonated with the idea of God. She was even glad to continue in a religious institution when she attended Hamline University, a Methodist school and the oldest college in the state, just an hour away from her home in Anoka. When she graduated in 1922 with a degree in English, Hedgeman became the first Black graduate in the school's history.[32]

Hedgeman taught for a couple of years at Rust College in Mississippi. There she learned just how vicious racism in the United States could be. Growing up in the Midwest and as the daughter of a well-respected man in the community, Hedgeman had experienced relatively few instances of racism—a wispy cloud compared to the storms of segregation she was about to endure. When she traveled by train from Chicago to Mississippi, a Black train porter escorted her from the white car to the "colored" car once they reached Cairo in the southern part of Illinois. The car was separate and anything but equal to the one white people occupied. "How could the railroad company permit such disgraceful service to any American?" she asked herself.[33] Hedgeman struggled to relate to other Black people at first. Having grown up as the only Black family in their Midwestern town, Hedgeman had had only sporadic contact with other Black people. She also grew up solidly middle class and did not know how to relate to the masses of poor Black people in the South, who seemed so different from her. When she finally arrived in Holly Springs, Mississippi, where the college was located, she couldn't even get a taxi at the train station. At Rust, she learned the startling realities of inequality in education. The college had few facilities and depended on white missionary donations and money from the impoverished Black community for its survival. Most of the students the college served had received a woefully inadequate education up to that point, and most could not fully afford their private school tuition. She frequently used money from her own paycheck to help meet the basic needs of her students. After just two years, Anna Arnold Hedgeman left Rust College. She saw too few opportunities for Black advancement in the South, but her brief time there had instilled in her a lifelong passion for racial justice.

After various leadership roles in the Northeast, Hedgeman got a new job. The National Council of Churches was the largest interdenominational network of churches at the time, representing more than thirty Christian denominations and forty million members.[34] In July 1963, they convened a meeting where they recommitted to the work of racial justice. In addition to several forthright statements about the obligation of Christians to work for racial harmony, the leadership also formed the Commission on Religion and Race (CRR). The commission's leader, Reverend Robert Spike, brought Anna Arnold Hedgeman on in a temporary role that soon became permanent. By this time Hedgeman was in her sixties and had four decades of experience working in various fields from teaching to local government.

She served in this position with the CRR at the same time she was part of planning the March on Washington for Jobs and Freedom. Hedgeman played a pivotal role as a bridge builder, orchestrating a meeting between A. Philip Randolph and Martin Luther King Jr. The two had been planning similar but separate marches, and this meeting enabled the two to coordinate and plan a massive demonstration together. Hedgeman was also instrumental in garnering organizational partnerships from women's groups to support the march. Although the male organizers of the march refused to heed her calls for greater female participation, she dutifully contributed her prodigious gifts to the march, bringing that same energy to her work with the CRR.[35]

In her role as coordinator of special projects with the Commission on Religion and Race, Hedgeman used her influence to recruit Protestants to participate in the March on Washington. Again, her skills as a bridge builder came into play. Black organizers of the march were understandably suspicious of white Christians—the people whom Martin Luther King Jr. called "white moderates" in his "Letter from Birmingham Jail" released just a few months prior.[36] Hedgeman shared their skepticism. "The church had a long history of race relations Sundays, prayer days, brotherhood pronouncements, conferences, seminars, workshops, statements, and resolutions, but action was too often another matter."[37] White people too had their reservations. Inculcated with messages about Black violence and aggression, many thought the march would end in bloodshed, mostly directed at white people. Yet Hedgeman worked with a fury. She made phone calls, organized events, and made appeals to everyone she could. In the end, her efforts proved immensely successful. She helped recruit more than 40,000 white Protestants to attend the march. One of the speakers on the platform that day was Eugene Carson Blake, chair of the CRR. Before that crowd of 250,000 demonstrators, Blake said, "[White Christians] come, late we come, but we come."[38]

After the March on Washington for Jobs and Freedom, Hedgeman continued her work with the Commission on Religion and Race, using her position to lobby for the passage of the Civil Rights Act of 1964. As euphoric as the march was, she understood it was only a beginning. There remained the tremendous challenge of harnessing all that interracial goodwill into policy change. A few weeks after the march, however, Hedgeman's faith was challenged. Four girls—Addie Mae Collins, Carole Robertson, Cynthia Wesley, and Denise McNair—were murdered when a white supremacist planted a bundle of dynamite at the 16th Street Baptist Church in Birmingham, Alabama, in September 1963. But Hedgeman's religious beliefs would not allow her to harbor bitterness toward anyone created in God's image, even if they were white supremacists. Through her grief and righteous anger, Hedgeman mobilized religious leaders to issue an interfaith statement in support of the pending legislation.[39] As with the March on Washington, Hedgeman wrote appeals, organized conferences, spoke at events nationwide, and formed coalitions of people to support the Civil Rights Act, including a provision that included sex as part of the nondiscrimination clause. When southern senators staged the longest filibuster in congressional history, Hedgeman organized a daily prayer meeting in Washington, DC, to pray for passage of the bill. When President Lyndon B. Johnson signed the Civil Rights Act into law on July 2, 1964, religious communities from every state had participated in some form of support for the action. Hedgeman was crucial to that support, and she was among the invitees President Johnson asked to attend a special ceremony at the White House commemorating the new law.[40]

Hedgeman continued her life of service in recognition of the intimate connection between faith and racial justice. Her difficult experiences confronting racism in Mississippi and the Deep South informed her conviction that she had to spend her life in support of Black equality. At the same time, her extensive contact with white people during her childhood and in her professional life helped her see the humanity in the people whose participation in the racial hierarchy made them oppressors. Some of her most enduring work came about while she was part of the National Council of Churches' Commission on Religion and Race. She translated the needs and concerns of white and Black Christians to each other. She put into practice a theology of racial justice that both prayed and worked for tangible change. Her often unheralded but indispensable efforts helped shape major events that led to some of the most significant racial progress of the twentieth century.

DOROTHY HEIGHT AND THE NATIONAL COUNCIL OF NEGRO WOMEN

Dorothy Height took her place as one of the few key women organizers and the only person representing a woman's organization during planning for the March on Washington for Jobs and Freedom.

She tirelessly pressed the necessity for women to be part of the program and highlighted their needs alongside issues of race. Her efforts went largely unrequited. Although she was an accomplished orator, she was not asked to speak. She and other women took seats on the platform near the podium during the march's proceedings, but that was largely a concession offered by the men for not allowing greater women's participation in the program. After the event, which many at the time hailed as a success, Height was part of a group of Black women who organized a meeting called "After the March . . . What?" That meeting helped cement the resolve of women in the movement to always elevate the concerns of women and families no matter what the men of the movement said or did.[41]

Height's role in the March on Washington came about because of her leadership in a seminal organization, the National Council of Negro Women (NCNW). Founded in 1935 by the inimitable Mary McLeod Bethune, the NCNW addressed a critical gap in the Black freedom struggle. While some entities focused on combating racism, and others focused on women's rights in general, few organizations homed in on the specific needs of Black women. McLeod Bethune stepped down from her role leading the NCNW in 1949, and after two other presidents, Dorothy Height took over and held the position for more than forty years. She led the NCNW throughout the civil rights movement and beyond. Through her faith, vision, and tenacity, she made this organization one of the most formidable and indispensable in the movement for racial and gender progress.

Height was born in 1912 in Richmond, Virginia, the former capital of the Confederacy. When she was still a child, her family moved north to a town near Pittsburgh, Pennsylvania. From her earliest days, her parents emphasized education, and she excelled as a student. As a teenager at an integrated high school, she began her organized pursuit of justice. She advocated for voting rights and antilynching campaigns.

While she was still in high school, she won a prestigious national speaking contest. Her topic focused on the Reconstruction Amendments, and although she was the only Black contestant, the all-white judges awarded her the victory and a full ride to college.[42] She applied and was accepted to Barnard College in New York City.

But before classes started in the fall of 1929, the dean called her to his office and told her that the school had already filled its quota of Black students and she could not attend. Height took her letter of acceptance to New York University and made her case there. They immediately accepted her, and she earned both a bachelor's and a master's degree there.[43]

Height never knew a time when faith was not a daily part of her life. Her family lived next door to Emmanuel Baptist Church, where they were members. Her father served as a deacon, superintendent of the Sunday school, and a choir leader and their family would often spend entire Sundays in church.[44] Height first exercised her leadership skills and honed her sense of justice in these church-related ministries—even as a child. At the segregated Rankin Christian Center, Height came up with a proposal that the noisy kindergartners needed something to occupy them in the early morning. The center's director agreed, and Height, at only twelve years old, began teaching Bible lessons to the all-white group of squirmy, cacophonous kids.[45]

In her twenties she became an officer in the United Christian Youth Movement. This brought her to the attention of longtime civil rights leader A. Philip Randolph, who appointed her to the National Youth Congress of the National Negro Congress.[46] Shortly after graduating from college, she started attending meetings hosted by the United Youth Front, which brought in speakers and ideas friendly to socialism and communism. This was during a season when Height was learning much more about systemic injustice and economic inequality. One day, a fellow participant demanded that she stop talking about God. Instead of backing down, she defended her belief. That moment became a turning point in her life. "I knew that my commitment to my faith and my work would never waver."[47]

Height's leadership abilities and organizational acumen made her the logical choice to become the fourth president of the NCNW, a position to which she was elected in 1957. While leading the NCNW, Height simultaneously served at the Young Women's Christian Association (YWCA) and was a key figure in their efforts to desegregate in the mid-twentieth century. She began working in the Harlem branch of the YWCA in 1937. There she first met her mentor and inspiration,

Mary McLeod Bethune, as well as Eleanor Roosevelt, who accompanied her. Height's long tenure with the YWCA included a year teaching in India at the Delhi School of Social Work.

Height helped the YWCA adopt a set of resolutions and principles called "The Interracial Charter and Related Policy." The pamphlet edited by Height stated, "Wherever there is injustice on the basis of race, whether in the community, the nation or the world, our protest must be clear and our labor for its removal, vigorous and steady."[48] As the civil rights movement gained momentum, the YWCA formed the Action Program for Integration and Desegregation of Community YWCAs in 1963. Height took on the role of leading the two-year initiative. The program evolved into a permanent office—the Office of Racial Justice—and Height served as its first director.[49] She retired from the YWCA in 1977 with an appointment as a lifetime national honorary board member.

Dorothy Height helped assemble a meeting among Black women held after the March on Washington for Jobs and Freedom. With the theme "After the March . . . What?" the women agreed that they needed to engage in more coordinated efforts that focused on Black women. They did not feel that existing women's rights groups gave sufficient attention to the role of racism, and many white women underappreciated the role poverty played in addition to other basic quality of life issues. "It took a while for women's movement leaders to understand that some of the issues in which they were more focused had less appeal to black women, who were caught up in bread and butter issues."[50] Height was one of the foremost leaders in the twentieth century who explicitly and consistently linked Black civil rights and women's rights.

Height's belief about race relations was that segregation created false impressions and stoked prejudices. She therefore worked to foster closer relationships across racial lines through dialogue, small groups, and one-on-one interactions. In 1964, Height was one of the organizers of a secret meeting in Atlanta, Georgia, of women representing groups such as the YWCA, the National Council of Jewish Women, the National Council of Catholic Women, and Churchwomen United.[51] The interracial group, which broke local laws by holding an integrated meeting, supported efforts to come alongside existing justice organizations in Mississippi to aid their work. The result was an initiative called Wednesdays in Mississippi (WIM) that Height cofounded with a white NCNW volunteer named Polly Cowan. The effort facilitated interactions between northern and southern and Black and white women in Mississippi.

Groups traveled to Jackson from whence they made excursions to smaller towns in the state to speak with local women. Later renamed Workshops in Mississippi, the program offered educational sessions where local leaders such as Fannie Lou Hamer taught. The NCNW continued its work in Mississippi, including purchasing pigs for the "pig bank" that Hamer started on her Freedom Farm. The NCNW bought fifty-five pigs in 1968, which grew to a population of over 3,000 five years later. Poor people—both Black and white—could come to the pig bank and borrow a pig as long as they later contributed a piglet as interest.[52]

Dorothy Height continued working until weeks before her death at ninety-eight years old. She never married and never had children, instead focusing her nearly boundless energy on promoting the cause of justice in society. For her efforts she was recognized with the Congressional Gold Medal and the Presidential Medal of Freedom. President Barack Obama offered remarks at her funeral, and as he reflected on Height's nearly 100 years of life, he said, "We remember her for all she did over a lifetime, behind the scenes, to broaden the movement's reach. . . . To make us see the drive for civil rights and women's rights not as a separate struggle, but as part of a larger movement to secure the rights of all humanity, regardless of gender, regardless of race, regardless of ethnicity."[53]

PRATHIA HALL AND THE DREAM

Substantial evidence from oral history suggests that Martin Luther King Jr.'s famous "I have a dream" line originated with a young Black college student named Prathia Hall. In 1962, Hall suspended her formal education to become part of the Student Nonviolent Coordinating Committee (SNCC) and the Black freedom struggle. At a vigil in remembrance of four Black churches that had recently been burned by

white supremacists, she was called on to offer the opening prayer. In
her invocation she repeated the phrase "I have a dream." The nation's
most prominent civil rights leader at the time, Martin Luther King
Jr., attended that event and heard Hall's prayer. The phrase left an
impression on King. He looked for Hall after the vigil to ask permission
to use the phrase—a request she granted without asking for recognition.
King then began incorporating the phrase into his speeches, the most
well-known of which occurred at the March on Washington for Jobs
and Freedom.[54] According to Hall's biographer, Courtney Pace, Hall's
use of a "dream" as a metaphor was an example of her sophisticated
theologizing informed by the pursuit of liberation and her Black church
roots. "The repetition of 'dream' guided her listeners into reflection on
what was and what could be, what had been promised and what had
already been fulfilled, what God actually said and what people did in
the name of God."[55]

Prathia Hall
Frank Lennon / Getty Images

Born in Philadelphia on June 29, 1940, Hall grew up as a
preacher's kid. Her father founded Mt. Sharon Baptist Church in
1938 and remained its pastor until his death in 1960. The church
was a family affair. In its early days, the congregation met in the Hall
home. Prathia and her siblings participated in the church's ministries

including a food pantry and visits to the sick and shut-in. As was true of many women of the time, Hall's mother bore many of the responsibilities of raising children, and she left a deep impression of piety and critical thinking on her daughter. When it came to Hall's church leadership and preaching, her father was her main influence. He never thought being a woman would diminish her ability to serve God or make a difference in the world. She even carried his handkerchief in her Bible as a reminder of his impact.[56] As an adult she described her sense of calling in this way:

> Well it sounds presumptuous to say you were born with a mission, but I have always had a deep passion for justice. I was raised by my parents in what I believe to be the central dynamic in the African-American religious tradition. That is, an integration of the religious and the political. It is a belief that God intends us to be free, and assists us, and empowers us in the struggle for freedom. So the stories of our history helped me to understand that we were called to be activists in this struggle for justice.[57]

In high school and college, Hall participated in the Fellowship Hall, a community dedicated to social justice from a Christian perspective. Fellowship Hall in Philadelphia hosted Mordecai Johnson, the same meeting Martin Luther King Jr. attended where he first heard about Gandhian nonviolence.[58] In her teenage years and early twenties, Hall was already experienced in putting her faith to work for social transformation. Hall practiced what she called "freedom faith": "the belief that God wants people to be free and equips and empowers those who work for freedom."[59] In her theological work she was a pioneer of what is now called womanism—theology rooted in the experiences and perspectives of Black women.

Throughout her time in college and as an activist in SNCC, Hall wrestled with her sense of calling. She strongly desired to become an ordained pastor, but she knew "almost no ordained women ministers were taken seriously."[60] So she kept searching for ways to get involved in the hands-on, frontline work of the movement. Her moment of decision finally arrived in the form of a personal calamity.

Hall's father died tragically when a trolley hit his car. Hall's earthly hero had gone home to heaven, and his passing left her devastated. Around this same time in 1960, students in Greensboro, North Carolina, started the sit-in movement. Although she was still a college student at Temple University, Hall found ways to participate in the movement including boycotts and picketing. In 1961, she and several others were arrested for a sit-in demonstration at a restaurant in Baltimore.

At the same time, students began organizing themselves into a new venture called the Student Nonviolent Coordinating Committee. Hall kept close tabs on the group and determined that she wanted to be part of it. The pull she felt toward active involvement in the movement only grew. Hall struggled to maintain her focus on her studies in her senior year of college, and as soon as she finished classes, she journeyed south and showed up unannounced at SNCC's office in Atlanta. They assigned her to Albany in southwest Georgia.

Even though SNCC eschewed strict hierarchies, Hall soon became the second-in-command to leader Charles Sherrod. She had a hand in training new participants, which was a critical and delicate task since she had to teach white northerners about the strict racial codes of the South and prepare everyone for the very real danger of attempting to disrupt the racial status quo. She was assigned to Terrell County in southwest Georgia. Because of the acute poverty of its residents and the merciless racial terrorism inflicted upon the Black community by the white population, the county earned the nickname "Terrible Terrell" and "Tombstone Territory."[61]

One night, when Hall was staying in the home of a local host, the house was shot up by white racial terrorists. Hall sustained minor wounds, but it was a major episode for her. "That night any and all romantic thoughts about our freedom adventure dissolved as we came face-to-face with the real and present possibility of death."[62] Though such violence tested the faith of Hall and her compatriots, they withstood the trial. Hall remained in Terrell and continued to work for voting rights amid constant danger.

She also blossomed as a preacher. Many witnesses to her orations were stunned at such maturity and sophisticated theology coming from a young woman. Even Martin Luther King Jr., with whom she frequently interacted through her work with the Albany movement, said, "Prathia Hall is the one platform speaker I would prefer not to follow."[63] Eventually Hall relented to the still, small voice of God in her spirit and pursued ordained ministry. In 1977, she became one of the very first women ordained by her denomination, the American Baptist Church. She also pastored Mt. Sharon Baptist Church, the church started by her father. In time, she earned a constellation of advanced degrees: an MDiv, a ThM, and a PhD from Princeton Theological Seminary. She taught in several capacities and ended her career as the Martin Luther King Jr. Chair in Social Ethics at the Boston University School of Theology.[64]

Hall summarized her sense of calling to social justice and a lifetime of activism by saying that every time a person willingly took the risk of standing up against racism, "that was a religious statement, as profoundly religious as saying a prayer or doing any kind of religious discipline."[65] Hall understood what many other people of faith in the movement would come to realize—worship did not begin or end in the hallowed halls of a church sanctuary. Faith had to be lived. It had to be exercised in the face of risk, danger, and uncertainty. What we call the spirit of justice, Prathia Hall called "freedom faith"—God's work through the community of faith "to set the oppressed free" (Luke 4:18).

UNITA BLACKWELL, THE MAYOR OF MAYERSVILLE

Little in Unita Blackwell's background foreshadowed that she would become the first Black woman mayor elected in Mississippi. Born in 1933 during the depths of the Great Depression to sharecropping parents, Blackwell initially attained only an eighth-grade education. She was in her thirties before she even knew she could vote, let alone run for office. But Blackwell's enduring dedication to rural communities in the Delta and her steely commitment to justice positioned her to gain the trust of local people, who chose her to lead their small town of Mayersville in 1976. She held the position of mayor for more than twenty years and achieved significant milestones for the impoverished town. Reflecting on her historic achievement, she said, "Nothing is set up for me to be the mayor of Mayersville, Mississippi. Nothing has been laid out for me to be that, 'cause everything was against us, you see. But you learn how to move, no matter what."[66]

Unita Blackwell
William Patrick Butler/CC BY 2.0

Born as U. Z. Brown, a teacher later told her she needed names, not just initials, so they settled on Unita (u-NEE-tuh) Zelma. Blackwell said she grew up "poor, black and barefooted in a loving churchgoing family in the Mississippi Delta."[67] Blackwell's mother was serious about churchgoing. She left her husband, Blackwell's father, because she wanted him to go to church more often, and he just wasn't interested. Her mother moved Blackwell and her siblings from Memphis to West Helena, Arkansas, where she could attend school for most of the year instead of just two or three months at a time. Even so, Blackwell stopped her formal schooling after eighth grade and went to work—mostly sharecropping for barely any money at all.[68]

Church was the center of Black life in those days. "Church was the only place we could go that was not controlled by white people, and it completed our needs in every part of our lives. The church was our anchor. It held us together. It kept us going."[69] Blackwell spent countless days in the church, not just Sundays. She was there throughout the week attending programs or in preparation for programs. This immersion into the life and language of the Black church would serve her well during her years of activism. Many of the hymns and gospel songs she grew up singing were adapted to become "movement songs." A word or phrase would be replaced with something appropriate to civil rights activities. The familiar rhythms and melodies came back to strengthen her in times of severe persecution. At church, Blackwell learned about the Golden Rule, to treat others as you would have them treat you. That lesson applied to how she was taught to view white people. Racism and segregation were embedded in the cracks of life in the Delta. She daily saw the injustices heaped upon Black people by white racists. A white plantation owner shot and killed her grandfather. But she learned from the church that she should not hate. "Without my church and my faith that God would pull me through, I don't think I could have survived those days or been prepared to face the future."[70] Those lessons from that community of faith enabled her to fulfill her role as a civil rights activist.

One hot Sunday in 1964, two out-of-towners came to Moon Lake Missionary Baptist Church. Unita Blackwell attended the church, and she had seen these newcomers the day before and suspected they might be Freedom Riders or on some similar initiative. Louis Grant and Bob Wright were, in fact, from the Student Nonviolent Coordinating Committee, and they had come to tell rural Black Mississippians how to register to vote. Blackwell had been giving a Sunday school lesson on the theme "God helps those who help themselves," and when one of the SNCC members got up to address the congregation, he repeated the phrase to encourage the congregation to get out and register. The next Wednesday they had another meeting at the church for interested parties. When the organizers asked for volunteers, Blackwell and her husband stood up. Later Blackwell said, "I've been standing up ever since."[71]

Standing up did not prevent others from trying to strike Unita Blackwell down. When a small group went to register to vote, white men with guns surrounded them in a show of intimidation. In addition, the local registrars were still adhering to the old Jim Crow stand-by—literacy tests. They gave each person a passage of the Mississippi Constitution to interpret. But the odds were stacked against Black people. Chronic undereducation limited literacy. Even though Blackwell could read and write, it didn't help. The white registrar always came up with some excuse to say a Black person failed the test. Soon after, Blackwell, already stuck in the depths of poverty, lost her job working in the fields. Overnight she found herself unemployed with no prospects for income. But she remained undaunted, becoming a field organizer for SNCC. Through this work she met other women committed to the cause such as Fannie Lou Hamer, who became a dear friend. She also got involved in the Mississippi Freedom Democratic Party (MFDP) and was one of the delegates when they went to the 1964 Democratic National Convention to attempt to unseat the all-white regular Mississippi delegation. Although her initial attempt to register to vote was unsuccessful, that action stirred the spirit of justice deep within her. "I couldn't get enough of it. I couldn't learn enough. Being a freedom fighter didn't just become part of my life; it *was* my life."[72]

The world of organizing is a small one, and it is even smaller for Black women. Blackwell knew and worked for Dorothy Height with the National Council of Negro Women. Height personally called on Blackwell for help in the NCNW's housing program. Blackwell served as housing coordinator for the NCNW from 1967 to 1975, a position that had her frequently on the road traveling to different parts of the country.[73] In 1973, Blackwell was invited by the Hollywood actor Shirley MacLaine to be one of twelve women who took a trip with her to China. They went to investigate life under Communist rule while MacLaine recorded a documentary about the trip. Blackwell would later take sixteen more trips to China throughout her life.[74]

By 1976, Blackwell had gained extensive experience in organizing and leadership. She had a lifetime of lessons since she began her civil rights activism in 1964, and she was ready to put them to use in ways that could have a long-term impact. She ran for and won election as mayor of the small town of Mayersville where she had been living for many years. Only about 500 people lived there, and the infrastructure of the town had yet to catch up to the late twentieth century. Many Black people in town did not have indoor plumbing, several roads were still made of packed dirt, and poor-quality housing plagued the residents. Blackwell's first order of business as mayor was to officially incorporate the town. That would open the community up to much-needed government funding. The community was about 80 percent Black, and the committee Blackwell formed was biracial, a new experience for most of the town's inhabitants.[75]

Utilizing the same mass meeting and canvassing tactics she had learned in her campaigns for voting rights, Blackwell's effort to incorporate the town was successful. That opened the way for significant projects including several public housing units that vastly improved the living conditions of poor Black people, along with paved roads, streetlights, and sewers. Her work kept her in office until 2001.[76] Blackwell's creativity and tenacity in bringing solutions to her poor rural community garnered her national recognition. In 1992 she earned a grant from the MacArthur Foundation, commonly referred to as the "genius grant." "*U.Z. Brown, the little fast girl from Lula, Mississippi, got a 'genius grant'!*"[77] She used the unrestricted funds from the grant to buy a brick house, put her grandson through private school, and purchase a Cadillac for herself.

Blackwell came a long way from her grade school days to accomplish much for others in her life. It all began with an organizing meeting in a small rural church in the Mississippi Delta. "In 1964, I was stuck in poverty and trapped by the color of my skin in a pointless existence. Then the movement came along, and my mind opened up. . . . My skin was as black as it had ever been, but my life had meaning."[78] For Unita Blackwell, as for many other Black women, getting involved in the civil rights movement gave her the opportunity to develop skills, exercise leadership, and improve the lives of her people. For Black women, in particular, the movement became a community where they could meet, learn from, and become friends with other women who would become like sisters in a new family.

CONCLUSION

Throughout the civil rights movement, Black women labored under what Mary Church Terrell dubbed "the double handicap of race and sex."[79] Activist Pauli Murray, herself a Christian, termed this systemic injustice at the intersection of race and gender "Jane Crow."[80] Like its twin, Jim Crow, it relegated an entire population—in this case, Black women—to second-class status in US society. But Black women transcended intense social boundaries to act as indispensable foot soldiers and leaders in the movement. Not only did Black women comprise a majority of participants during the civil rights era, but they also set forth sophisticated organizing philosophies, a collaborative form of decision-making, and an inspirational example through their stalwart resilience in the face of both sexism and racism. The civil rights movement simply would not have happened if not for Black women who tapped into the spirit of justice for the progress of their people and the nation.

CHAPTER
NINE

BLACK *AND* CHRISTIAN

The civil rights movement of the 1950s and 1960s did much to topple the legalized system of Jim Crow. Yet the promise of the civil rights movement remained distant, especially to the masses of Black people trapped in urban environments racked by poverty, crime, drugs, and joblessness. After more than a decade of nonviolent protest, embodied in the life and work of Martin Luther King Jr. and other Black Christians, many people pushed back against such tactics in favor of alternative stances against racism and inequality. In 1966, SNCC activist Stokely Carmichael popularized the term *Black power* during a march in Mississippi. The juxtaposition of *Black* and *power* catalyzed young people and others who bristled against the expectation that they should "turn the other cheek" in the face of white racism, police brutality, and acute poverty. On that same humid Mississippi night, Carmichael also said, "The only way we gonna stop them white men from whippin' us is to take over."[1] In the face of continued white racism and resistance to change, the tone of the movement was beginning to shift. It was entering a new phase of struggle focused on the lingering legacies of Jim Crow and white supremacy.

Black frustration with the status quo reached a peak during several urban uprisings in the late 1960s. These conflagrations often began with incidents of police brutality and resulted in mass arrests, injuries, property damage, and even death. In 1965, nearly 30 percent of Black people lived below the poverty line, compared to just 8 percent of white people.

The unemployment rate for Black people was 8.5 percent, nearly double the unemployment rate for white people at 4.3 percent. In August of that year, the Watts community in Los Angeles erupted in protest after Marquette Frye and his brother Ronald were pulled over. Marquette had been drinking and driving. Ronald went to get their mother just a few blocks away. When the mother saw the scene with her son and the officers, the situation escalated to physical blows and arrests. By that time a crowd had gathered, and rumors began to spread. Then local community members, filled with anger and frustration, broke car windows, assaulted white people in the vicinity, and engaged in several days of looting and clashes with law enforcement.[2]

The summer of 1967 brought more historic urban rebellions. In Newark, New Jersey, a Black cabdriver named John Smith drove around a double-parked police cruiser. The officer in the car pulled him over and assaulted him before taking him to a nearby police station. An untrue rumor spread that Smith had been killed, and a crowd of Black people gathered at the police station throwing rocks and bottles. The situation escalated into four days of blood, fire, and destruction.[3] Also in 1967, Detroit erupted into the deadliest of the uprisings. Early on the morning of July 23, police raided an unlicensed bar called a "blind pig." As the officers made the arrests, a crowd gathered in a tense standoff. After someone threw a brick and shattered the back window of a police cruiser, the rebellion began. It took five days and the deployment of federal troops to quell the unrest, and by the end forty-three people had been killed.[4]

In the aftermath of these devastations, President Lyndon B. Johnson established the National Advisory Commission on Civil Disorders, better known as the Kerner Commission after its chairman, Illinois governor Otto Kerner. The committee was charged to answer three questions: What happened? Why did it happen? And what can prevent it from happening again? After seven months of site visits, interviews, and research, the committee released its findings in February 1968. The most-referenced sentence of the report stated, "Our Nation is moving toward two societies, one black, one white—separate and unequal."[5]

The commissioners upended the prevailing narrative about Black pathology as the cause of the uprisings. Instead, they pointed to the responsibility of white Americans. "What white Americans have never fully understood but what the Negro can never forget—is that white society is deeply implicated in the ghetto. White institutions created it, white institutions maintain it, and white society condones it."[6] The report pointed to a constellation of causes such as inadequate housing, joblessness, voter suppression, and police brutality. The recommendations of the commission included providing more opportunities for community input on policies, financial assistance, federal programs for the poor, and reviews of local police practices to reduce brutality. Almost none of the recommendations were supported or implemented by federal or community officials.

All of this occurred within the milieu of a resurgent far-right politics. Republican Richard Nixon won the presidency after Lyndon B. Johnson made the surprising decision not to run for reelection. He appealed to the "silent majority"—an amorphous group of moderate, suburban (white) Americans—whose opinions were allegedly being drowned out by voices on the far-left political extreme.[7] Nixon also implemented the so-called "southern strategy" to recruit white "backlash" voters upset with the social unrest of the 1960s, especially efforts at racial desegregation.[8] The Religious Right emerged as a politically conservative movement organized to resist the liberal turn in national sociopolitical life and to return America to "traditional" values. Eventually, Jerry Falwell would go on to form the "Moral Majority" in 1979 to mobilize conservative Christians in support of the Republican Party. The Moral Majority, in turn, used emerging forms of mass media such as mailing lists with hundreds of thousands of addresses to help get Ronald Reagan elected.[9] The political ascendancy of the far right would result in tax breaks for the wealthiest citizens, a rollback of social support programs, and increases in "law and order" policies that precipitated the crisis of mass incarceration.

In response to the unmet promises of democracy, the Constitution, and the civil rights movement, Black people mobilized. In Oakland in 1966, two Black men, Huey P. Newton and Bobby Seale, formed the Black Panther Party for Self-Defense. They created the group with a focus on preventing police brutality in urban Black communities. They donned black berets and leather jackets and armed themselves with pistols, rifles, and other firearms. They set up patrols to follow police officers and monitor interactions with community members. Contra the accusations that the Black Panthers and similar groups did not have coherent agendas, they put together a ten-point program that included demands such as: "We want freedom. We want power to determine the destiny of our Black Community," "We want an immediate end to POLICE BRUTALITY and MURDER of Black people," and "We want education that teaches us our true history and our role in present-day society."[10]

The Panthers, along with other groups such as the Revolutionary Action Movement (RAM) and the Republic of New Afrika, prioritized systemic injustice, structural inequality, and class solidarity over racial integration or moral suasion. Integral to these efforts was a growing identification with blackness and Africa. The Black power movement, as this era was called, influenced social and political realms as well as religious ones. Black Christians drew on the spirit of justice during the Black power era to insist on the beauty of blackness and the necessity of deeper structural changes.

THE NCBC AND THE STATEMENT ON BLACK POWER

Scarcely a month after Stokely Carmichael uttered, "Black power," in Mississippi, a group of Black ministers gathered in New York City to address this new spirit in the civil rights movement. In January 1966, Reverend Benjamin Payton became the director of the Commission on Religion and Race of the National Council of Churches, the same group Anna Arnold Hedgeman had once led. He gathered with noted ministers Gayraud S. Wilmore, a Presbyterian, and Henderson R. Hughes, an AME minister. In short order the men had formed a new organization: the National Committee of Negro Churchmen (later the National Commission of Black Churchmen, or NCBC). Their positions in these denominations primed them for the cry of "Black power" and spoke to their desire to translate the slogan into theological and ethical terms that resonated with Black Christians.[11]

Just a few weeks after the creation of the NCBC, the organizers released a statement on Black power. They wanted it to be as widely read as possible, so they published it as an ad in the *New York Times*. The statement included forty-eight signatories, all Black men except Anna Arnold Hedgeman, whose previous position with the Commission on Religion and Race afforded her the unique privilege of participation. The name of the National Council of Black Churchmen speaks to the patriarchy embedded in Black church practice, the same patriarchy that Black Christian women had to confront before and during the civil rights movement and beyond. The supporters, all of whom had their names printed in the paper, came from historically white mainline denominations as well as historically Black denominations. As another sign of a new focus of the civil rights movement, most of the Black ministers who signed the statement came from the North, not the South, and represented a spectrum of traditions, not just Baptists.[12]

The ministers supported and interpreted the term *Black power* for a broad audience. They began by framing the problem. "The fundamental distortion facing us in the controversy about 'black power' is rooted in a gross imbalance of power and conscience between Negroes and white Americans."[13] They pointed out that white people seemed like they were permitted to use power to meet their desired ends, but Black people could only rely on moral suasion through suffering and patience. This tacit social arrangement deceived white people into thinking that inordinate power was their right and tricked Black people into thinking they had no ability to resist it. "We are faced now with a situation where conscienceless power meets powerless conscience, threatening the very foundations of our nation," they wrote.[14]

The statement proceeded to address four groups in turn: the leaders of America, white churchmen, Negro citizens, and the mass media. To the political leaders of the nation, they explained that a concern with power was not the problem. "At issue in the relations between whites and Negroes in America is the problem of inequality of power." The crux of the issue was not with a slogan nor the concept of power itself—the ability to achieve one's goals and desires. The heart of the matter was that white people hoarded power and Black people had much less power for self-determination and fewer opportunities.

To the white clergy, they explained that integration as it had often been practiced was no longer the order of the day. "It is not enough to answer that 'integration' is the solution. . . . The Negro Church was created as a result of the refusal to submit to the indignities of a false kind of 'integration' in which all power was in the hands of white people."[15] They inveighed against the abuse of concepts such as "Christian love" to pacify Black people and silence their demands for justice. Then the authors turned their attention to Black people and encouraged them to take inventory of their existing assets. "'Black power' is already present to some extent in the Negro church, in Negro fraternities and sororities, in our professional associations."[16] While they spoke strongly against racism, these Christian ministers still supported the universal equality of all people. "For in the final analysis, we are *persons* and the power of all groups must be wielded to make visible our common humanity."[17] Black power did not mean white disempowerment but the right of all people to exercise agency for themselves.

In their words to the mass media, the ministers recognized the solemn charge of journalists to spread truth. They had performed admirably in covering the brutality of the Jim Crow South during the civil rights movement, but "the truth that needs revealing today is not so clear-cut in its outlines, nor is there a national consensus to help you form relevant points of view."[18] The ministers recognized that the landscape of the Black freedom struggle had been reshaped by the shift in attention from primarily the rural South to the urban North. The problems Black people faced in urban ghettos were complex and interwoven. Many well-meaning people differed sharply on what should be done and how to do it. Therefore, journalists had to work much harder to hear a variety of perspectives and report accurately.

The Black Power Statement by the National Council of Black Churchmen stood as one of the first and most public interactions with the changing landscape of the Black freedom struggle during the Black power era. Instead of repudiating or softening the term *Black power*, they laid out its ethical and social implications. They sought to harness the increasing energy and race-consciousness in the national discourse. The group continued to issue statements and convene meetings. Although the churchmen still exhibited similar forms of patriarchy as previous generations, they also represented a new vanguard of Black Christians who embraced change and pushed for the structural and economic progress necessary to uplift Black people. For them Black power was an expression of faith, not a denial of it.

ALBERT CLEAGE JR. AND THE SHRINE OF THE BLACK MADONNA

On Easter Sunday, March 26, 1967, Reverend Albert Cleage Jr. unveiled an eighteen-foot-tall painting of the Black Madonna at his church in Detroit. She stands serenely and powerfully, covered in white, sky blue, and lavender cloth. Her eyebrows slope downward to eyes that stare fixedly ahead, and her face is adorned by a broad nose and full lips. Only her arms and face—a deep shade of dark chocolate—are visible. In her arms she holds an infant of the same hue as his mother, swaddled in pale pink cloth.

Albert Cleage Jr. in front of Black Madonna
Detroit Historical Society

This was not the first depiction of Mary or her son Jesus the Christ as African-descended, but in the context of the Black power movement, it was more than an aesthetic choice. It was an act of resistance. "Instead of a sermon, we could just sit here and look at the chancel mural of the

Black Madonna which we unveiled on Easter Sunday," Cleage intoned.[19] Cleage was not merely asserting his artistic sensibilities. On that Easter morn, he attempted to radically redefine Christianity in a way that supported the contemporary Black movement for political and economic power. "We issue a call to all black Churches. Put down this white Jesus who has been tearing you to pieces. Forget your white God," Cleage preached that Sunday.[20]

The Black Madonna mural served as a visual illustration of Cleage's central intellectual contribution to the Black power movement and Black Christianity in that era—that Jesus was Black. Cleage's ideas of Black independence, pride, and separatism were influenced by Malcolm X, whom he greatly admired. Cleage developed the theology of Black Christian Nationalism (BCN) as a new way of conceiving of a Christianity decoupled from the Eurocentric and white interpretations of the faith that he believed many Black people had uncritically adopted.

Born in Detroit in 1911, Cleage was the son of a medical doctor who was well-respected in the community. Both his mother, Pearl Reed Cleage, and his father were Christians, but his mother did more than anyone else to shape Cleage Jr.'s beliefs about God from a young age. She was a small woman with a big presence. She kept all seven of the Cleage children in line. But she also instilled in them a sense of the divine. "The advice I had for him is the same for all his life, was to take your troubles to God."[21]

Cleage followed a circuitous route that finally ended up with his pastorate in Detroit. But for years he searched for an environment that would allow him to adequately express his Black nationalist ideas and work for his people. He enrolled at Wayne State University but transferred before he graduated to Oberlin College in Ohio. He eventually earned degrees from both institutions.

Right after graduating from Oberlin in 1943, Cleage accepted a position as assistant pastor of Chandler Memorial Congregational Church in Lexington, Kentucky. But a short time later he and his wife, Doris, moved to San Francisco so he could accept a temporary appointment at a new church there. It was called the Church for the Fellowship of All Peoples—one of the first intentionally racially integrated churches of the era. Cleage was there to fill the role of copastor along with a white minister, Albert Fisk, until the renowned theologian Howard Thurman could take up the position full-time.[22]

The conflicts between Cleage and his white copastor started almost at once. Fisk thought that Cleage was too focused on community matters and not on pastoral care of the congregation or preaching. He thought Cleage came across as "very blunt" and "tactless." To Fisk, Cleage's sermons were "ethical, rather than religious" and "defeatist."[23] For his part, Cleage held little respect for Fisk. He believed that Fisk avoided the necessary conflict that comes with putting people of different races together. In Cleage's view, Fisk "didn't want to raise racial tensions in his heaven." When Thurman came to San Francisco in June 1944, Cleage was ready to leave.

Cleage and his wife left the church after only a few months. He then took on the role of pastor at the historic Saint John's Church in Springfield, Massachusetts. The church had a long record of racial justice and had served as a stop along the Underground Railroad in the antebellum period. Cleage had finally found a position where he could begin to focus on social justice issues. He made an especially vigorous effort to serve the area's youth through sports leagues, Bible studies, and other initiatives. He wanted them to understand a kind of Christianity that opened its arms in welcome amid a world that had crossed its arms against them.

In 1951, Albert Cleage Jr. and his family (by this time he had two daughters) returned to Detroit, Michigan. Cleage accepted the call to pastor Saint Mark's United Presbyterian Community Church. It was a new congregation formed by the United Presbyterian Church denomination in response to the ongoing influx of Black residents in the city due to the Great Migration and specifically "to serve the growing northwest Negro residential area."[24] His blunt communication style and uncompromising tactics in pursuit of Black uplift once again led to conflict with other religious leaders. By March of 1953, leaders in the United Presbyterian Church denomination had determined that Cleage could not continue as pastor of Saint Mark's. He was dismissed by the Committee of Missions, part of the Detroit Presbytery. In the end, Cleage proved very popular and 300 of Saint Mark's congregants, nearly the entire congregation, left to form a new church. The church they launched was first called Saint Mark's Congregational Church, then Central Congregational Church, but it would eventually become the Shrine of the Black Madonna.

The church Cleage led moved into a building that featured a large stained-glass window at the front of the sanctuary. The scene depicted a pilgrim named William Brewster, a British man on the run from religious persecution in Europe. As the only college-educated member of the landing party, he became the ruling elder and spiritual leader of the Pilgrim colony. In the stained-glass window towering within Pilgrim Congregational Church's sanctuary, Brewster is shown getting off of the *Mayflower* and giving a Bible to a group of grateful indigenous people. One journalist wrote, "As you look to the altar you see a magnificent twenty to twenty-five foot stained glass window. It is truly a masterpiece. The coloring is so tremendous that even when the sun isn't shining on it, it still maintains vivid color life."[25] When the church's original white congregation sold the building to the budding Black congregation led by Cleage, the mural remained.

As Cleage grew in his Afrocentric focus, he determined that a different visual representation was needed for the church sanctuary. The church's leaders commissioned a Black artist named Glanton Dowdell to paint the mural. Dowdell was a formerly incarcerated man who served ten years in prison on a second-degree murder charge. He used a local Black woman, Rose Waldron, as his model and inspiration for the Black Madonna. Dowdell saw in the Black Madonna the plight and strength of the Black women he had encountered in Detroit and his personal life. "I can't divorce the Madonna from black women," he said. "I don't think that any of the experiences of the Madonna were more poignant or dramatic than those of any negro mother, an ADC [Aid to Dependent Children] mother, a mother whose child goes wrong, anyone."[26] In the most personal of ways, the Black Madonna symbolized the burdens many Black women and mothers faced in a world filled with sexism and malice toward the Black babies they bore.

By March 26, 1967, Easter Sunday, Cleage and his congregation were primed for his most visible and decisive demonstration of a new vision of Christianity in light of the long history of the social, political, and economic struggles of Black people. The unveiling of the Black

Madonna and child mural gave an artistic demonstration of Cleage's conviction that Christianity must be completely reimagined in light of their suffering. But Cleage did not stop at visual depictions of a Black Messiah. He incorporated his beliefs into a new theological system he called Black Christian Nationalism.

Cleage thought Black Christians could excise the white supremacist concepts often embedded in US Christianity and thus get back to the true religion of Jesus. He said that the church could serve Black people only if it could "rediscover the fact that Christianity began as a Black religion for Black people."[27] The core of Black Christian Nationalism was Cleage's notion of a Black nation. Cleage emphasized the formation of a Black "nation within a nation" because integration into a society where white people still controlled most resources and maintained their grip on the levers of power was an impossibility. The only way for Black people to gain the power to control their own lives and destinies was by creating communities that operated as independently from the larger white society as possible. While other religions such as the Nation of Islam were making inroads with some Black people, Cleage remained committed to Christianity—not one that began with a white Jesus, but with a Black Messiah and a Black nation.

Cleage's ideas about Christianity continued to evolve. He eventually moved on from Black Christian Nationalism to form the Pan-African Orthodox Church. In 1978, he changed his name to Jaramogi Abebe Agyeman—an African name derived from a blend of Luo, Amharic, and Akan words meaning "liberator," "holy man," and "savior of the nation."[28] Albert Cleage Jr. conducted his ministry the way he thought any Black Christian would if they knew they were truly free. He intended for his life, ministry, and theology to be a model for all Black people, especially Black Christians, of how to transcend the whiteness that distorted Christ and Christianity.

JAMES CONE AND BLACK LIBERATION THEOLOGY

James Cone had been watching the events of the Black revolution closely as they unfolded throughout the civil rights movement of the 1960s.

But when the Detroit uprising in 1967 turned into the deadliest urban rebellion of the era, it killed something in Cone too. "My explosion shook me at the core of my racial identity, killing the 'Negro' in me and resurrecting my black self."[29] The spirit of justice rose within him and gave him new life. Some marched in the streets, others belted on bandoliers, and many preached against prejudice. Young Dr. James Cone decided to use the tools of his trade—theology—to fight oppression.

James Cone
Union Theological Seminary

James Cone is typically cited as the founder of Black Liberation Theology. In his project of theological reimagination, he wanted to "make it unquestionably clear that the God of Moses and of Jesus makes an unqualified solidarity with the victims, empowering them to fight against injustice."[30] Cone placed the suffering of Black people and the oppressed more generally at the center of the gospel and built a theological framework outward from that core. He explored what Christianity meant when it took seriously the pleas, prayers, and priorities of a people who suffered under anti-Black racism. He dedicated his prolific writing and teaching career as a theologian to this work.

Cone was born in Arkansas in 1940. He grew up under the segregated conditions of the Jim Crow South and knew from experience the white-fisted grip that racism could hold over entire communities. He attended the historically Black Philander Smith College in Little Rock and was in the city during the historic showdown to desegregate Central High School. From there he went on to earn his PhD in systematic theology from Garrett Theological Seminary at Northwestern University near Chicago, Illinois. He taught briefly at Philander Smith then took a job at Adrian College in Michigan.[31] This was the time when the "Negro" in him died, and he was reborn as a Black liberation theologian. He spent the remainder of his career at Union Theological Seminary in New York City where he cemented his legacy as a seminal theological thinker of the twentieth century.

When the term *Black power* became the new banner under which activists marched in 1966, it provided the catalyst for him to shift his theological perspective. Unlike many other Christians, even some Black Christians, Cone resonated with the term *Black power*. He felt it captured the rage and frustration that Black people had been feeling ever since being forcibly removed from their homelands in Africa centuries ago. To him Black power meant that the children of Africa would no longer be made to feel humiliated by their melanated skin. Nor would they any longer accept a whitewashed Christianity that either remained silent in the face of racism or was used as a tool to articulate and reinforce it.

Cone published the seminal *Black Theology and Black Power* in 1969 as an explanation of how Black power related to Christianity and the academic study of theology. His burden was to articulate a theology that was liberated from white theology and centered on the Black experience. Like Albert Cleage Jr., Cone declared, "Jesus is black."[32] Cone explained that Jesus was Black because Jesus always identifies with the most marginalized, oppressed, and despised people in a society. That, he said, is the meaning of Jesus' incarnation as a Jew in first-century Palestine. The Jewish people were situated in a politically and religiously marginalized position—first as enslaved people in Egypt and then, in Jesus' lifetime, as the subjects of the Roman Empire. Jesus' ethnic particularity as a Jew pointed to his universal identification with the poor and powerless in all times and places. "To say that Christ is black means that black people are God's poor people whom Christ has come to liberate."[33] It was not Jesus' skin pigmentation or African genealogy at the core of Cone's assertion that Jesus is Black; rather, it was Jesus' status as poor and his eternal solidarity with the outcast that mattered.

Decades later, Cone would revise and refine the ideas he initially presented in *Black Theology and Black Power*. He came to realize the sexism in his early formulations of Black theology after Black womanist theologians critiqued his silence on the ways sexism combined with racism in the oppression of Black women. He also heard other Black theologians who pointed out that even in his critique of white theology he tended to rely on white theologians and the neo-orthodoxy espoused by European theologians for his theoretical frameworks. Though subject to critique, Cone's black liberation theology opened corridors of opportunity in the academy for new disciplines such as Latin American, Asian, and womanist theology. He constantly disputed with white academics in an effort to demonstrate the legitimacy of a Christian theology that took the Black experience as its point of departure. Regardless of how white Christians responded to or repudiated his work, Cone remained faithful to his calling to be a "theological witness to the black freedom struggle" and helped spark a revolution in Christian theology in the United States.[34]

SHIRLEY CHISHOLM'S FAITH IN POLITICS

Shirley Chisholm is best remembered as the first Black woman to run for presidential nomination on a major party ticket.[35] What is less appreciated is how her faith undergirded her politics and helped her maneuver as a Black woman in a field dominated by men. In her long and distinguished career as a public servant, she privately drew on the faith she had learned as a child and held onto as an adult for the fortitude to remain "unbought and unbossed."[36]

Chisholm lived most of her life in the United States, but she always considered herself a Barbadian American. Shirley St. Hill was born in Brooklyn in 1924 to a father from Guyana and a mother from Barbados.

Shirley Chisholm

After just a few years in the United States, her mother took young Shirley and her two siblings back to Barbados, but their stay was only temporary until the family could save enough money for a decent place to live in the United States and to put their children through school. Her mother went back to the United States and left the children in the care of their grandmother, Emily Seale. Although she was stern, "there were endless hugs, laughter, tears, and chatter."[37] After a few idyllic years growing up on a farm and learning the basics in elementary school, she and her siblings moved back to Brooklyn. It was 1934 and the nation was caught in the depths of the Great Depression. Her family was poor but proud. Chisholm's parents brought the pride of having grown up in places where Black people were a majority. Her father was a follower of Marcus Garvey, a fellow West Indian, and the Universal Negro Improvement Association.[38]

Sundays meant three treks to church for various services. Other children used to laugh at their piety, but Chisholm's mother told her children, "You're going to grow up to be good Christians."[39] Chisholm grew up going to a Brethren church. Instead of a typical church service featuring a sermon, the congregation sat on benches arranged in con-centric circles. They would sing a song a cappella since no instruments were allowed. Then they would sit in silence until someone felt the Holy Spirit move them to preach a message or share a song. A spirited child like Shirley Chisholm did not necessarily enjoy these services, but she respected religion and took to heart the lessons she learned at church and from her mother.

Chisholm did well in high school. When she graduated in 1942, she had been accepted by Vassar College and Oberlin College. Her parents could not afford to pay for room and board at these schools, so she stayed closer to home and attended Brooklyn College. The school was more than 90 percent white. Even though the college was progressive for the time, Chisholm began to see more clearly how pervasive racism was. "Things were organized to keep those who were on top up there. The country was racist all the way through."[40] She graduated cum laude and became a teacher, one of the few professional pathways open to Black women at the time.

For seven years Chisholm worked as a teacher in Harlem. While working, she took night classes at Columbia Teachers College and earned a master's degree in education. She met a Jamaican immigrant, and they married in 1949. She continued working as an educator in various roles and rose up the ranks to lead several daycare centers. Her formal political activity began when she worked on election campaigns and joined an advocacy group called the Bedford-Stuyvesant Political League. From her earliest days of political participation, she worked to expand opportunities for Black people and women. She ran for and won her first political office in 1964 and became a sitting member of the New York State Assembly. In 1968, Chisholm set her sights on the US Congress. She ran and won the election with the campaign slogan "Fighting Shirley Chisholm—Unbought and Unbossed."[41] She gained her victory in an upset over James Farmer, the former leader of the Congress of Racial Equality (CORE). Shirley Chisholm had become the first Black woman elected to Congress.

But she wasn't done. In January 1972, Chisholm announced yet another audacious goal. Standing before a crowd of 700 at Concord Baptist Church, she launched a bid for the Democratic Party nomination for president of the United States. The reaction was predictably sensational and skeptical. Because she was a Black woman, few had any confidence she could win, and many were bewildered as to why she would even try. She said she was "literally and figuratively the dark horse."[42] But with characteristic boldness, Chisholm forged ahead. Her faith in God aided her boldness. "I only look to God and my conscience for approval of what I am doing."[43] If Chisholm had waited for popular support, she probably never would have run for local office, let alone president. But in her labors to serve the poor, Black people, and women, she did not seek the approbation of other people. She had cultivated a conscience sensitive to the issues of justice, and she had faith in the God of justice. This was the key to the credibility of her campaign slogan: unbought and unbossed. She did what she did for an audience of One.

Despite her faith, the odds of winning were not in Chisholm's favor. For starters, she only had a fraction of the financial resources the other Democratic candidates boasted. She simply could not match the expenditures typical of a nomination bid. She did earn the endorsement of groups such as the Black Panther Party, and she received enthusiastic support from women and the poor and working class of the nation.[44]

To win the highest office in the nation, however, one needs supporters from within the establishment, and Chisholm faced obstacles both as a woman and as a Black person. Even Black leaders, especially men, were conspicuously silent or outright critical of Chisholm's campaign. Reverend William Jones of Operation Breadbasket and the SCLC said her ambition was "purely symbolic rather than substantive."[45] The 1972 National Black Political Convention in Gary did not invite her to speak, nor did they endorse her. Neither did the liberal white women of the women's movement support her wholeheartedly. They saw her campaign as risky and did not approach issues of Black economic empowerment with the urgency Chisholm thought the problem required. Hounded by a lack of resources, a disorganized campaign on the ground, and infighting between constituents of the diverse coalition she tried to form, Chisholm did not win the nomination. The lack of support from Black men stung, and while she did not shrink back from her public duties afterward, she refocused her attention on her local constituents.

Chisholm continued to serve in Congress for several more years until 1981. During her time in elected office as the first Black woman member of Congress, she was also a founding member of the Congressional Black Caucus and the Democratic Women's Caucus. She opposed the war in Vietnam, and she constantly pushed for more resources and better living conditions for her constituents. That was what she wanted to be remembered for, not her demographics but her work. Undergirding all her efforts was a faith that she did not "wear on her sleeve" but that animated her actions and her belief that the nation could be better than it was.[46] "America has the laws and the material resources it takes to ensure justice for all its people. What it lacks is the heart, the humanity, the Christian love that it would take."[47]

MYRLIE EVERS-WILLIAMS, A LIFETIME OF JUSTICE

The National Association for the Advancement of Colored People (NAACP) was not doing well. A series of scandals and missteps had tarnished the venerable institution that had been at the center of the Black freedom struggle for nearly a century. Some said the organization and its leadership were out of step with the times. Benjamin Hooks had been the executive director since 1972, and by the end of his term in the 1990s, critics said that the NAACP was "a dinosaur whose national leadership is still living in the glory days of the civil rights movement."[48] The next leader of the NAACP, Ben Chavis Jr., served for just sixteen months when his own board ousted him for numerous controversies including an incident where he used NAACP funds to settle a sexual harassment case.[49] The troubles did not end with character issues. An external audit of the civil rights organization released in 1995 revealed that it was nearly $4 million in debt.[50] It would take an incredible leader to bring an institution like this—one that relied on the public's good faith for its effectiveness—back from the brink. That is when Myrlie Evers-Williams once again took her place as a leader in the ongoing movement for racial justice.

She didn't want to do it. Evers-Williams, who had remarried after Medgar Evers's assassination, had no designs on leading the NAACP. But her second husband, Walter Williams, was dying of prostate cancer.

With just weeks to live, he insisted that Myrlie run for board chair. "Run and win," he said.[51] Reluctantly, but with a sense of obligation to both Medgar, who served as the first field secretary for the NAACP in Mississippi, and her dying husband, whose final wishes included a request for her intervention, in 1995 Myrlie Evers-Williams ran for leadership of the board and won . . . by one vote.

She served for a whirlwind three years, and according to the NAACP, in that time she was able to increase their cash balances by more than $1 million, reduce their debt by $665,000, decrease their expenses by nearly $7 million, and bring in $2 million in revenue and contributions.[52] She was able to use her powerful reputation as an activist, her years of accumulated leadership experience, and her deep reservoirs of energy to steer the organization back into good standing. It was a feat that simply served as the latest evidence of her faith in God and steely will in the face of obstacles.

Myrlie Evers-Williams (née Beasley) was born on Saint Patrick's Day, March 17, 1933, in Vicksburg, Mississippi. In the segregated town, Myrlie Beasley's world was Black, Christian, and mostly female. Her mother was sixteen years old when she had her, and Myrlie's father was a twenty-eight-year-old truck driver.[53] Her parents broke up when she was about one year old, and her mother moved away. But her paternal grandmother, whom she called "Mama," raised her, while her father came in and out of her life. She also grew up with her great-great-grandmother, "Grandma," who had been born into slavery. After Grandma died, they also lived with her aunt Myrlie, after whom young Myrlie was named. These Black women left an indelible mark on her developing mind. They were educated, industrious, and well-respected. They were also women of faith. Like many other Black people of the time, Myrlie grew up in a Christian household. She remembers her mama singing gospel songs such as "Pass Me Not, O Gentle Savior" when Myrlie was a child.[54] In high school, Myrlie had the rare experience of interracial worship. For a few months, their Black pastor managed to get Myrlie's all-Black youth group together for occasional meetings with a youth group from a local white Baptist church. The meetings themselves occurred without incident, but the segregationist culture meant they were forced to stop meeting after just a few months.[55]

Like Coretta Scott King, Myrlie Beasley excelled in music. Her chosen instrument was the piano. She intended to major in music in college, but no Black college in Mississippi had a music major. She applied for a special grant from the state that would give her the funds to attend a school out-of-state that offered such a program. Segregationist states often paid out-of-state tuition for Black students to send them off and keep them from enrolling in all-white local colleges and universities. In this way, the state could technically abide by the "separate but equal" clause of *Plessy v. Ferguson*. But they refused Myrlie a grant, and she had to settle for a major in education and a minor in music at Alcorn A&M (now Alcorn State University). Myrlie was angry with the administrators who refused to allow her to study the major she wanted, but she recalled, "It is one of the ironies of my life that I probably would never have met Medgar but for the way Mississippi cheats its Negroes."[56]

Myrlie met Medgar Evers her first day on campus. In 1950, Medgar was eight years older than Myrlie, a junior in school, on the football team, and a World War II veteran. Right away, her grandmother and aunt criticized the pairing. They didn't want an older GI taking advantage of this naive college freshman. The couple's love, however, was genuine and deep. "I had prayed for months about Medgar and me, and by this time I was sure we were right for each other."[57] They married on Christmas Eve 1951. Although Medgar graduated, Myrlie's time to study quickly eroded due to household tasks, her duties as a wife, and financial constraints. She stopped going to school before she obtained her degree.[58]

Soon the couple relocated to Mound Bayou, an all-Black town founded by Isaiah T. Montgomery in 1887, and began raising a family. Medgar took a job selling insurance, which took him to all parts of the Mississippi Delta region and brought him face-to-face with the plight of Black people like never before. Already restive with a sense that he needed to be working for the good of his people, Medgar was spurred on by this experience to get involved with local civil rights organizations. Working with prolific civil rights leaders such as Amzie Moore and T. R. M. Howard, Medgar became a founding member of the Regional Council of Negro Leadership (RCNL), and his formal work for justice in Mississippi began.[59]

In January 1954, Medgar Evers applied to enroll as a student at the all-white University of Mississippi, the state's pride and joy when it came to public universities. Myrlie, who was pregnant with their second child and concerned about both the financial and physical risks, called her husband's decision "selfish and foolish."[60] When Evers was rejected, as predicted, he appealed to the NAACP for support in a lawsuit against the university. Instead, the NAACP suggested that he become the organization's first field secretary in Mississippi. Myrlie said she was "scared to death, but if that's what you want to do, let's try, because it also means that we come as a package, and that I will have a job."[61] Throughout his tenure with the NAACP, Myrlie served as his secretary and coworker in voter registration drives, boycotts, and other demonstrations. The couple moved to Jackson, Mississippi, where Myrlie would reside until shortly after her husband's assassination.

The bullet that killed Medgar Evers on June 12, 1963, didn't stop in his chest. It ripped through his body and through the wall of his home, denting the refrigerator inside where his wife and three children—Darrell, Reena, and Van—were still awake. Fortunately, the Evers family had trained for just such an occasion. They instantly dropped to the ground for cover. Unfortunately for Medgar Evers, when he dropped to the ground, he would never get up again. Years later, Myrlie recalled, "Whenever I closed my eyes, I saw Medgar, I felt his body, I felt the warmth of his kisses, and I relived his death in all its terrible vividness—the shot, the sight of his body, his blood oozing into the armful of white 'Jim Crow Must Go' t-shirts he had been carrying, my screams, the lights, the sirens."[62]

In the moments immediately following the shot, Myrlie relied on the faith that her mama and grandma had instilled in her. She said she "prayed for God's will to be done and I sobbed and I prayed that whatever happened I would be able to accept it."[63] After her husband died, living with that reality was not a simple matter. Now a single mother wracked by grief, Myrlie shared in her memoir, "I seriously contemplated taking my life."[64] She had been pregnant with her fourth child when Medgar was shot, but she miscarried. She took it as a blessing that she did not have to care for an infant when she could hardly care for herself or her family. Whether it was driving recklessly on dark two-lane highways in Mississippi or stockpiling sleeping pills so that she could take enough to never wake up, Myrlie did not think she could bear the pain. One day she came close to ending it all. When two of her children were at school and the youngest was napping, she raised a handful of pills to her mouth but could not bring herself to ingest them. "For some reason—divine intervention I'm sure—I simply couldn't act on my intention."[65] In the faces of her children and the face of God, Myrlie found a reason to keep living.

A year later, the young widow took her children and moved to Claremont, California, where they could begin anew. With the determination that comes from necessity, she enrolled at Pomona College and completed the educational journey she had started at Alcorn. Now the sole breadwinner for the family and armed with a college degree, Evers reentered the working world. She got a job working with the Claremont Colleges in recruitment and later worked in publicity and advertising. In 1975, she worked as the national director for community affairs at the Atlantic Richfield Company (ARCO) in Los Angeles. In 1976, she opened herself up to love again and married Walter Williams, a longshoreman and union organizer. They remained married until he died of pancreatic cancer in 1995.

Amid all the changes in her life, Evers made time to publish the book *For Us, the Living* in 1967. It told the story of how Medgar and Myrlie met and fell in love. In it she wrote, "Somewhere in Mississippi lives the man who murdered my husband."[66] Her husband's murderer, Byron De La Beckwith, was not convicted of the crime. He had been tried twice before, and both times the trial ended with an all-white hung jury. Myrlie Evers-Williams persisted in seeking justice.[67] The case finally came to trial again in 1994. After the jury deliberated, Myrlie and her children assembled in the courtroom a few dozen feet from her husband's unremorseful killer. After interminable moments when the history of Mississippi's racism and the promise of racial progress hung in the balance, the verdict was read: "The jury finds the defendant, Byron De La Beckwith, guilty as charged."[68] That moment came as a welcome and needed expression of the spirit of justice. It meant that with persistent effort and hope, accountability is possible.

Evers-Williams accumulated many distinguished feats during her long life. She helped found the National Women's Political Caucus. She ran for Congress in California twice. In 1987, Tom Bradley, the first Black mayor of Los Angeles, appointed her to the prestigious Board of Public Works. She was the first Black woman to serve as a commissioner on the board.[69] She published her autobiography, *Watch Me Fly*, and coedited *The Autobiography of Medgar Evers*. She started the Medgar and Myrlie Evers Institute in 1989. In 2013, fifty years after her husband's murder, she delivered the invocation at the second inauguration of President Barack Obama. She was the first woman and the first layperson to do so. She was instrumental in seeing that their home in Jackson, where Medgar was shot, was made into a national park and then into a national monument in 2023.[70]

Throughout her life, Evers-Williams remained active in the NAACP, the organization to which her husband had devoted the last of his energies. She spoke nationwide on behalf of the group and offered her wisdom and guidance. In the 1990s, when the organization teetered on the edge of ignominy, she stepped up to help. All of her exploits thus far had prepared her for the difficulties of righting a listing ship. In recognition for her service, the NAACP presented her with their highest honor, the Spingarn Medal, in 1998. As of this writing she is still alive, and lives by a notion that has carried her through many difficult days: "Though tragedy has shattered my world more than once, I have kept on keeping on. My faith in God and the strength of my forebears are like pillars holding up my soul, giving me an inner reserve of courage and hope to draw from."[71]

SISTER THEA BOWMAN

By June 1989, the breast cancer had spread to her legs, hips, arms, shoulder blades, and skull. But the most excruciating pain came from the cancer in her spine. It made her body feel at times like it was on fire. It rendered walking impossible, and she was confined to a wheelchair. Yet even nearing the end of her life, and especially on that day in June at the United States Conference of Catholic Bishops, she was resplendent.

Sister Thea Bowman
Franciscan Sisters of Perpetual Adoration / fspa.org/theabowman

The nun from the Franciscan Sisters of Perpetual Adoration began as she often did—with a song. In answer to her own question about how it felt to be Black in the church and in society, she sang, "Sometimes I feel like a motherless child. . . . A long way from home, a long, long way from home."[72] She asked her audience of black-clad Catholic clergy what it meant to be Black in the United States. To address her own query, she described in brief, colorful strokes the history of people of African descent from their time in Africa to the Middle Passage to slavery. But it was not merely a story of victimhood. Instead, she emphasized how Africans brought their whole selves to North America. "Here in an alien land African people clung to African ways of thinking, of proceeding, of understanding values, of celebrating life, of walking and talking and healing and learning and singing and praying."[73] She was putting the majority white crowd on notice that Black people had much to offer, and their culture should be valued in the church.

But, she explained, to be Black and Catholic also felt "like being a second or third class citizen of the Holy City."[74] Too often the white clergy and religious orders sent to Black communities insulated themselves from the local people. They did not take the time to learn from Black people. This isolation allowed racism, stereotypes, and prejudices to persist. White Catholics imposed religious practices and solutions on the community without input from the people who were suffering, poor, and marginalized. Black Catholics had not been afforded a seat at the decision-making table, and both Black and white people suffered for it.

Sister Bowman told these austere priests that a new era had dawned. Black Catholics were not merely wards of a predominantly white US clergy. They had a rich spirituality and a communal solidarity that the church needed. "And now our Black-American bishops in the name of the church universal have publicly declared that we as people of faith, as a Catholic people of God, have come of age, and it is time for us to be evangelizers of ourselves."[75] Black people had leaders and ideas of their own. They did not need to be dictated to but empowered.

Toward the close of her talk, Bowman cast a vision of the true Catholic Church. One racially, ethnically, and culturally diverse yet united—the church as a "family of families."[76] A church that because of its unity would be a powerful force for good in the world. The true church, able to overcome: "Overcome the poverty—overcome the loneliness—overcome the alienation and build together a Holy city, a new Jerusalem, a city set apart where they'll know that we are here because we love one another." Then she ended as she began. She led this group of mostly white priests in an old song that had found new life in the civil rights movement, "We Shall Overcome."

Sister Thea Bowman has been called "the most well-known African American religious sister in U.S. Catholic history."[77] Her notoriety comes from a combination of factors, not least of which was her dedication to the cause of racial justice. Born as Bertha Bowman in 1937 in Mississippi, she exhibited an affinity for reading and music even as a toddler, which allowed her to skip first grade.[78] She was raised Protestant in a churchgoing household, and those early days of attending Black church taught her the "old time religion" and gave her a vision of growing up and becoming a preacher.[79] As a child she was sensitive to matters related to God and had a tender conscience. So when Catholics set up work in her town of Canton, Mississippi, she was drawn to them because of their good works and wanted to be part of what they were doing. In 1947 at the age of nine, Bertha Bowman was baptized into the Roman Catholic Church.

Bowman attended Holy Child Jesus Mission School in Mississippi. As a teenager she sensed a call to the Catholic sisterhood, and in 1953, after a visit to a chapel run by the Sisters of Perpetual Adoration, she formally declared her intent to enter the religious order. It was somewhat of a sensation that a Black teenage girl from Mississippi would become Catholic, let alone a nun. Yet Bowman sensed an inner call from God to devote her life to faith and service. At the start of her novitiate year in 1956, Bertha Bowman became Sister Thea Bowman. Two years later, she officially took her vows as a sister in the Catholic Church.

At this time, the civil rights movement was gaining momentum. Bowman continued her education by enrolling at Viterbo College, a higher education institution run by the sisterhood. But she always paid close attention to the news of the Black freedom struggle. She retained a strong pull to her own people, one that was made even more acute by her presence in a Catholic and white environment. She began her teaching career at the age of twenty-one, when the order assigned her to instruct fifth- and sixth-grade students at Blessed Sacrament Elementary School in La Crosse, Wisconsin. She went on to teach at the same Catholic school she had attended in Mississippi and at Viterbo College and Xavier University in New Orleans. She also continued her education by earning a master's degree and eventually a PhD in English from the Catholic University of America.

After Bowman had taught for more than a decade, the Catholic bishop of Jackson, Mississippi, called her to be the Consultant for Intercultural Awareness for the diocese. In this role she often worked with children and incorporated her love and talent for the arts. She taught them to sing songs, play games, and perform plays. She tried to help them have a "better understanding of their own heritage, the values and ways of thinking that made them who they are." Her ability to connect with an audience and communicate her love of the church while also challenging people to put their faith into action made her an in-demand speaker. She traveled all over the United States and internationally to places such as Nigeria, Kenya, and the Virgin Islands.[80]

In 1983, Bowman was diagnosed with breast cancer. Even with an aggressive treatment regimen, the cancer advanced and spread. Nevertheless, Bowman kept a packed speaking and traveling schedule even as her body deteriorated. "Part of my approach to my illness has been to say I want to choose life, I want to keep going, I want to live fully until I die." After she died in 1990, those who knew her best remarked how Bowman did more than simply live. Her friend Margaret Walker Alexander, a renowned Black writer, educator, and poet, expressed a sentiment many others held as well: "I think Sister Thea is a modern-day saint."[81]

CONCLUSION

The civil rights movement emerged as one of the most significant social movements in US history. But it left much unfinished concerning racial justice. It even engendered a staunch defense of the status quo in the form of the rise of the Religious Right and conservative political platforms that rolled back or halted efforts to create a social safety net. Racism never goes down without a fight. But even as racism adapts, so does the resistance to racism. The Black power movement emerged as the next phase of the Black freedom struggle. New movements that self-consciously and proudly embraced Black identity emerged. Within Christianity, Black people asserted their right to be both Black and Christian simultaneously without compromising one for the other. They embraced different forms of resistance to racism. They still marched and protested, but they also won elections, registered voters, and engaged in the long, tedious work of crafting laws and policies that would lead to more equity among all people groups. The spirit of justice remained at work during the Black power era, empowering people to continue the fight against injustice.

CHAPTER
TEN

THE NEXT JUSTICE GENERATION

A group of men gathered from around the country to kneel in prayer in preparation for what they were about to do. The day was overcast and in the forties, so many of them had layered T-shirts under sweatshirts and hoodies. A few wore winter jackets—most wore black, some wore camouflage. Many of them sported backpacks. Those wearing caps took them off as the prayer began.

"Dear Lord, we come to you today and we ask for protection and wisdom," the prayer leader opened.[1] He continued, "We ask for the rest of our fellow Americans, Lord. . . . We understand that the ideas and the ideologies that come out of some of these value systems and socialism . . . are antithetical to you and what you would wish for us, Lord." The prayer then turned patriotic as he thanked God for the "wonderful nation we've all been blessed to be in." Moving on from thanksgiving, the prayer leader made supplication to God for the resources they needed for their task: "We pray that you would invite all of us with courage and strength to both represent you and represent our culture well. In Jesus' name we pray."[2] And they all said amen.

Assured of God's blessing, the men stood up and stormed the Capitol. It was January 6, 2021—the day of an attempted insurrection in Washington, DC. Just after the prayer ended, someone from the group yelled for everyone to get their masks on—not for fear of spreading the COVID-19 virus, but because someone was about to start a live video, and they presumably did not want to be identified. They were later identified as members of a group called the Proud Boys.

Proud Boys marching in Washington, DC, on January 6, 2021.
Elvert Barnes/CC BY SA 2.0

The Proud Boys describe themselves as a "pro-Western fraternal organization for men who refuse to apologize for creating the modern world, aka Western Chauvinists."[3] A watchdog organization offers an even more explicit description. They describe the Proud Boys as a far-right hate group started in 2016 that regularly pronounces white nationalist, anti-Muslim, anti-Semitic, and anti-Black ideas.[4] Before January 6, the Proud Boys frequently appeared at rallies in Washington and Oregon as well as the deadly "Unite the Right" rally, a protest against removing a statue of Confederate general Robert E. Lee from Charlottesville, Virginia, in 2017.

The Proud Boys' prayer wasn't the only sign of Christianity at the January 6 insurrection. Once the mob had broken into the chambers of Congress, the so-called QAnon Shaman, Jacob Chansley—shirtless and adorned with face paint and a fur hat with horns—shouted, "Let's all say a prayer in this sacred space." He was grateful that God had allowed them to "exercise our rights, to allow us to send a message to all the tyrants, the communists and the globalists that this is our nation, not theirs." He shouted, "Jesus Christ, we invoke your name!"[5] Outside the Capitol, a huge wooden cross stood, and someone with black gloves with a printed image of finger bones on them clutched a Bible to his chest. People held signs reading, "Jesus is my Savior. Trump is my President." They had all gathered in support of the lie that the 2020 presidential election had been stolen from the incumbent, Donald J. Trump. They wanted to overturn the election results and keep him as their leader. The Christian symbolism at the insurrection made it clear that this was not a wholly secular event, and some of the most ardent protesters claimed Christianity as their religion. Implicit in their messages about religion and nationalism was an ideology about race.

Cross being carried at protest outside US Capitol building, January 6, 2021.
lev radin/Shutterstock.com

Many of those who stormed the Capitol on January 6 represented a set of beliefs and commitments called white Christian nationalism, an ethnocultural ideology that uses Christian symbolism to create a permission structure for the acquisition of political power and social control.[6] While it is often unspoken, the word *white* should be presumed as a prefix of Christian nationalism because racial bigotry is inherent to and inseparable from this belief system. To give just one example, the most notorious racist terrorist group in the United States, the Ku Klux Klan, operates from a white Christian nationalist framework. The founder of the second major wave of Klan activity, William J. Simmons, wrote in 1922 that the KKK only admits "native born, white, Gentile, Protestant Americans."[7] The white Christian nationalist view of "true" Americans has always centered on people deemed white and has labeled anyone else—Jews, Blacks, or immigrants—as "other."[8]

White Christian nationalism is the greatest threat to democracy and the witness of the church in the United States today. As we have seen throughout US history, racism has taken on different faces from slavery to Jim Crow. Now it goes by the name of white Christian nationalism. The goal of this movement is to institute an authoritarian, fascist political state that uses Christianity to legitimate its ideas. It relies on a strict social hierarchy that places white people at the top and Black people at the bottom. Also inherent to this belief system is the promotion of patriarchy and the subjugation of women, as well as xenophobia and homophobia.[9] White Christian nationalists believe that the United States is specially favored by God, and in order to maintain God's blessing on the nation, its citizens must adhere to a strict, conservative interpretation of Christianity. To the extent that the nation has lost its way, it is due to "others" such as Muslims, Jews, the LGBTQIA community, and people of color who promote supposedly godless social justice ideas. The spirit of justice in the present day resists authoritarian and antidemocratic impulses that proceed under the banner of religion.

THE RISE OF THE TEA PARTY

White Christian nationalism, on full display during the attempted January 6 insurrection, did not crop up from nowhere. It had antecedents in prior years that coalesced into the violent mob action that took place just before a new president was to be inaugurated. In 2008, a US senator from Illinois and relative newcomer to politics named Barack

Obama made history when he became the first Black president of the United States. People in the crowd on the day his victory was announced in Grant Park in Chicago stood in the frigid winter temperatures with tears streaming down their faces.[10] The prayers and hopes of prior generations culminated in this moment as a Black person became the most powerful political official and leader of the nation. It was, for many, a hopeful sign that the country, founded with race-based chattel slavery at its inception, had finally moved beyond racism and had lived up to the ideals espoused in the Declaration of Independence and the Constitution.

But even before his election, Obama faced racist headwinds. Trump, who would later be elected forty-fifth president of the United States, spread the "birther" conspiracy that said Obama had not been born in the United States and thus could not be president.[11] A short time into Obama's presidency, a new political insurgency showed up called the Tea Party, named after the Boston Tea Party that had protested British rule over North American colonies. Formed in 2009 to oppose Obama and promote far-right politicians, the Tea Party spoke out against government programs such as the Affordable Care Act ("Obamacare") and in support of "small government."

Yet as the movement gained more popularity and public attention, its true origins became clearer. "Tea Party concerns exist within the context of anxieties about racial, ethnic, and generational changes in American society."[12] The NAACP explicitly decried the racism of the Tea Party in a 2010 resolution, noting that only 1 percent of Tea Partiers identified as Black while 89 percent identified as white. They said, "Whereas, these Tea Party protesters have engaged in explicitly racist behavior, displayed signs and posters intended to degrade people of color generally and President Barack Obama specifically."[13] Then they called upon Tea Party leaders and other politicians to "to publicly and privately repudiate the racism within the Tea Party, and to stand in opposition to its drive to push our country back to the pre-civil rights era."[14]

The Tea Party helped mobilize voters to bring Republicans massive electoral gains in the 2010 midterms. But when Donald Trump announced his bid for the Republican presidential nomination in 2015, much of the energy the Tea Party had generated shifted to Trump and

Trumpism. "The Tea Party still exists—except now it's called Make America Great Again," Trump once said to a journalist.[15] Trumpism represented not only a political shift but also a shift against another growing movement for racial justice, one that often marched under the banner of "Black Lives Matter."

A NEW CENTURY, A NEW MOVEMENT FOR RACIAL JUSTICE

Black Lives Matter emerged as a slogan and a social movement in 2013, the year after a neighborhood vigilante shot and killed Trayvon Martin, a seventeen-year-old Black teenager who was walking home one night wearing a hoodie. Martin's killer was acquitted by a jury under Florida's controversial "Stand Your Ground" law. In response, a Black woman named Alicia Garza wrote a post on Facebook that said, "Black people. I love you. I love us. Our lives matter." Her friend Patrisse Cullors adapted that wording into a hashtag that read #blacklivesmatter.[16] The phrase "Black lives matter" drew widespread public attention the next year after a white police officer killed a Black teenager named Mike Brown in Ferguson, Missouri. Thousands marched and protested using the words "Black lives matter." Following the numerous incidents of Black people being brutalized or killed by police officers that have been caught on video, the protests have often been done in the name of Black Lives Matter.

Just as with the term *Black power*, Christians have had to respond to Black Lives Matter. Activist and Christian minister Michelle Higgins gave a keynote address at a large evangelical conference hosted by the InterVarsity Christian Fellowship. She told her audience of young college students, "Black Lives Matter is not a mission of hate, Black Lives Matter is a movement on mission in the truth of God."[17] But some responded to her message with vitriol. A senior leader of InterVarsity shared with a journalist that they had received "blowback from just about every side" about the talk and about the conference's overall support of the Black Lives Matter movement.[18] Despite the pushback, however, a new movement of Christians across the racial and ethnic spectrum is responding to the spirit of justice active in the twenty-first century and taking action to fight against racism wherever it exists today.

RESISTING WHITE CHRISTIAN NATIONALISM

Amanda Tyler, a lifelong Christian, sat before the US House of Representatives subcommittee on civil rights and civil liberties and told the members that her religion is not what brings people in the country together. "Christianity does not unite Americans. Our belonging in American society must never depend on how we worship, what we believe or how we identify religiously."[19] Tyler, also a lawyer and the head of the Baptist Joint Committee for Religious Liberty (BJC), had been studying white Christian nationalism before it made national headlines in the aftermath of the January 6 insurrection. She and her team started an initiative called Christians against Christian Nationalism (CACN) in 2019 and have been warning politicians and Christians about the harmful ideology ever since.

A signature resource of CACN is a statement about white Christian nationalism that is addressed to Christians. It describes the ideology and explains why it is contrary to both a healthy democracy and the kind of religion that Jesus Christ taught. The document contains a series of belief statements designed to clarify and affirm Christian stances that contradict Christian nationalism and affirm a different set of Christian convictions. As an organization dedicated to religious freedom for all, they make clear that "government should not prefer one religion over another or religion over nonreligion."[20] They also explain how Christian nationalism's distorted view of faith and politics is harmful to all, especially the disempowered. "Conflating religious authority with political authority is idolatrous and often leads to oppression of minority and other marginalized groups." The statement ends with a charge to Christians: "America has no second-class faiths. . . . As Christians, we must speak in one voice condemning Christian nationalism as a distortion of the gospel of Jesus and a threat to American democracy." As of this writing, the statement has garnered more than 30,000 signatures.

The BJC also partnered with the Freedom from Religion Foundation to create a report called "Christian Nationalism and the January 6, 2021, Insurrection." The report is "the most complete accounting to date of how Christian nationalism contributed to the events leading up to January 6 and the day of the attack itself."[21] Released in February 2022, it reveals evidence of how Christian nationalism was present on the day of the insurrection and tells the story of which organizations and individuals led the effort in the months prior. It also contains commentary from sociologists, historians, lawyers, and other experts to help further illuminate Christian nationalism's influence in the attempted insurrection.[22]

Doug Pagitt believes small changes can make a big difference. Pagitt founded Vote Common Good in 2018 on the premise that there exists a small percentage of white evangelical voters in every election who can be persuaded that white Christian nationalism and its political representatives are not good for democracy and can be convinced to vote differently. He and his organization believe there are at least "5–10% [of evangelical voters] who are looking for an 'exit ramp' from supporting Republicans who sacrifice the common good."[23] Vote Common Good seeks to directly address those voters, and they have conducted cross-country tours to engage with conservative evangelicals who may have conflated their religion with a political party and need to hear a different narrative. They also train political candidates and elected officials on how to talk to evangelical voters. Pagitt believes all politicians, even Democratic officials who have often shied away from addressing religion directly, should "take religiously motivated voters seriously."[24] Vote Common Good advances the simple but difficult-to-practice ideal that Jesus' call to "love your neighbor as yourself" is also a call to vote for the common good.

Another organization active in opposition to Christian nationalism is Faithful America. In 2019, the board of directors of Faithful America searched for a new leader at a time when the "soul of our country is at stake," and they turned to Reverend Nathan Empsall.[25] The veteran digital campaign organizer took the reins of the organization (which was founded in 2004) in the midst of the Trump presidency. In his first few weeks, Empsall led a campaign to protest Trump's immigration policies and called on a Christian publishing company to cut ties with James Dobson, who was spreading racist ideas about immigrants. The advocacy organization says they are "fighting for social, economic, and racial justice, standing with the Black Lives Matter movement and upholding the Gospel's values of love, equality, and dignity." They realize the danger of Christian nationalism and have made fighting it one of their central initiatives. Faithful America recognizes the danger that Christian nationalism poses to people of color and the pursuit of a multiracial democracy. "In reality, it is Christian nationalism that marginalizes the Black Church tradition, mainline Protestants, Roman Catholics, progressive evangelicals, and millions of other members of the Body of Christ."[26] In fighting against Christian nationalism, they are also fighting against racism in one of its contemporary forms.

RACIAL JUSTICE ORGANIZATIONS

With the advent of Black Lives Matter and a renewed urgency to address racism, Black people and other people of color are forming organizations to resist racism. No longer satisfied trying to work exclusively within existing white evangelical institutions, they are creating nonprofits that have antiracism embedded in the DNA of their culture and work. The people running these organizations go beyond the typical Black-white racial binary and incorporate the concerns of other racial groups in their work. Yet they all realize the ongoing importance of addressing anti-Black racism.

I started what later became "The Witness" in October 2011. At the time I was a seminary student at a conservative seminary in Jackson, Mississippi. The school was nondenominational but had close ties to southern Presbyterianism and Reformed theology, traditions that typically resisted efforts at racial progress including desegregation attempts during the Jim Crow era. As an intern at a theologically conservative Presbyterian church and with intentions of becoming an ordained pastor, I believed we needed a voice for Black Christians within evangelical and Reformed circles. We began as the Reformed African American Network (RAAN), a name that signified our location within predominantly white Christian circles. But the Black Lives Matter movement, as well as ongoing incidents of racism within Reformed and evangelical spaces, compelled us to pivot.

In 2017, our leadership team met in Jackson, and we decided to change the name from RAAN to The Witness, a Black Christian

Collective. Our actions represented more than a branding shift. They signaled a self-conscious and unapologetic centering of Black people in our work. No longer would we prioritize making a defense for racial justice, especially to those who refused to see its importance or impact on the Black people in their midst. In 2019, we announced the creation of The Witness Foundation, a philanthropic branch of the organization that offers individual grants of $100,000 and advanced organization leadership training to a cohort of emerging Black Christian racial justice leaders. Through our podcasts, and especially *Pass the Mic*, which I cohost with Pastor Tyler Burns of Pensacola, Florida, our online articles, and our commentary on social media, The Witness reveals the richness of the expansive Black Christian tradition.

Chasing Justice, cofounded by Sandra Maria Van Opstal, is another example of the new wave of racial justice organizations. Van Opstal is a Latina raised in a Catholic family, but she knows white evangelicals well, having spent fifteen years with InterVarsity Christian Fellowship and serving as the director of worship for their Urbana missions conference, among other roles. As a worship leader, she engaged with one of the most important and personal forms of multicultural engagement: music. Van Opstal knew from experience and study that "culture shapes worship . . . [and] worship expression is inextricably linked with one's own culture." Yet she often faced resistance or skepticism from white evangelicals when she introduced worship music that went beyond their cultural comfort level. As a church leader she also recognizes the role of faith in the work of justice. She cofounded Chasing Justice, "a movement led by people of color to mobilize a lifestyle of faith and justice."[27] Their work includes providing expert racial justice speakers for events; consulting with organizations on diversity, equity, and inclusion and cultural competencies; and forming cohorts of leaders for training and collaboration.

Some racial justice efforts more explicitly address objections to Christianity as a belief system. Lisa Fields grew up as a "PK"—preacher's kid—but in college she nearly gave up her belief in God. A course on the New Testament at the University of North Florida challenged the beliefs about Scripture that she had been taught from childhood. Fields held on to her faith because she learned that questions were not antithetical to a strong faith but essential to it. She founded the Jude 3 Project (the name refers to a verse in Jude, "Contend for the faith that was once for all entrusted to God's holy people") to engage in Christian apologetics from a Black-centered perspective. Apologetics is the branch of theology concerned with defending the faith by addressing questions and conundrums through logical reasoning. Yet apologetics has historically been dominated by white male theologians. "A lot of this material wouldn't appeal to a lot of people in black churches because the illustrations aren't relevant, and some of the issues aren't as relevant," Fields said.[28] The Jude 3 Project responds to questions that arise from within the Black experience. Is Christianity the white man's religion? Is the church still relevant for young people and to the justice work of today? The Jude 3 Project hosts an annual conference called "Courageous Conversations" that brings together Black scholars and practitioners who may hold different theological convictions for dialogue and education. Fields has also produced films, including *Juneteenth: Faith and Freedom*.[29]

Other organizations are broadening the fight for racial justice to include additional people of color. At the beginning of the COVID-19 pandemic in 2020, wild rumors flew around the internet and on news channels about the origins of the virus—and some of those rumors were racist. When the virus was traced to China, many people in the United States started targeting Asian Americans for hate. They called it the "Chinese virus" and said all Asians should "go back home." Some of these incidents even became physical with assaults on Asian Americans increasing in that period.[30] Ray Chang, a pastor and organizer who is Korean American, started the Asian American Christian Collaborative (AACC) to respond to growing anti-Asian racism and contribute to the broader movement for racial and social justice.

The AACC is "committed to representing the voices, issues, and histories of Asian Americans in the church and society at large."[31] They are also engaged in work with other racial and ethnic groups to pursue the mission of justice. In June 2020, during the height of racial justice demonstrations protesting the murders of George Floyd, Breonna Taylor, and Ahmaud Arbery, the AACC partnered with an Asian American church and a historically Black church for a march for Black lives. About 1,000 people marched from a church in Chinatown in Chicago to the historically Black Bronzeville neighborhood. "Our deep hope is that . . . the healing will drive from the church to the rest of the communities, and that we'll start to build bridges from the work that we're doing," said Chang.[32]

RACIAL JUSTICE LITERATURE

By 1895, Ida B. Wells-Barnett had become well-known for her investigative journalism and her writing that uncovered the heinous lynchings that white people inflicted on Black people throughout the country. People all over the North invited her to speak at events and share her findings. At these events, people invariably asked her some version of the same question: "What can I do to help the cause?" Her reply to them never varied. "The answer always is: 'Tell the world the facts.'" Wells-Barnett believed that if people of conscience, especially Christians, knew the truth about racism, they would be moved to act. While this approach did not sway everyone, Wells-Barnett's dedication to truth-telling did leave an indelible impression on some, and it is why we still speak of her today.

What Ida B. Wells-Barnett said nearly 130 years ago remains relevant today. Those who would resist racism must tell the truth about it. As with Wells-Barnett, some have chosen to employ the written word to share the reality of their experiences with racism. In the 2010s and beyond, a bevy of books written by Black authors and others have reshaped our understandings of racism and what to do about it. Michelle Alexander, a civil rights lawyer and professor at Union Theological Seminary, published her book *The New Jim Crow: Mass Incarceration in the Age of Colorblindness* in 2010. It has since spent 250 weeks on the *New York Times* bestseller list and has been called the "secular bible of a new social movement."[33] Alexander argued that mass incarceration creates a permanent second-class citizen—those who have been caught up in the United States legal system. Jim Crow, then, did not go away. It was simply redesigned. Alexander points to the inviolable dignity of the human person as the impetus to change the system of incarceration in this country. "My motivation really needed to come from a place of deep commitment to honor the dignity and value of each and every one of us no matter who we are, where we come from, and what we may have done."[34]

Ida B. Wells

Her work has amplified similar endeavors in the field of criminal legal reform such as the documentary *13th* directed by Ava DuVernay and the work of Bryan Stevenson and his team at the Equal Justice Initiative.

While Michelle Alexander's work had a national impact far beyond the church, others have focused on speaking to Christians with great effect. Dominique DuBois Gilliard, director of racial righteousness and reconciliation for the Evangelical Covenant Church (ECC), published *Rethinking Incarceration: Advocating for Justice That Restores* in 2018. He describes the role of Christians in embracing "law and order" policies that ballooned the population of incarcerated individuals. He then explains from the Bible why a restorative approach to justice is needed. Mark Charles and Soong-Chan Rah published *Unsettling Truths: The Ongoing, Dehumanizing Legacy of the Doctrine of Discovery* in 2019. They reach back to the fifteenth century and the "doctrine of discovery" as the root of the racism and white supremacy that still mar the North American sociopolitical landscape. Esau McCaulley, a professor of New Testament at Wheaton College, published *Reading While Black: African American Biblical Interpretation as an Exercise in Hope* in 2020. He walks through stories from the Bible and shows how they relate to and inform the historical Black experience in the United States. Robert Chao Romero, a lawyer and historian, published *Brown Church: Five Centuries of Latina/o Social Justice, Theology, and Identity* in 2020 to describe how people of Latin American descent have understood the Bible and faith as a force for social transformation. My own book *The Color of Compromise: The Truth about the American Church's Complicity in Racism*, published in 2019, tells the history of many Christians in the United States who chose compromise and complicity with racism instead of courageous confrontation.

Other Christian authors have adopted the approach of writing in the tradition of the slave narrative—exposés that reveal the truth of the racism they've experienced, usually at the hands of other Christians. *I'm Still Here: Black Dignity in a World Made for Whiteness*, published in 2018 by Austin Channing Brown, tells the story of her upbringing as a Black girl in mostly white spaces and then her experience as a Black woman in mostly white professional and evangelical settings. The book became a *New York Times* bestseller, and actor Reese Witherspoon selected it for her very popular book club. Author Danté Stewart was, at one point, deeply embedded in conservative evangelical circles. But when Trumpism began its march through Christian churches, he realized the depths of racism in the pews. That set him on a journey to discover both Black authors and Jesus Christ in a new way. Stewart chronicles that journey in his 2021 book, *Shoutin' in the Fire: An American Epistle*, a book written in the tradition of James Baldwin—incisive criticism infused with a heartfelt sensitivity for the human condition. Lisa Sharon Harper journeyed deep into her family's personal history to write *Fortune: How Race Broke My Family and the World and How to Repair It All*, published in 2022. The author goes back through ten generations of her family history to demonstrate how race affected not just one family but the entire globe, and then she offers responses to the most intractable issues of racism today. Ally Henny wrote her first book, *I Won't Shut Up: Finding Your Voice When the World Tries to Silence You*, in 2023 specifically to help Black women embrace their unique voice. She takes up the historic call of Black women freedom fighters who simultaneously battled racism and sexism to build a better nation and a healthier church. Cole Arthur Riley, in her 2022 debut book, *This Here Flesh: Spirituality, Liberation, and the Stories That Make Us*, wrote, "Some theologies say it is not an individual but a collective people who bear the image of God. I quite like this, because it means we need a diversity of people to reflect God more fully. Anything less and the image becomes pixelated and grainy, still beautiful but lacking clarity. If God really is three parts in one like they say, it means that God's wholeness is in a multitude."[35] Riley had already built up a significant social media following through her *Black Liturgies* writing, which incorporates spirituality with Black literature, history, and experience. But her soulful exploration of the spiritual life and race made this new book a bestseller as well.

Other authors take a practical approach to fighting racism. They offer implementable solutions and road maps for people to resist racial prejudice today. *Be the Bridge: Pursuing God's Heart for Racial Reconciliation* was published in 2019 by Latasha Morrison and gains its name from the nonprofit company she founded to foster racial reconciliation in the church. The book provides a biblical rationale for why Christians should pursue racial reconciliation and urges people to build bridges of understanding rather than walls of prejudice. It became a *New York Times* bestseller, and the educational materials her organization produces are used in churches across the country. Brenda Salter McNeil has been doing racial reconciliation and justice work for more than thirty years as a consultant, professor, and minister. In her 2020 book, *Becoming Brave: Finding the Courage to Pursue Racial Justice Now*, she explains how a purely individual emphasis on racism is a truncated view and why our definition of racism must expand to include systemic injustice. In the books *Rediscipling the White Church* by David Swanson and *White Awake* by Daniel Hill, two white pastors instruct their fellow white Christians on the ways racism wreaks havoc on the souls of not just Black folk but white people as well, and they unpack the responsibility of white people to fight racism. Sheila Wise Rowe, a professional counselor, makes a critical intervention in racial justice literature with her 2020 book, *Healing Racial Trauma: The Road to Resilience*. She explains how racism inflicts trauma on the psyche and how to pursue repair for our hearts and souls. And in a creative three-author work, the women of the *Truth's Table* podcast published a book in 2022 called *Truth's Table: Black Women's Musings on Life, Love, and Liberation.* Their book centers on the intersection of being Black, Christian, and women. In a triphonic chorus, they address topics such as colorism, divorce, multiethnic church worship, and the spiritual value of protest. Their work offers a tangible way to listen to, learn from, and act on the voices of those who have been marginalized in society.

These are just a few examples of the proliferation of books about race and racism filling shelves today, from pastor's studies to home libraries to seminary classrooms and beyond. Social media, video, newsletters, and other media provide great ways to share information, but no other form of communication has the longevity and power of a book to challenge long-held perspectives and stir souls to new ways of thinking and being in the world.

THE CREATIVES

Though books are powerful resources in the fight against racism, they are still just one of many instruments that today's racial justice advocates and activists utilize to cultivate change. The arts—including poetry, music, and video—have never been more accessible or shareable. Smartphones can record voices, videos, or images that can be shared in seconds with thousands of people. This technology has given rise to a new class of people who access contemporary multimedia tools to address contemporary justice concerns—the creatives.

Garrison Hayes has amassed a TikTok following of more than 300,000 people for his informative and entertaining videos about history and current events. Using a combination of savvy video editing and deeply researched content, several of his videos have garnered over one million views. Some of his videos include "Will Racism Die Off?" and "Whiteness and Fictional Characters."[36] Hayes served as a pastor and developed his skills as a creative while leading his church's digital strategy during the 2020 COVID-19 pandemic. In 2022, he was selected for the new Creator in Residence position at Mother Jones news organization.[37] He blends history, race, and faith to inform an upcoming generation about the importance of the past and their responsibilities to work for justice in the present.

Danielle Coke Balfour does her public work as an illustrator, advocate, and entrepreneur under the business name and social media handle "Oh Happy Dani." She's always been an artist, but she got her professional start as a social media manager and a graphic designer for mission-driven organizations.[38] Her work started to gain widespread attention in 2020 when she posted an illustration on social media about Martin Luther King Jr. She spent the next month creating illustrations speaking to the realities she experienced as a Black woman in the United States. People really started to discover her work in the summer of 2020 when the entire nation's attention was focused on race, and she gained 300,000 social media followers in a single week. She has since been tapped as a consultant for brands such as Adobe, Toms, and Comcast and also has a signature collection at Target stores.[39] Coke Balfour believes that art accesses the human heart in an indispensable way, and she uses her illustrations to promote justice. "Art invokes emotion, but activism encourages action, so when you put them both together, you're encouraging action by invoking emotion," she said.[40]

André Henry probably couldn't have resisted becoming a musician even if he wanted to. His father was a reggae musician and filled his home with music and musicmaking. The content of his father's songs also sank in. They were tunes about protest, justice, and defiance. Henry's racial justice awakening came in 2016 when a police officer shot and killed Philando Castile near Minneapolis. Henry was studying theology at the time and knew he had to ask different questions and seek different answers than what his white professors were teaching him. So as a work of artistic activism, Henry dragged a 100-pound boulder around in a cart. When people inevitably stopped him to ask what he was doing, he explained, "The boulder represents the burden that racism places on the Black psyche."[41] He describes his music as "anthems of resilience and revolution."[42] Although Henry has left evangelicalism behind, he has reconstructed a faith that exhibits tenderness, compassion, hope, and justice.

THE ACTIVISTS

Much of today's racial justice work takes place in the educational sphere, but some groups and individuals engage in hands-on activism.

They carry on the tradition of protest by lobbying for policy change and systemic reforms. Their work includes the sharing of information but also the hands-on labor of making tangible changes in policies and institutions.

Terence Lester experienced being houseless when he was a teenager. By the age of sixteen he had dropped out of high school and joined a gang. An accumulation of events had him living on the streets, and at one point his situation became so overwhelming that he contemplated taking his own life. When he was twenty years old, police arrested Lester. In jail, someone shared the gospel of Jesus Christ with him, and it changed his life. Years later, Lester and his wife, Cecilia, started Love beyond Walls to move beyond walls of division, raise awareness about those experiencing poverty and homelessness, and mobilize people to act on behalf of others. His work involved national campaigns such as "Love Sinks In," which distributed portable sinks for people who didn't have homes to wash their hands and stay healthy during the COVID-19 pandemic. He also started the Dignity Museum, the first museum completely dedicated to the history of homelessness, which is run out of a refurbished shipping container.[43]

Stanley Frankart was also involved in the criminal legal system. During an attempted robbery in 2013, Frankart shot the victim in the head. The victim survived, but Frankart's fate was all but sealed. He was facing a sentence of twenty-five years to life, but a merciful judge sentenced him to only ten years. While he was incarcerated, three other incarcerated men, all of whom had been in prison for twenty years or more, began discipling him in the ways of Jesus.[44] While he was still in prison, Frankart and his compatriots formed what became Young Christian Professionals (YCP), a group dedicated to teaching incarcerated men the skills they need in society upon reentry to reduce their chances of ending up back in prison. Upon his release, Frankart held a few different jobs but still felt the tug to be involved in YCP full-time. He pivoted and now leads the organization as president and CEO. Through an eight-week curriculum geared toward individuals involved in the legal system, YCP teaches character development and business etiquette and has expanded to serve nine different prisons throughout the state of Ohio.[45] Their work directly reduces the recidivism rate of formerly incarcerated people who have been recently released by helping them navigate life on the outside with personal integrity and job skills.[46]

Common Hymnal is a group of musicians who formed to create "praise and protest" music.[47] Throughout the civil rights movement and other phases of the Black freedom struggle, people have relied on music for lament, encouragement, and joy. They sang songs such as "We Shall Overcome" and "This Little Light of Mine" as they marched, picketed, and demonstrated. While still claiming this historical lyrical legacy, Common Hymnal asks, "What are the new protest songs tailored for the current generation?" They are creating music for what they call the "spiritual underground"—the people of faith who, in all kinds of ways, seek to subvert the status quo and pursue justice. "Our hope is that the marriage of the two will catalyze God's people to become a real and transformative prophetic voice in the corrupt and unjust systems in which we live."[48] Some of their recent work includes recording an updated version of the hymn "Amazing Grace" on the song's 250th anniversary. They have also written a song called "Stars and Stripes" as a response to the prevalence of white Christian nationalism. In 2020, they partnered with pastor Otis Moss III of Trinity United Church in Chicago to write and record a song for a "get out the vote" campaign. Their music played in a video about Moss's grandfather, who walked eighteen miles to three different polling locations in the 1940s to attempt to register to vote. He was denied everywhere he went.[49] When new legs march to protest age-old injustices, they may well sing songs from the Common Hymnal.

CONCLUSION

White Christian nationalism remains a threat to the longevity of a stable democracy. The danger is not only to the political system but to the church too. As long as an antidemocratic, authoritarian movement more concerned with power than people masquerades as Christianity, people will continue to turn away from religion. Yet there is another witness. People of faith from all races and ethnicities have seen the danger and are doing the work to counteract it. Through literature, music, advocacy, Black- and people-of-color-led institutions, and more, they are working to dismantle harmful racial ideas that continue to proliferate today. The spirit of justice is more than a historical phenomenon of the past. It lives on today through a new generation of individuals and organizations adapted to the shifting racial landscapé of the twenty-first century.

CHAPTER
ELEVEN

THE SPIRIT OF
JUSTICE SPEAKS

The stories of faith, race, and resistance in this book are both instructive and inspiring. The people who came before us speak through their legacies. They have bequeathed to us boundless narratives that tell of a people who stood unbowed in the face of racial oppression and injustice. Their stories offer us an expanded vocabulary of courage and justice. The threats they faced in previous eras may differ, but the call to resist racism remains constant. It remains for us this day to meditate on their lives and actions so that we can honor their memories and work for progress in our day.

Surveying how people were empowered through the spirit of justice in the past allows us to glean lessons for righteous living in the present. While much can be learned through their individual and collective examples, four virtues have been consistently exhibited by those who followed the spirit of justice and found remarkable strength to resist injustice. These virtues are faith, courage, imagination, and resilience. We need to cultivate each virtue to continue the legacy of justice today.

FAITH

The true stories featured in *The Spirit of Justice* differ in a multitude of ways, but what binds them together is the role of faith. We too often pass over the role religion plays in the story of the Black freedom struggle. The actions we scrutinize—the protests, the boycotts, the imprisonments—are often the outward manifestation of inward faith. Before engaging in the work that put their jobs, safety, and lives on the line, people prayed, sang, and worshiped. Their understanding of religion, especially Christianity, provided the moral and spiritual force to resist racial oppression.

The Bible says, "For our struggle is not against flesh and blood, but against the rulers, against the authorities, against the powers of this dark world and against the spiritual forces of evil in the heavenly realms" (Ephesians 6:12). The women and men of faith who confronted racism in their day believed that their work was not merely earthly. The forces arrayed against them were not simply unjust, but evil. John Wesley once said a requirement for salvation was avoiding evil, "especially that which is most generally practiced, such as . . . slaveholding; buying or selling slaves."[1] Decrying the twin evils of racism and sexism, Prathia Hall declared, "Racism is a sin we love to 'pounce' upon. Sexism is no less evil, divisive, or sinful. The time is now for atonement."[2] Abolitionists understood that "the unlimited power of one man over another was morally and spiritually unacceptable, that it led to sin, both physical and moral."[3] Marcus Garvey proclaimed, "Jesus was the greatest radical the world ever saw. He came and saw a world of sin and his program was to inspire it with spiritual feeling."[4]

If there exists a spirit of justice, then there also exists a spirit of injustice. A great cloud of witnesses who fought against racism conceived of their battle as both material and spiritual. They drank deeply from the wells of faith to sustain their struggle. Yet today many people question the role of faith communities, especially the Christian church, in the pursuit of justice. A report from Pew Research reported that just 13 percent of Black people thought that Black churches or other religious organizations had "done the most to help Black people in recent years."[5] They listed Black Lives Matter as the most helpful (39 percent) and the NAACP as the second most helpful (17 percent). Their skepticism is understandable. Racism, homophobia, sexism, greed, scandal, and more all provide ample reason to think that churches are being overcome by the world rather than overcoming evil in the world. But it would be a mistake to believe that the church today is any more wayward than churches in centuries past. Faith communities in the nineteenth and the sixteenth centuries were subject to the same temptations as churches are in the twenty-first century.

The individuals we've met in *The Spirit of Justice* may have had their own issues with organized religion as well. But they also heard the message of liberation in the words of Jesus Christ. They saw in the Hebrew people in Egypt a reflection of their own experience in the United States. They understood that suffering for the sake of righteousness was a powerful witness against the racism they endured. This is not to say that one must be Christian or believe in any religion at all to strive valiantly against injustice. Indeed, when it comes to fighting racism, many people who do not claim a religion have outpaced those who do. Yet the story of resistance to the ideology of racism would not be complete without attending to the faith in God so many cherished.

COURAGE

I have written elsewhere about the witness of Fannie Lou Hamer and how she stands as a symbol of courage.[6] She was born as the twentieth of twenty children to a poor sharecropping family in the Mississippi Delta in 1917. She followed the same path as many of her peers. She married Perry "Pap" Hamer, a sharecropper, and they became a sharecropping couple. Yet all that changed when she went to an SNCC organizing meeting at her church and heard about voting rights. She volunteered to attempt to register to vote, and as soon as the owner of the plantation where she worked heard about it, he ordered her to stop. When she refused, the owner fired her. Already poor, Fannie Lou Hamer was now also unemployed.

When Hamer explained why she raised her hand to go register to vote in church that day, she said, "I guess if I'd had any sense I'd've been a little scared, but what was the point of being scared? The only thing they could do to me was kill me, and it seemed like they'd been trying to do that a little bit at a time ever since I could remember."[7]

Fannie Lou Hamer

Hamer's words recall the words of Jesus. "Do not be afraid of those who kill the body but cannot kill the soul" (Matthew 10:28). Jesus offered his disciples an eternal perspective by explaining that the worst another human being could do was take their physical life. Only God has power to affect both body and soul. Therefore, they could courageously confront evil and injustice in this world knowing the power of racism in this world was no match for the power of God.

When it comes to fighting racism, we don't have a how-to problem; we have a want-to problem. It is not that we lack strategies, tactics, or methods to fight racism. Give almost anyone a paper, a pen, and five minutes and they will come up with suggestions for how we can push back against racism. The missing element in our journey of racial justice is courage. That is why in the hundreds of addresses I have given to crowds of people who want to commit themselves or become more committed to the cause of racial justice, I constantly emphasize courage. Courage is not the absence of fear but the resolve to move forward in the face of it. Courage can be cultivated. The more you exercise it, the more of it you have.

The people in this book have all demonstrated courage. Many of them faced ostracism, physical violence, and emotional trauma for standing up for righteousness. People like Martin Luther King Jr. and Medgar Evers were killed for their commitment to justice. Even those who survived the struggle did so at great cost to themselves, their families, and their friends. But they found through the spirit of justice the temerity to confront their trepidations and move forward.

In many cases, these women and men had nothing left to lose. They counted their present estate as so detestable that no matter what risks they undertook, the consequences could not be worse than their present reality. For many of us today, we will have to come to the point in our lives where the pain of the status quo is greater than the fear of confronting it. Those who continually insist on recreating racist patterns will find themselves arrayed against a people who have already lost much and figure they cannot lose much more. The fight is fiercest in those whose backs are against the wall. That is also when courage shows up and change becomes possible.

IMAGINATION

We cannot get through an annual MLK holiday or a Black History Month celebration without hearing the words "I have a dream" quoted ad infinitum. While the phrase is highly quotable and filled with meaning, it deserves analyzing just why the notion of a dream has such resonance. King's repeated intonation of the dream evoked more than a flurry of ephemeral images conjured by a sleeping mind. The dream he spoke of referred to a new reality that one day might be possible if people leaned into the spirit of justice. It spoke to the unuttered yearnings that welled up within any person who had ever hungered and thirsted for righteousness. The dream spoke of a world where the problems of the present could become a melancholy memory. To say, "I have a dream," is to say, "I have imagination."

Ponder the imagination it took for Robert Smalls to contrive a plan to steal a Confederate slave ship. He had to envision every phase of the risky plan—the hour when the white sailors would depart, which of his fellow enslaved people would accompany him, the signals necessary to pass through the naval defenses, and countless contingencies in the very likely case that something went wrong. Harriet Tubman had to imagine all kinds of ways to disguise herself and evade slave catchers on her numerous sojourns back to the land of slavery on a mission to liberate others. Charles Hamilton Houston had the imagination to come up with a legal strategy to challenge the jurisprudence that enshrined racial segregation as the law of the land. Those who contended with racism had to imagine new realities that might be possible. They had to envision days beyond the slave ship, beyond the plantation, beyond the abuse, beyond the exclusion.

It is not enough to point out the problems of an unjust system. The people who become the greatest agents of change also convey a notion of a better future. It is not sufficient to decry what is. We must also craft an image of what might be. Proverbs says, "Where there is no vision, the people perish" (Proverbs 29:18 KJV). It is possible to become so consumed by cynicism and despair as to become blind to what is possible. A person can lose the mental vision to see how their current circumstances might be different. Oppression suppresses imagination. Justice cultivates creativity. The spirit of justice allows us to be refreshed by the wellspring of imagination that brings us to the mountaintop and lets us see a promised land beyond the valley of oppression.

RESILIENCE

Jarena Lee's conscience was so sensitive that she was tempted to take her own life from the despair of contemplating her imperfections. When all else seemed to fail her, Lee returned again and again to prayer. Like the persistent widow who kept pleading with the judge, "Grant me justice against my adversary" (Luke 18:3), Lee kept going to God for justice and relief. This persistence enabled Lee to become the first woman authorized to preach in the AME denomination and later to become the first Black woman in the United States to have her autobiography published.

Resilience characterizes the people filled with the spirit of justice. In every era of history, the people who make the most progress resisting racism are the people who simply won't quit. At some level every admirable example in the annals of history is a story of resilience. It is a tale about people confronted with multitudinous challenges, obstacles, and deprivations who kept pushing ahead. No matter how daunting the forces arrayed against you are, they cannot ultimately prevail when you refuse to give up.

Coretta Scott King would have been justified in retreating from the public eye to craft a quiet life and simply raise her family after her husband's murder. But she kept going. The spirit of justice in her stirred a desire to make sure what happened to her family would not happen to others. As a result, she became a living example of how to chase racial justice, and she motivated others to follow her path. Even today, veterans of the Black freedom struggle survey the political, social, and economic landscape and see a world that still traffics in the vile ideology of racism. But talk to any one of them and you will find that the spirit of justice still grants them breathtaking resilience. Many of them are still writing, speaking, mentoring, and praying for a reality they may never live to see. From one perspective, the ongoing necessity of their resilience is a tragic commentary on a people whose hearts have been hardened toward their fellow human beings. From another vantage point, we can take heart that the strength in us is greater than the powers of hatred assembled against us. Nothing can stop a people who refuse to stop.

THE SPIRIT OF JUSTICE SPEAKS

In church history there are martyrs and there are confessors. Martyrs die for the sake of their faith. They endure imprisonment, physical abuse, and privation because they refuse to deny their devotion to Jesus and justice. For that fidelity, they pay with their lives. Confessors endure all the same hardships, but they live.

Myrlie Evers-Williams is a confessor of the civil rights movement. She went through pain and loss that no one should have to bear. With the crack of a gun, her husband became a martyr of the movement, and she became a widow and a single parent. In the face of this devastating theft of life, she continued her work for justice. Evers-Williams managed the first state office of the NAACP in Mississippi, a visible role that left her vulnerable to constant threats and intimidation. She persevered for thirty years while her husband's killer walked free until a jury finally convicted him in 1994. She went back to school and earned her bachelor's degree, wrote books, remarried, raised a family, and became national chair of the board for the NAACP, leading the organization her husband once worked for.

Now in her ninth decade of life, Myrlie Evers-Williams has earned her rest. But racism never goes away; it adapts. In the past several years, Evers-Williams has witnessed attacks on racial justice in the form of anti–Critical Race Theory and anti-woke efforts. The Supreme Court of the United States rolled back a key provision of the Voting Rights Act in 2013, a cause that she and her husband had dedicated their lives to advance. She has seen the nation's first Black president get elected and then the subsequent president stoke the basest racist tropes, creating a context for an insurrection. At the precise time when successive generations should be gifting her the progress made possible because of her work, she once again must tap into the spirit of justice to continue the fight against racism.

The same spirit of justice that empowered generations past is available to you today. It has been there for people across time whenever they needed it. It is here when you need it too. And, lamentably, it is always needed. So pause for a moment. Listen intently to the sound of your soul and the echoes of your ancestors. Listen closely enough and you will hear a still, small voice encouraging you to declare your dignity and stand up for righteousness.

The spirit of justice still speaks.

NOTES

Chapter 1: The Spirit of Justice

1. DeNeen L. Brown and Cleve R. Wootson Jr., "Trump Ignores Backlash, Visits Mississippi Civil Rights Museum and Praises Civil Rights Leaders," *Washington Post*, December 9, 2017.
2. Michael Vinson Williams, *Medgar Evers: Mississippi Martyr* (Fayetteville, AR: University of Arkansas Press, 2011), 7–11.
3. C. Eric Lincoln and Lawrence H. Mamiya, *The Black Church in the African American Experience* (Durham: Duke University Press, 1990), 15.
4. See my first book, *The Color of Compromise* (Grand Rapids: Zondervan Reflective, 2019), for a historical survey of Christian complicity with racism.
5. Andrew Cohen, "The Speech That Shocked Birmingham the Day after the Church Bombing," *The Atlantic*, September 13, 2013, https://www.theatlantic.com/national/archive/2013/09/the -speech-that-shocked-birmingham-the-day-after-the-church-bombing/279565/.
6. Charles Morgan Jr., *A Time to Speak: The Story of a Young American Lawyer's Struggle for His City—and Himself* (New York: Harper & Row, 1964; repr., Tuscaloosa: University of Alabama Press, 2022), 173.
7. Roy Reed, "Charles Morgan Jr., 78, Dies; Leading Civil Rights Lawyer," *New York Times*, January 9, 2009, https://www.nytimes.com/2009/01/10/us/10morgan.html.
8. Carol Anderson, *White Rage: The Unspoken Truth of Our Racial Divide* (London: Bloomsbury, 2016), 4.
9. Martin Luther King Jr., *Where Do We Go from Here: Chaos or Community?*, rev. ed. (Boston: Beacon, 2010), 11.

Chapter 2: Becoming African American

1. Mark Charles and Soong-Chan Rah, *Unsettling Truths: The Ongoing, Dehumanizing Legacy of the Doctrine of Discovery* (Downers Grove, IL: InterVarsity Press, 2019), 19.
2. "The Doctrine of Discovery, 1493," Gilder Lehrman Institute of American History, https:// www.gilderlehrman.org/history-resources/spotlight-primary-source/doctrine-discovery-1493.
3. "The Doctrine of Discovery, 1493."
4. Christina Proenza-Coles, *American Founders: How People of African Descent Established Freedom in the New World* (Montgomery, AL: NewSouth, 2019), 13.
5. For more information, see Michael A. Gomez, *Exchanging Our Country Marks: The Transformation of African Identities in the Colonial and Antebellum South* (Chapel Hill: University of North Carolina Press, 1998).
6. Anthony Chiorazzi, "The Spirituality of Africa," *The Harvard Gazette*, October 6, 2015, https://news.harvard.edu/gazette/story/2015/10/the-spirituality-of-africa/.

7. Howard Thurman, *Jesus and the Disinherited* (Boston: Beacon, 1976), xix.
8. See Thomas C. Oden, *How Africa Shaped the Christian Mind: Rediscovering the African Seedbed of Western Christianity* (Downers Grove, IL: InterVarsity Press, 2007); and Vince Bantu, *A Multitude of All Peoples: Engaging Ancient Christianity's Global Identity* (Downers Grove, IL: InterVarsity Press Academic, 2020).
9. It is true that African leaders participated in the slave trade by supplying Africans to Europeans. Not to excuse their greed, but most of the Africans involved in this commerce in people had little conception of the type of slavery Europeans practiced. Slavery and varying forms of unfree labor were common throughout the world for much of human history. But what evolved into race-based chattel slavery was a novel and particularly heinous practice.
10. Darlene Clark Hine, William C. Hine, and Stanley C. Harrold, *The African-American Odyssey*, vol. 1, 7th ed. (Boston: Pearson, 2016), 36.
11. Hine, Hine, and Harrold, *African-American Odyssey*, 1:44.
12. Harcourt Fuller, "Maroon History, Music, and Sacred Sounds in the Americas: A Jamaican Case," *Journal of Africana Religions* 5, no. 2 (2017): 278, https://doi.org/10.5325/jafrireli.5.2.0275.
13. W. T. M. Riches, "White Slaves, Black Servants and the Question of Providence: Servitude and Slavery in Colonial Virginia 1609–1705," *Irish Journal of American Studies* 8 (1999): 7.
14. Alden T. Vaughan, "Blacks in Virginia: A Note on the First Decade," *The William and Mary Quarterly* 29, no. 3 (1972): 475, https://doi.org/10.2307/1923875.
15. Riches, "White Slaves, Black Servants and the Question of Providence," 3.
16. Beth Austin, "1619: Virginia's First Africans," Hampton History Museum, revised December 2019, 13, https://hampton.gov/DocumentCenter/View/24075/1619-Virginias-First-Africans?bidId=.
17. Austin, "1619: Virginia's First Africans," 19.
18. Katharine Gerbner, *Christian Slavery: Conversion and Race in the Protestant Atlantic World* (Philadelphia: University of Pennsylvania Press, 2018), 12.
19. Historian John Donoghue argues that a more accurate term for indentured servitude is "bond slave." John Donoghue, "'Out of the Land of Bondage': The English Revolution and the Atlantic Origins of Abolition," *The American Historical Review* 115, no. 4 (2010): 943–74.
20. "9th July, 1640," in *Minutes of the Council and General Court of Virginia 1622–1632, 1670–1676: With Notes and Excerpts from Original Council and General Court Records into 1683, Now Lost*, ed. H. R. McIlwaine, 2nd ed. (Richmond: Virginia State Library, 1979), 466.
21. Theodore W. Allen, *The Invention of the White Race*, vol. 2, *The Origin of Racial Oppression in Anglo-America*, 2nd ed. (Brooklyn, NY: Verso, 2012), 238–40.

Chapter 3: The Language of Liberty

1. Julian P. Boyd, ed., *The Papers of Thomas Jefferson*, vol. 1, 1760–1776 (Princeton, NJ: Princeton University Press, 1950), 243–47.
2. For more about Thomas Jefferson's record as a slaver and about Sally Hemings, see Annette Gordon-Reed, *The Hemingses of Monticello: An American Family* (New York: Norton, 2009).
3. Isaac Kramnick, "Lockean Liberalism and the American Revolution," Gilder Lehrman Institute of American History, https://ap.gilderlehrman.org/history-by-era/road-revolution/essays/lockean-liberalism-and-american-revolution.
4. John Locke, "A Letter Concerning Toleration," trans. William Popple (London, 1740), 10.
5. John Locke, "Second Treaties on Civil Government," in *The Works of John Locke*, 4 vols., 7th ed. (London, 1768), 250.
6. Hezekiah Niles, *Principles and Acts of the Revolution in America: or, An Attempt to Collect and Preserve Some of the Speeches, Orations, and Proceedings, with Sketches and Remarks on Men and Things, and Other Fugitive or Neglected Pieces, Belonging to the Men of the Revolutionary Period in the United States* (Baltimore: W. O. Niles, 1822), 189.
7. Jupiter Hammon, "An Evening Thought: Salvation by Christ with Penitential Cries," in

America's First Negro Poet: The Complete Works of Jupiter Hammon of Long Island, ed. Stanley Austin Ransom Jr. (Port Washington, NY: Kennikat,1970), 45.

8. NPR Staff, "Student Finds New Work by First Published African-American Poet," *Tell Me More*, NPR, March 12, 2013, https://www.npr.org/2013/03/12/174100708/first-african -american-poet-still-showing-new-work.

9. Cedrick May and Julie McCown, "'An Essay on Slavery': An Unpublished Poem by Jupiter Hammon," *Early American Literature* 48, no. 2 (2013): 464–65.

10. May and McCown, "An Essay on Slavery," 467.

11. Phillis Wheatley, "On Being Brought from Africa to America," Poetry Foundation, https:// www.poetryfoundation.org/poems/45465/on-being-brought-from-africa-to-america.

12. Wheatley, "On Being Brought from Africa to America."

13. Phillis Wheatley, "To the Right Honorable William, Earl of Dartmouth," in *The Collected Works of Phillis Wheatley*, ed. John Shields (New York: Oxford University Press, 1988), 74.

14. Wheatley, "To the Right Honorable William, Earl of Dartmouth."

15. Wheatley, "To the Right Honorable William, Earl of Dartmouth."

16. Benjamin Banneker, letter to Thomas Jefferson, August 19, 1791, Baltimore County, Maryland, Founders Online, National Archives, https://founders.archives.gov/documents /Jefferson/01-22-02-0049.

17. Banneker, letter to Thomas Jefferson, August 19, 1791.

18. Banneker, letter to Thomas Jefferson, August 19, 1791.

19. Thomas Jefferson, letter to Benjamin Banneker, August 30, 1791, Philadelphia, Pennsylvania, Founders Online, National Archives, https://founders.archives.gov/documents/Jefferson/01 -22-02-0091.

20. David Hackett Fischer, *African Founders: How Enslaved People Expanded American Ideals* (New York: Simon & Schuster, 2022), 94.

21. "Prince Hall: Bound for Greatness," Medford Historical Society and Museum, https://www .medfordhistorical.org/medford-history/africa-to-medford/prince-hall/.

22. Massachusetts Historical Society, "To the Honorable Counsel & House of [Representa]tives for the State of Massachusetts Bay in General Court assembled, Jun. 13, 1777," *Collections of the Massachusetts Historical Society*, vol. 3, series 5 (Boston: Massachusetts Historical Society, 1877), 436.

23. "To the Honorable Counsel," 436.

24. Roy E. Finkenbine, "Belinda's Petition: Reparations for Slavery in Revolutionary Massachusetts," *The William and Mary Quarterly* 64, no. 1 (2007): 98.

25. "Belinda Sutton's 1783 Petition," transcription, Royall House and Slave Quarters, https:// royallhouse.org/belinda-suttons-1783-petition-full-text/.

26. "Belinda Sutton's 1783 Petition."

27. "The General Rules of the Methodist Church," *The Book of Discipline of the United Methodist Church* (Nashville: United Methodist Publishing House, 2016), https://www.umc.org/en /content/the-general-rules-of-the-methodist-church.

28. Richard Allen, *The Life, Experience, and Gospel Labours of the Rt. Rev. Richard Allen. To Which Is Annexed the Rise and Progress of the African Methodist Episcopal Church in the United States of America. Containing a Narrative of the Yellow Fever in the Year of Our Lord 1793: With an Address to the People of Colour in the United States* (Philadelphia: Martin & Boden, 1833), 16, https://docsouth.unc.edu/neh/allen/allen.html.

29. Purifoy, "The Methodist Antislavery Tradition, 1784–1844," 3–16.

30. Lewis M. Purifoy, "The Methodist Antislavery Tradition, 1784–1844," in *Methodist History*, 3–4, https://archives.gcah.org/bitstream/handle/10516/1445/MH-1967-07-%20Purifoy -%205-18.pdf?sequence=1&isAllowed=y.

31. Society of Friends, Germantown, PA, "Germantown Friends' Protest against Slavery, 1688," facsimile, https://www.loc.gov/item/rbpe.14000200/.

32. John Woolman, *The Journal of John Woolman* (1774; Stadium Publishing, 2018), loc. 282, Kindle.

33. Woolman, *The Journal of John Woolman*, loc. 474, Kindle.

34. John Woolman, "Some Considerations on the Keeping of Negroes" (Philadelphia: Tract Association of Friends, 1757), 3.

Chapter 4: The Antislavery Movement

1. Frederick Douglass, *Narrative of the Life of Frederick Douglass, an American Slave* (1845; repr., Overland Park, KS: Digireads, 2011), 48.

2. Douglass, *Narrative of the Life*, 48.

3. Douglass, *Narrative of the Life*, 91.

4. David W. Blight, *Frederick Douglass: Prophet of Freedom* (New York: Simon & Schuster, 2018), 93.

5. Douglass, *Narrative of the Life*, 91.

6. "Cotton Gin and Eli Whitney," History, A&E Television Networks, last up October 10, 2019, https://www.history.com/topics/inventions/cotton-gin-and-eli-whitney.

7. Joan Brodsky Schur, "Eli Whitney's Patent for the Cotton Gin," Educator Resources, National Archives, last updated December 16, 2021, https://www.archives.gov/education/lessons/cotton -gin-patent/.

8. James Walvin, *The Zong: A Massacre, the Law, and the End of Slavery* (New Haven, CT: Yale University Press, 2011), 1–12.

9. Walvin, *The Zong*, 1–12.

10. "1783 Quaker Petition to Parliament," letter, June 16, 1783, The Abolition Project, last edited January 15, 2008, http://gallery.nen.gov.uk/image77385-abolition.html.

11. When the British Parliament passed the Slavery Abolition Act in 1833, they agreed to pay £20,000,000, or 40 percent of the national budget, to compensate enslavers. Slaveholders received reparations in exchange for emancipating enslaved Africans. It took British taxpayers until 2015 to pay off the fee to slaveholders. See Kenan Malik, "Let's Put an End to the Delusion That Britain Abolished Slavery," *The Guardian*, February 10, 2018, https://www .theguardian.com/commentisfree/2018/feb/11/lets-end-delusion-britain-abolished-slavery.

12. Elena Abbott et al., "Religion and Reform," ed. Emily Conroy-Krutz, in *The American Yawp*, ed. Joseph Locke and Ben Wright (Stanford, CA: Stanford University Press, 2018), https:// www.americanyawp.com/text/10-religion-and-reform/.

13. Abbott et al., "Religion and Reform."

14. For more information, see Jemar Tisby, *The Color of Compromise: The Truth about the American Church's Complicity in Racism* (Grand Rapids: Zondervan Reflective, 2019), 52–54.

15. David Walker, *David Walker's Appeal, in Four Articles, Together with a Preamble, to the Coloured Citizens of the World, but in Particular, and Very Expressly, to Those of the United States of America* (1829; rev. 1830; repr., n.p.: Affordable Classics Limited, 2021), 76.

16. George Washington Williams, *A History of Negro Troops in the War of Rebellion, 1861–1865* (New York: Fordham University Press, 2012), 32.

17. Philippe R. Girard, *The Memoir of General Toussaint Louverture* (New York: Oxford University Press, 2014), 22.

18. Girard, *The Memoir of General Toussaint Louverture*, 22.

19. Philippe R. Girard and Jean-Louis Donnadieu, "Toussaint before Louverture: New Archival Findings on the Early Life of Toussaint Louverture," *The William and Mary Quarterly* 70, no. 1 (2013): 66, https://doi.org/10.5309/willmaryquar.70.1.0041.

20. Charles Forsdick and Christian Hogsbjerg, *Toussaint Louverture: A Black Jacobin in the Age of Revolutions* (London: Pluto, 2017), 157–58.

21. Forsdick and Hogsbjerg, *Toussaint Louverture*, 157–58.

22. The discovery of David Ingraham's journal eventually led to a book, a short documentary, and a suite of resources for the church to study abolition and anti-racism. For more on Ingraham,

James Bradley, and Nancy Prince, see *Awakening to Justice: Faithful Voices from the Abolitionist Past* (Downers Grove, IL: InterVarsity Press, 2024).

23. The Africans from the *Ulysses* were freed but still faced harsh conditions. Many of them quickly died from disease and the ordeal of the transatlantic trip. Others were forced to work on plantations. For more, see Christopher P. Momany, "Address before the International Symposium on Black Slavery from the 16th to the 19th Century," paper, Cotonou, Benin, December 1, 2022.

24. David Ingraham, journal entry, June 19, 1840, Belleville, NJ, https://www.raceandfaithproject.com/historical-docs-1.

25. William Hall, "Jury Instructions," October 1855, 2–3, https://www.famous-trials.com/images/ftrials/Celia/documents/JuryInstructions.pdf.

26. The literature on Black nationalism is expansive, and the ideology is variously defined by different scholars and activists. For more, see Jeffrey O. G. Ogbar, *Black Power: Radical Politics and African American Identity* (Baltimore: Johns Hopkins University Press, 2005); Peniel Joseph, *Waiting 'til the Midnight Hour: A Narrative History of Black Power in America* (New York: Henry Holt, 2007); Eddie S. Glaude Jr., ed., *Is It Nation Time?: Contemporary Essays on Black Power and Black Nationalism* (Chicago: University of Chicago Press, 2002); Keisha N. Blain, *Set the World on Fire: Black Nationalist Women and the Global Struggle for Freedom* (Philadelphia: University of Pennsylvania Press, 2018), to name a few.

27. "Paul Cuffe, a Brief Biography," Paul Cuffe, an African American and Native American Heritage Trail, website, https://paulcuffe.org/biography/.

28. "Petition Signed by John Cuffe and Paul Cuffe regarding Taxation," December 19, 1780, National Museum of African American History and Culture, https://nmaahc.si.edu/object/nmaahc_2009.26.1.

29. "Paul Cuffe, a Brief Biography."

30. Sally Loomis, "The Evolution of Paul Cuffe's Black Nationalism," *Negro History Bulletin* 37, no. 6 (1974): 298–302.

31. "Biography," Paul Cuffe: An African American and Native American Heritage Trail, https://paulcuffe.org/biography/.

32. Walker, *David Walker's Appeal, in Four Articles*, 80.

33. Walker, *David Walker's Appeal, in Four Articles*, 82.

34. Walker, *David Walker's Appeal, in Four Articles*, 82.

35. Walker, *David Walker's Appeal, in Four Articles*, 81.

36. Walker, *David Walker's Appeal, in Four Articles*, 84.

37. Walker, *David Walker's Appeal, in Four Articles*, 84.

38. Walker, *David Walker's Appeal, in Four Articles*, 84.

39. Walker, *David Walker's Appeal, in Four Articles*, 84.

40. Frederick Knight, "The Many Names for Jarena Lee," *Pennsylvania Magazine of History and Biography* 141, no. 1 (2017): 59, https://doi.org/10.5215/pennmaghistbio.141.1.0059.

41. Jarena Lee, *Religious Experience and Journal of Mrs. Jarena Lee, Giving an Account of Her Call to Preach the Gospel* (Philadelphia, 1849; repr., Miami: Hardpress, 2017), 3.

42. Lee, *Religious Experience and Journal*, 5.

43. Lee, *Religious Experience and Journal*, 8.

44. Lee, *Religious Experience and Journal*, 10.

45. Lee, *Religious Experience and Journal*, 11.

46. Lee, *Religious Experience and Journal*, 11.

47. Lee, *Religious Experience and Journal*, 11.

48. Lee, *Religious Experience and Journal*, 11.

49. Lee, *Religious Experience and Journal*, 17.

50. Knight, "The Many Names for Jarena Lee," 59–68.

51. Lorraine Boissoneault, "The Hidden History of Anna Murray Douglass," *Smithsonian*

Magazine, March 5, 2018, https://www.smithsonianmag.com/history/hidden-history-anna-murray-douglass-180968324/.

52. Rosetta Douglass Sprague, "Anna Murray Douglass: My Mother as I Recall Her," delivered before the Anna Murray Douglass Union, WCTU, May 10, 1900, Washington, DC, 8.

53. Sprague, "Anna Murray Douglass," 10.

54. Sprague, "Anna Murray Douglass," 16.

55. Frederick Douglass Papers, "Articles and Essays, 1836 to 1846," *Library of Congress*, https://www.loc.gov/collections/frederick-douglass-papers/articles-and-essays/frederick-douglass-timeline/1836-to-1846/.

56. Sprague, "Anna Murray Douglass," 20.

57. Sprague, "Anna Murray Douglass," 20.

58. Leigh Fought, *Women in the World of Frederick Douglass* (London: Oxford University Press, 2017), 262.

59. Frederick Douglass, "West India Emancipation," speech, August 3, 1857, Canandaigua, NY, in *Frederick Douglass: Selected Speeches and Writings*, ed. Philip S. Foner, abridged by Yuval Taylor (Chicago: Lawrence Hill, 1999), 367.

Chapter 5: Fighting for Freedom

1. Jemar Tisby, *The Color of Compromise: The Truth about the American Church's Complicity in Racism* (Grand Rapids: Zondervan Reflective, 2019), 78.

2. Tisby, *The Color of Compromise*, 77–80.

3. "Fugitive Slave Act," The Avalon Project: Documents in Law, History, and Diplomacy, Yale Law School, https://avalon.law.yale.edu/19th_century/fugitive.asp.

4. "Fugitive Slave Act."

5. Abraham Lincoln, "Abraham Lincoln Papers: Series 2, General Correspondence, 1858–1864: Abraham Lincoln to Horace Greeley, Friday, August 22, 1862 (Clipping from Aug. 23, 1862 *Daily National Intelligencer*, Washington, D.C.)," https://www.loc.gov/item/mal4233400/.

6. "Declaration of the Immediate Causes Which Induce and Justify the Secession of South Carolina from the Federal Union," The Avalon Project: Documents in Law, History, and Diplomacy, Yale Law School, https://avalon.law.yale.edu/19th_century/csa_scarsec.asp.

7. "An Act to Provide for Calling Forth the Militia to Execute the Laws of the Union, Suppress Insurrections, and Repel Invasions and to Repeal the Act Now in Force for Those Purposes," Philadelphia, 1795, https://www.loc.gov/item/rbpe.22201300/.

8. Thomas Wentworth Higginson, *Army Life in a Black Regiment and Other Writings* (1870; repr., New York: Penguin Random House, 2004), electronic edition, loc. 52–66.

9. Higginson, *Army Life in a Black Regiment*, loc. 360.

10. Higginson, *Army Life in a Black Regiment*, loc. 3719.

11. Edward L. Pierce, "The Contrabands at Fortress Monroe," *Atlantic Monthly*, November 1861, 626–40, https://www.americanantiquarian.org/Freedmen/Intros/contrabands.html.

12. "Second Confiscation Act," *Freedmen and Southern Society Project*, University of Maryland, http://www.freedmen.umd.edu/conact2.htm, sec. 9.

13. "Robert Smalls," Fort Sumter and Fort Moultrie National Historical Park, Reconstruction Era National Historical Park, National Park Service, https://www.nps.gov/people/robert-smalls.htm.

14. C. G. Woodson, "Robert Smalls and His Descendants," *Negro History Bulletin* 11, no. 2 (1947): 27, http://www.jstor.org/stable/44174742.

15. "Robert Smalls," National Park Service.

16. Cate Lineberry, *Be Free or Die: The Amazing Story of Robert Smalls' Escape from Slavery to Union Hero* (New York: St. Martin's, 2017), 121.

17. Edward A. Miller Jr., *Gullah Statesman: Robert Smalls from Slavery to Congress, 1839–1915* (Columbia, SC: University of South Carolina Press, 1995), 228.

18. Lineberry, *Be Free or Die*, 221.

19. Lineberry, *Be Free or Die*, 231–32.

20. Robert L. Harris Jr., "H. Ford Douglas: Afro-American Antislavery Emigrationist," *The Journal of Negro History* 62, no. 3 (1977): 222–24, https://doi.org/10.2307/2716951.

21. H. Ford Douglas, "Speech of H. Ford Douglass [*sic*]," *The Liberator* 30, no. 28 (July 13, 1860), https://ark.digitalcommonwealth.org/ark:/50959/5h742p085.

22. Matthew Norman, "The Other Lincoln-Douglas Debate: The Race Issue in a Comparative Context," *Journal of the Abraham Lincoln Association* 31, no. 1 (Winter 2010): 1–10, http://hdl .handle.net/2027/spo.2629860.0031.103.

23. Harris, "H. Ford Douglas," 229.

24. Roger D. Cunningham, "Douglas's Battery at Fort Leavenworth: The Issue of Black Officers during the Civil War," *Kansas History* 23 (Winter 2000–2001): 209.

25. Valeria Lira-Ruelas, "H. Ford Douglas," in *Black Organizing in Pre–Civil War Illinois: Creating Community, Demanding Justice*, ed. Kate Masur, for the Colored Conventions Project, coloredconventions.org/black-illinois-organizing/delegates/ford-douglas/.

26. Cunningham, "Douglas's Battery at Fort Leavenworth," 210.

27. Cunningham, "Douglas's Battery," 210.

28. Cunningham, "Douglas's Battery," 216.

29. Lira-Ruelas, "H. Ford Douglas."

30. Lira-Ruelas, "H. Ford Douglas."

31. Lira-Ruelas, "H. Ford Douglas."

32. "The Beginning of the End," *Harper's Weekly*, September 14, 1861, http://www.sonofthesouth .net/leefoundation/the-civil-war.htm.

33. Eric Foner, *The Fiery Trial: Abraham Lincoln and American Slavery* (New York: Norton, 2010), 187.

34. Foner, *The Fiery Trial*, 206.

35. "DC Compensated Emancipation Act," *The Civil War: The Senate's Story*, United States Senate, https://www.senate.gov/artandhistory/history/common/civil_war /DCEmancipationAct_FeaturedDoc.htm.

36. Sarah Pruitt, "5 Things You May Not Know about Abraham Lincoln, Slavery and Emancipation," History.com, September 21, 2012, updated June 23, 2020, https://www.history .com/news/5-things-you-may-not-know-about-lincoln-slavery-and-emancipation.

37. David W. Blight, *Frederick Douglass: Prophet of Freedom* (New York: Simon & Schuster, 2018), 383.

38. Blight, *Frederick Douglass*, 383.

39. Blight, *Frederick Douglass*, 383.

40. Karsonya Wise Whitehead, "Beyond Myths and Legends: Teaching Harriet Tubman and Her Legacy of Activism," *Meridians* 12, no. 2 (2014): 199, https://doi.org/10.2979/meridians.12.2 .196.

41. Jean M. Humez, "In Search of Harriet Tubman's Spiritual Autobiography," *NWSA Journal* 5, no. 2 (1993): 170, http://www.jstor.org/stable/4316258.

42. Humez, "In Search of Harriet Tubman's Spiritual Autobiography," 176.

43. Kate Clifford Larson, *Bound for the Promised Land: Harriet Tubman, Portrait of an American Hero* (New York: One World Ballantine, 2004), 250–51.

44. Larson, *Bound for the Promised Land*, 259.

45. Larson, *Bound for the Promised Land*, 259–61.

46. Humez, "In Search of Harriet Tubman's Spiritual Autobiography," 174.

47. For more on women in the plantation economy, see Thavolia Glymph, *Out of the House of Bondage: The Transformation of the Plantation Household* (New York: Cambridge University Press, 2003).

48. Nancy Wartick, "Overlooked No More: Elizabeth Keckly, Dressmaker and Confidante to Mary Todd Lincoln," *New York Times*, December 12, 2018, https://www.nytimes.com/2018 /12/12/obituaries/elizabeth-keckly-overlooked.html.

49. Elizabeth Keckley, *Behind the Scenes, or Thirty Years a Slave, and Four Years in the White House* (repr., n.p.: Eno, 2016), 9.
50. Keckley, *Behind the Scenes*, 10.
51. Keckley, *Behind the Scenes*, 10.
52. Keckley, *Behind the Scenes*, 11.
53. Jennifer Fleischner, *Mrs. Lincoln and Mrs. Keckly: The Remarkable Story of the Friendship between a First Lady and a Former Slave* (New York: Broadway, 2004), 4.
54. Keckley, *Behind the Scenes*, 36.
55. William T. Sherman, *Memoirs of General William T. Sherman*, 2nd ed., 2 vols. (New York: Appleton, 1913; repr., New York: Penguin Classics, 2000), 799.
56. Sherman. *Memoirs of General William T. Sherman*, 570.
57. Sherman, *Memoirs of William T. Sherman*, 797.
58. Sherman, *Memoirs of William T. Sherman*, 797.
59. Sherman, *Memoirs of William T. Sherman*, 797.
60. "Fort Pulaski," National Park Service, US Department of the Interior, 16–18, https://www.nps.gov/fopu/learn/education/upload/Resources.pdf#page=16.
61. "Fort Pulaski," 19.
62. "Fort Pulaski," 19.
63. "Fort Pulaski," 19.
64. Barton Myers, "Sherman's Field Order No. 15," *New Georgia Encyclopedia* (online), last updated September 30, 2020, https://www.georgiaencyclopedia.org/articles/history-archaeology/shermans-field-order-no-15/.
65. "Negroes of Savannah," *New York Daily Tribune*, February 13, 1865, Consolidated Correspondence File, ser. 225, central records, quartermaster general, record group 92, National Archives, 20.

Chapter 6: Building Black Institutions

1. William J. Simmons, *Men of Mark: Eminent, Progressive and Rising* (Cleveland: Rewell, 1887), 8.
2. "13th Amendment to the U.S. Constitution: Abolition of Slavery (1865)," Milestone Documents, National Archives, https://www.archives.gov/milestone-documents/13th-amendment.
3. "Civil Rights Act of 1866, 'An Act to Protect All Persons in the United States in Their Civil Rights, and Furnish the Means of Their Vindication,'" National Constitution Center, April 9, 1866, https://constitutioncenter.org/the-constitution/historic-document-library/detail/civil-rights-act-of-1866-april-9-1866-an-act-to-protect-all-persons-in-the-united-states-in-their-civil-rights-and-furnish-the-means-of-their-vindication.
4. "14th Amendment to the U.S. Constitution: Civil Rights (1868)," Milestone Documents, National Archives, https://www.archives.gov/milestone-documents/14th-amendment.
5. Eric Foner, *A Short History of Reconstruction* (New York: Perennial Library, 1990), 184.
6. Todd E. Lewis, "Elias Camp Morris," *The Encyclopedia of Arkansas* (online), last updated July 11, 2023, https://encyclopediaofarkansas.net/entries/elias-camp-morris-433/.
7. I lived and worked in Helena, Arkansas, for over fifteen years.
8. Mark Twain, *Life on the Mississippi* (New York: Grosset & Dunlap, 1917), 260.
9. "Centennial Baptist Church," National Register of Historic Places, Arkansas Heritage, 2, https://www.arkansasheritage.com/docs/default-source/national-registry/ph0119-pdf.
10. "Centennial Baptist Church," 3–5.
11. Lewis, "Elias Camp Morris."
12. Paula J. Giddings, *Ida, a Sword among Lions: Ida B. Wells and the Campaign against Lynching* (New York: Amistad, 2008), 603.
13. Ida B. Wells-Barnett, *The Arkansas Race Riot* (Chicago: self-published, 1920), 63.
14. *Our Cornerstone: Centennial Baptist Church*, dir. Nolan Dean, Helena, AR, Cherry Street Productions, 2023.

15. Wells-Barnett, *The Arkansas Race Riot*, 4.

16. Jemar Tisby, *The Color of Compromise: The Truth about the American Church's Complicity in Racism* (Grand Rapids: Zondervan Reflective, 2019), 114.

17. Marne L. Campbell, "Race, Class, Ethnicity, and the Origins of the Pentecostal Movement, 1906–1913," *Journal of African American History* 95, no. 1 (2010): 12.

18. Campbell, "Race, Class, Ethnicity, and the Origins," 1.

19. Campbell, "Race, Class, Ethnicity, and the Origins," 16.

20. Larry Martin, *Charles Fox Parham: The Unlikely Father of Modern Pentecostalism* (New Kensington, PA: Whitaker, 2022), 205.

21. Estrelda Y. Alexander, *Black Fire: 100 Years of African American Pentecostalism* (Downers Grove, IL: InterVarsity Press, 2011), 115–16.

22. Martin, *Charles Fox Parham*, 206–10.

23. Martin, *Charles Fox Parham*, 219.

24. Martin, *Charles Fox Parham*, 221.

25. Alexander, *Black Fire*, 55.

26. Alexander, *Black Fire*, 56.

27. Alexander, *Black Fire*, 165.

28. Alexander, *Black Fire*, 220.

29. Alexander, *Black Fire*, 91.

30. James M. O'Toole, "Passing: Race, Religion, and the Healy Family, 1820–1920," *Proceedings of the Massachusetts Historical Society* 108 (1996): 1–34, http://www.jstor.org/stable/25081113.

31. O'Toole, "Passing," 12.

32. Cyprian Davis, "Black Catholics in Nineteenth Century America," *U.S. Catholic Historian* 5, no. 1 (1986): 12, http://www.jstor.org/stable/25153741.

33. Shannen Dee Williams, *Subversive Habits: Black Catholic Nuns in the Long African American Freedom Struggle* (Durham, NC: Duke University Press, 2022), 72.

34. Williams, *Subversive Habits*, 74–76.

35. Taylor Lewis, "Here's What You Need to Know about the Plight of HBCUs (and It's Getting Worse)," *Essence*, October 27, 2020, https://www.essence.com/news/hbcus-black-colleges-closing-plight/.

36. "HBCUs Punching above Their Weight: A State-Level Analysis of Historically Black College and University Enrollment and Graduation," UNCF Frederick D. Patterson Research Institute, United Negro College Fund, 2018, 5, https://cdn.uncf.org/wp-content/uploads/PATW_Report_FINAL0919.pdf.

37. "How HBCUs Can Accelerate Black Economic Mobility," McKinsey Institute for Black Economic Mobility, July 30, 2021, https://www.mckinsey.com/industries/education/our-insights/how-hbcus-can-accelerate-black-economic-mobility.

38. C. G. Colen, N. P. Pinchak, and K. S. Barnett, "Racial Disparities in Health among College-Educated African Americans: Can Attendance at Historically Black Colleges or Universities Reduce the Risk of Metabolic Syndrome in Midlife?," *American Journal of Epidemiology* 190, no. 4 (2021): 553, https://doi.org/10.1093/aje/kwaa245.

39. William J. Simmons, *Men of Mark: Eminent, Progressive, and Rising* (Cleveland: Rewell, 1887), 33–34.

40. Simmons, *Men of Mark*, 34.

41. Albert Witherspoon Pegues, *Our Baptist Ministers and Schools* (Springfield, MA: Willey, 1892), 441.

42. Simmons, *Men of Mark*, 31.

43. Simmons, *Men of Mark*, 7.

44. Ida B. Wells, *Crusade for Justice: The Autobiography of Ida B. Wells*, 2nd ed. (Chicago: University of Chicago Press, 2020), 29.

45. Olivia M. Cloud, "The Harvard of Black Kentucky," *Courier-Journal*, June 23, 2007, H1, H4.

46. Simmons, *Men of Mark*, 33.
47. Cloud, "Harvard of Black Kentucky," H4.
48. "Simmons College Named to Official List of Historically Black Colleges," WDRB.com, April 13, 2015, -https://www.wdrb.com/news/simmons-college-named-to-official-list-of-historically -black-colleges/article_3812a96c-3218-5cb6-b1b6-12827e425e84.html.
49. Pegues, *Our Baptist Ministers and Schools*, 445.
50. Pegues, *Our Baptist Ministers and Schools*, 452–53.
51. Tony Martin, *Race First: The Ideological and Organizational Struggles of Marcus Garvey and the Universal Negro Improvement Association* (Dover, MA: Majority, 1976), ix.
52. Ula Yvette Taylor, *The Veiled Garvey: The Life and Times of Amy Jacques Garvey* (Chapel Hill: University of North Carolina Press, 2002), 41.
53. Martin, *Race First*, 23.
54. For more on the Universal Negro Improvement Association, especially the vital role of women, see Keisha Blain, *Set the World on Fire: Black Nationalist Women and the Global Struggle for Freedom* (Philadelphia: University of Pennsylvania Press, 2018); and Taylor, *Veiled Garvey*.
55. "Negroes Acclaim a Black Christ," *New York Times*, August 6, 1924, 3.
56. "Negroes Acclaim a Black Christ," 3.
57. George A. McGuire, *Universal Negro Catechism: A Course of Instruction in Religious and Historical Knowledge Pertaining to the Race* (New York: Universal Negro Improvement Association, 1921), 3, https://hdl.handle.net/2027/emu.010000685445.
58. Martin, *Race First*, 70–74.
59. Lauren Prestileo, "There Are 13 Quotations in a U.S. Passport. Guess How Many Are from Men?," *New York Times*, February 28, 2020, https://www.nytimes.com/2020/02/28/travel /american-passport-quotes-women.html.
60. Beverly Guy-Sheftall, "Black Feminist Studies: The Case of Anna Julia Cooper," *African American Review* 43, no. 1 (2009): 11–15, http://www.jstor.org/stable/27802555.
61. Mark S. Giles, "Special Focus: Dr. Anna Julia Cooper, 1858–1964; Teacher, Scholar, and Timeless Womanist," *The Journal of Negro Education* 75, no. 4 (2006): 623, http://www.jstor .org/stable/40034662.
62. Derrick P. Alridge, "Of Victorianism, Civilizationism, and Progressivism: The Educational Ideas of Anna Julia Cooper and W. E. B. Du Bois, 1892–1940," *History of Education Quarterly* 47, no. 4 (2007): 429, http://www.jstor.org/stable/20462186.
63. Alridge, "Of Victorianism, Civilizationism, and Progressivism," 435n51.
64. Alridge, "Of Victorianism, Civilizationism, and Progressivism," 624–26.
65. Anna Julia Cooper, *A Voice from the South* (Xenia, OH: Aldine, 1892; repr., Seattle: Amazon Classics, 2016), 172.
66. Cooper, *A Voice from the South*, 172.
67. Cooper, *A Voice from the South*, 172. Italics in original.
68. Cooper, *A Voice from the South*, 172.
69. Anna Julia Cooper, "The Ethics of the Negro Question," speech, September 5, 1902, Society of Friends General Conference, Asbury Park, NJ, 16.
70. Cooper, "The Ethics of the Negro Question," 17.
71. Cooper, "The Ethics of the Negro Question," 21.
72. Cooper, "The Ethics of the Negro Question," 23.
73. Alridge, "Of Victorianism, Civilizationism, and Progressivism," 427.
74. Giles, "Special Focus: Dr. Anna Julia Cooper," 627.
75. Genna Rae McNeil, *Groundwork: Charles Hamilton Houston and the Struggle for Civil Rights* (Philadelphia: University of Pennsylvania Press, 1983), 41.
76. "Charles Hamilton—Biography," Howard University School of Law, https://web.archive.org /web/20150905080154/http://www.law.howard.edu/1397.
77. McNeil, *Groundwork*, 76.

78. McNeil, *Groundwork*, 21–23.

79. Charles H. Houston. "An Approach to Better Race Relations," speech, May 5, 1934, National YWCA Convention, Philadelphia, https://www.law.cornell.edu/houston/ywcatxt.htm.

80. Robert L. Carter, William T. Coleman Jr., Jack Greenberg, Genna Rae McNeil, and J. Clay Smith Jr., "In Tribute: Charles Hamilton Houston," *Harvard Law Review* 111, no. 8 (1998): 2175n8, http://www.jstor.org/stable/1342456.

81. Carter, Coleman, Greenberg, McNeil, and Smith, "In Tribute: Charles Hamilton Houston," 2175n8.

Chapter 7: Beyond the Quotable King

1. Richard Lischer, *The Preacher King: Martin Luther King Jr. and the Word That Moved America* . (Oxford: Oxford University Press, 1995, 2020), xvii.

2. For thorough biographies of King that highlight his political and cultural significance, see Taylor Branch's trio of books: *Parting the Waters*; *Pillar of Fire*; and *At Canaan's Edge* (New York: Simon & Schuster, 1989, 1999, 2007); Jonathan Eig, *King: A Life* (New York: Farrar, Straus and Giroux, 2023); David J. Garrow, *Bearing the Cross: Martin Luther King, Jr., and the Southern Christian Leadership Conference* (New York: William Morrow, 1987); Stephen B. Oates, *Let the Trumpet Sound: A Life of Martin Luther King, Jr.* (New York: HarperCollins, 1982); among many others.

3. "King, Alberta Williams," *The King Encyclopedia*, Martin Luther King, Jr. Research and Education Institute, Stanford University, https://kinginstitute.stanford.edu/king-alberta -williams.

4. Martin Luther King Jr., "An Autobiography of Religious Development," Martin Luther King, Jr., Papers, 1954–1968, Howard Gotlieb Archival Research Center, Boston University, https:// kinginstitute.stanford.edu/king-papers/documents/autobiography-religious-development.

5. King, "An Autobiography of Religious Development."

6. King, "An Autobiography of Religious Development."

7. King, "An Autobiography of Religious Development."

8. Lischer, *The Preacher King*, 14.

9. "Crozer Theological Seminary," *The King Encyclopedia*, Martin Luther King, Jr. Research and Education Institute, Stanford University, https://kinginstitute.stanford.edu/encyclopedia /crozer-theological-seminary.

10. More will be written about Coretta Scott King and her leadership in the following chapter.

11. Garrow, *Bearing the Cross*, 57.

12. Garrow, *Bearing the Cross*, 58.

13. Martin Luther King Jr., *Stride toward Freedom: The Montgomery Story* (1958; Boston: Beacon, 2010), 109.

14. King, *Stride toward Freedom*, 109.

15. King, *Stride toward Freedom*, 114.

16. King, *Stride toward Freedom*, 120.

17. King, *Stride toward Freedom*, 79.

18. Kate Clifford Larson, *Bound for the Promised Land: Harriet Tubman, Portrait of an American Hero* (New York: One World Ballantine, 2004), 133.

19. Ida B. Wells, *Southern Horrors: Lynch Law in All Its Phases* ([Charleston, SC]: Create Space, 2011), loc. 309.

20. Wells, *Southern Horrors*, loc. 309.

21. Maegan Parker Brooks, *A Voice That Could Stir an Army: Fannie Lou Hamer and the Rhetoric of the Black Freedom Movement* (Jackson: University of Mississippi Press, 2014), 103.

22. King, *Stride toward Freedom*, 118.

23. Eig, *King*, loc. 4352, Kindle.

24. Eig, *King*, loc. 4352, Kindle.

25. Eig, *King*, loc. 1310, Kindle.

26. Martin Luther King Jr., "I Have a Dream," speech, August 28, 1963, March on Washington for Jobs and Freedom, Washington, DC, The Martin Luther King, Jr. Research and Education Institute, Stanford University, https://kinginstitute.stanford.edu/encyclopedia/i-have-dream.

27. Martin Luther King Jr., "Speech at the Great March on Detroit," speech, June 23, 1963, Detroit Walk to Freedom, https://www.mesaartscenter.com/download.php/engagement/jazz-a-to-z/resources/archive/2016-2017/teacher-resources/speech-at-the-great-march-detroit.

28. Garrow, *Bearing the Cross*, 283.

29. King, "I Have a Dream."

30. King, "I Have a Dream."

31. Hajar Yazdiha, *The Struggle for the People's King: How Politics Transforms the Memory of the Civil Rights Movement* (Princeton, NJ: Princeton University Press, 2023), 8.

32. King, "I Have a Dream."

33. Martin Luther King Jr., *Why We Can't Wait* (Boston: Beacon, 1964), 158.

34. King, *Why We Can't Wait*, 158.

35. King, "I Have a Dream."

36. Martin Luther King Jr., "Will Capitalism Survive?," Four Papers on Preaching Issues, The Martin Luther King, Jr. Research and Education Institute, Stanford University, https://kinginstitute.stanford.edu/king-papers/documents/four-papers-preaching-issues.

37. Martin Luther King Jr., "Jobs Are Harder to Create Than Voting Rolls," *The Nation*, March 14, 1966, https://www.thenation.com/article/economy/last-steep-ascent/.

38. King, "Jobs Are Harder to Create Than Voting Rolls."

39. Martin Luther King Jr., "A New Sense of Direction," speech, 1967, Southern Christian Leadership Conference, Frogmore, SC.

40. King, "A New Sense of Direction."

41. King, "A New Sense of Direction."

42. Michael K. Honey, *To the Promised Land: Martin Luther King and the Fight for Economic Justice* (New York: Norton, 2019), 123.

43. A similar effort had been attempted in 1932 amid the Great Depression. It was called the Bonus Army and consisted of more than 40,000 people, many of them veterans of World War I who demanded immediate redemption of their certificates received for their service in the military. The protest ended with the US military violently forcing the protesters away, killing two of them in the process.

44. Honey, *To the Promised Land*, 184.

45. Harry Enten, "Americans See Martin Luther King Jr. as a Hero Now, but That Wasn't the Case during His Lifetime," CNN, January 16, 2023, https://edition.cnn.com/2023/01/16/politics/martin-luther-king-jr-polling-analysis/index.html.

46. Enten, "Americans See Martin Luther King Jr. as a Hero Now."

47. Martin Luther King Jr., *The Autobiography of Martin Luther King, Jr.*, ed. Clayborne Carson (New York: Grand Central, 1998), loc. 2016, Kindle.

48. Michael K. Honey, "Remembering the Courage of Martin Luther King, Jr.," *History News Network*, January 17, 2011, https://historynewsnetwork.org/article/135486.

49. For a comprehensive study of the FBI and Hoover's surveillance of MLK, see Lerone A. Martin, *The Gospel of J. Edgar Hoover: How the FBI Aided and Abetted the Rise of White Christian Nationalism* (Princeton, NJ: Princeton University Press, 2023).

50. Eig, *King*, loc. 5541, Kindle.

51. Beverly Gage, "What an Uncensored Letter to M.L.K. Reveals," *New York Times Magazine*, November 11, 2014, https://www.nytimes.com/2014/11/16/magazine/what-an-uncensored-letter-to-mlk-reveals.html.

52. Gage, "What an Uncensored Letter to M.L.K. Reveals."

53. Arline T. Geronimus, "The Physical Toll Systemic Injustice Takes on the Body," *Time*

Magazine, March 28, 2023, https://time.com/6266329/systemic-injustice-health-toll
-weathering/.

54. King, *The Autobiography of Martin Luther King, Jr.*, loc. 4995, Kindle.
55. D. J. R. Bruckner, "Dozens Hurt during March in Chicago," *Chicago Tribune*, August 6, 1966, https://www.latimes.com/la-me-dozens-hurt-during-march-19660806-story.html.
56. King, *The Autobiography of Martin Luther King, Jr.*, loc. 6633, Kindle.
57. Garrow, *Bearing the Cross*, 600.
58. Garrow, *Bearing the Cross*, 600.
59. Martin Luther King Jr., "I've Been to the Mountaintop," speech, April 3, 1968, Mason Temple, Memphis, TN, https://www.americanrhetoric.com/speeches/mlkivebeentothemountaintop.htm.

Chapter 8: Women of the Movement

1. Barbara Ransby, *Ella Baker and the Black Freedom Movement: A Radical Democratic Vision* (Chapel Hill: University of North Carolina Press, 2003), 17.
2. Ransby, *Ella Baker and the Black Freedom Movement*, 3.
3. Ella Baker, interview by John Britton, June 19, 1968, Washington, DC, https://www.crmvet .org/nars/baker68.htm#baker68_ldsp.
4. Danielle L. McGuire, *At the Dark End of the Street: Black Women, Rape, and Resistance—A New History of the Civil Rights Movement from Rosa Parks to the Rise of Black Power* (New York: Knopf, 2010), xx.
5. Martha S. Jones, *Vanguard: How Black Women Broke Barriers, Won the Vote, and Insisted on Equality for All* (New York: Hachette, 2020), xi.
6. Faith S. Holsaert et al., eds., *Hands on the Freedom Plow: Personal Accounts by Women in SNCC* (Urbana: University of Illinois Press, 2010), loc. 167, Kindle.
7. Holsaert et al., *Hands on the Freedom Plow*, loc. 230, Kindle.
8. Coretta Scott King and Barbara Reynolds, *Coretta: My Life, My Love, My Legacy* (New York: Henry Holt, 2017), 1.
9. King and Reynolds, *Coretta*, 15.
10. King and Reynolds, *Coretta*, 16, 3.
11. King and Reynolds, *Coretta*, 19.
12. King and Reynolds, *Coretta*, 20.
13. King and Reynolds, *Coretta*, 28.
14. King and Reynolds, *Coretta*, 47.
15. King and Reynolds, *Coretta*, 4.
16. King and Reynolds, *Coretta*, 186.
17. Stevie Wonder, "Happy Birthday," *Hotter Than July*, Tamla, 1980.
18. "The 15 Year Battle for Martin Luther King, Jr. Day," Smithsonian National Museum of African American History and Culture, https://nmaahc.si.edu/explore/stories/15-year-battle -martin-luther-king-jr-day.
19. King and Reynolds, *Coretta*, 247.
20. Ossie Davis and Ruby Dee, *With Ossie and Ruby: In This Life Together* (New York: William Morrow, 1998), 4.
21. Sarah Halzack, "Ruby Dee, Actress and Civil Rights Activist, Dies at 91," *Washington Post*, June 12, 2014, https://www.washingtonpost.com/entertainment/celebrities/ruby-dee-actress -and-civil-rights-activist-dies-at-89/2014/06/12/d4c3e4d2-f250-11e3-9ebc-2ee6f81ed217 _story.html.
22. Davis and Dee, *With Ossie and Ruby*, 33–34.
23. Davis and Dee, *With Ossie and Ruby*, 6.
24. Ossie Davis, eulogy for Malcolm X, Faith Temple Church of God, Harlem, NY, February 27, 1965, https://web.archive.org/web/20141006110705/http://www.malcolmx.com/about/eulogy .html.

25. Taylor Branch, *Parting the Waters: America in the King Years, 1954–63* (New York: Simon & Schuster, 1988), 218.

26. King and Reynolds, *Coretta*, 285.

27. Associated Press, "Ruby Dee Memorialized at Riverside Church in NYC with Song and Dance," ABC News, WJLA, September 20, 2014, https://wjla.com/news/entertainment/ruby -dee-memorialized-at-riverside-church-in-nyc-with-song-and-dance-107347.

28. Diamond Sharp, "Ruby Dee: Advice from a Legend," *The Root*, June 13, 2014, https://web .archive.org/web/20160304034815/http://www.theroot.com/articles/culture/2014/06/ruby _dee_advice_from_a_legend.html?wpisrc=burger.

29. Jennifer Scanlon, *Until There Is Justice: The Life of Anna Arnold Hedgeman* (New York: Oxford University Press, 2016), 2.

30. Scanlon, *Until There Is Justice*, 2.

31. Scanlon, *Until There Is Justice*, 13.

32. "About Our Namesake: Dr. Anna Arnold Hedgeman," Hedgeman Center, Hamline University, https://www.hamline.edu/about/offices-services/hedgeman-center/namesake.

33. Scanlon, *Until There Is Justice*, 29.

34. Scanlon, *Until There Is Justice*, 154.

35. Scanlon, *Until There Is Justice*, 157.

36. Martin Luther King Jr., "Letter from Birmingham Jail," Martin Luther King, Jr. Research and Education Institute, Stanford University, https://kinginstitute.stanford.edu/encyclopedia /letter-birmingham-jail.

37. Scanlon, *Until There Is Justice*, 158.

38. Scanlon, *Until There Is Justice*, 167.

39. Scanlon, *Until There Is Justice*, 175.

40. Scanlon, *Until There Is Justice*, 183.

41. Bettye Collier-Thomas and V. P. Franklin, eds., *Sisters in the Struggle: African American Women in the Civil Rights-Black Power Movement* (New York: New York University Press, 2001), 85–87.

42. Margalit Fox, "Dorothy Height, Largely Unsung Giant of the Civil Rights Era, Dies at 98," *New York Times*, April 20, 2010, https://www.nytimes.com/2010/04/21/us/21height.html.

43. Fox, "Dorothy Height."

44. Dorothy I. Height, *Open Wide the Freedom Gates: A Memoir* (New York: Public Affairs, 2003), 13.

45. Height, *Open Wide the Freedom Gates*, 17.

46. Height, *Open Wide the Freedom Gates*, 59.

47. Height, *Open Wide the Freedom Gates*, 62.

48. "Interracial Charter and Related Policy," National Board of the Young Women's Christian Association of the U.S.A., adopted 1946, rev. 1955, 6, https://www.smith.edu/libraries/libs /ssc/ywca2/popups/pop4072.html.

49. "Biographical/Historical," Dorothy Height Papers, Sophia Smith Collection of Women's History Repository, https://findingaids.smith.edu/repositories/2/resources/814.

50. Height, *Open Wide the Freedom Gates*, 324.

51. Rebecca Tuuri, "Building the Collective 'Voice of Negro Women in Mississippi': The National Council of Negro Women in Mississippi in the 1960s and 1970s," *Mississippi History Now*, June 2020, https://www.mshistorynow.mdah.ms.gov/issue/building-the-collective -%E2%80%9Cvoice-of-negro-women-in-Mississippi%22-the-national-council-of-negro-women -in-mississippi-in-the-1960s-and-1970s.

52. Tuuri, "Building the Collective 'Voice of Negro Women.'"

53. Barack Obama, "Obama's Remarks at Dorothy Height's Funeral Service," *New York Times*, April 29, 2010, https://www.nytimes.com/2010/04/30/us/politics/30height-text.html.

54. Courtney Pace, *Freedom Faith: The Womanist Vision of Prathia Hall* (Athens: University Press of Georgia, 2019), 222–23.

55. Pace, *Freedom Faith*, 224.

56. Pace, *Freedom Faith*, 8.
57. "Prathia Hall," *This Far by Faith*, PBS, https://www.pbs.org/thisfarbyfaith/people/prathia _hall.html.
58. Pace, *Freedom Faith*, 13.
59. Pace, *Freedom Faith*, 1.
60. Holsaert et al., *Hands on the Freedom Plow*, 181.
61. Holsaert et al., eds., *Hands on the Freedom Plow*, 182.
62. Holsaert et al., eds., *Hands on the Freedom Plow*, 183.
63. "Prathia Hall," *This Far by Faith*.
64. Pace, *Freedom Faith*, 2.
65. Holsaert et al., eds., *Hands on the Freedom Plow*, 188.
66. Adam Ganucheau, "Unita Blackwell, Civil Rights Pillar and First Black Woman Mayor in Mississippi, Dies at 86," *Mississippi Today*, May 13, 2019, https://mississippitoday.org/2019/05 /13/unita-blackwell-civil-rights-pillar-and-first-black-woman-mayor-in-mississippi-dies-at-86/.
67. Unita Blackwell, *Barefootin': Life Lessons from the Road to Freedom* (New York: Crown, 2006), ix.
68. Blackwell, *Barefootin'*, 13.
69. Blackwell, *Barefootin'*, 40.
70. Blackwell, *Barefootin'*, 45.
71. Blackwell, *Barefootin'*, 75.
72. Blackwell, *Barefootin'*, 78.
73. Blackwell, *Barefootin'*, 177.
74. Peter T. Kilborn, "A Mayor and Town Rise Jointly," *New York Times*, June 17, 1992, https:// www.nytimes.com/1992/06/17/us/a-mayor-and-town-rise-jointly.html.
75. Blackwell, *Barefootin'*, 210.
76. Katharine Q. Seelye, "Unita Blackwell, 86, Dies; Rights Crusader and Winner of Historic Election," *New York Times*, May 17, 2019, https://www.nytimes.com/2019/05/17/obituaries /unita-blackwell-dead.html.
77. Blackwell, *Barefootin'*, 249. Emphasis original.
78. Blackwell, *Barefootin'*, 177.
79. Kyle Brooks, "The Morning After: Black Women and the March on Washington," *Black Perspectives*, December 12, 2022, https://www.aaihs.org/the-morning-after-black-women-and -the-march-on-washington/.
80. Brooks, "The Morning After."

Chapter 9: Black *and* Christian

1. Darlene Clark Hine, William C. Hine, and Stanley C. Harrold, *The African-American Odyssey*, combined vol., 7th ed., digital ed. (Boston: Pearson, 2016), 22.1.3.
2. "Watts Rebellion (Los Angeles)," Martin Luther King, Jr. Research and Education Institute, Stanford Institute, https://kinginstitute.stanford.edu/encyclopedia/watts-rebellion-los-angeles.
3. WNYC Newsroom, "50 Years after the Riots, a Newarker Looks Back on His Decision to Stay," *WNYC News*, July 10, 2017, https://www.wnyc.org/story/50-years-after-riots-newarker -looks-back-his-decision-stay.
4. "Uprising of 1967," *Encyclopedia of Detroit*, Detroit Historical Society, https://detroithistorical .org/learn/encyclopedia-of-detroit/uprising-1967.
5. Otter Kerner, chairman, "Report of the National Advisory Commission on Civil Disorders," Othering and Belonging Institute, University of California at Berkeley, 1, https://belonging .berkeley.edu/sites/default/files/kerner_commission_full_report.pdf?file=1&force=1.
6. Kerner, "Report of the National Advisory Commission on Civil Disorders," 1.
7. Richard Nixon, "Address to the Nation on the War in Vietnam," November 3, 1969, The American Presidency Project, University of California at Santa Barbara, https://www .presidency.ucsb.edu/documents/address-the-nation-the-war-vietnam.

8. Matthew Lassiter, *The Silent Majority: Suburban Politics in the Sunbelt South* (Princeton, NJ: Princeton University Press, 2006), 226.

9. Jemar Tisby, *The Color of Compromise: The Truth about the American Church's Complicity in Racism* (Grand Rapids: Zondervan Reflective, 2019), 166–67.

10. Clayborne Carson et al., eds., *Eyes on the Prize Civil Rights Reader: Documents, Speeches, and Firsthand Accounts from the Black Freedom Struggle* (New York: Viking Penguin, 1991), 346–47.

11. James Findlay Jr., *Church People in the Struggle: The National Council of Churches and the Black Freedom Movement, 1950–1970* (New York: Oxford University Press, 1993), 185.

12. Findlay, *Church People in the Struggle*, 185.

13. Milton C. Sernett, ed., *African American Religious History: A Documentary Witness*, 2nd ed. (Durham, NC: Duke University Press, 1999), 556.

14. Sernett, *African American Religious History*, 557.

15. Sernett, *African American Religious History*, 558.

16. Sernett, *African American Religious History*, 559.

17. Sernett, *African American Religious History*, 560, emphasis original.

18. Sernett, *African American Religious History*, 561.

19. Albert Cleage Jr., *The Black Messiah* (New York: Sheed and Ward, 1968), 85.

20. Cleage, *The Black Messiah*, 98.

21. Hiley Ward, *Prophet of a Black Nation* (Philadelphia: Pilgrim, 1969), 44.

22. Peter Eisenstadt, *Against the Hounds of Hell: A Life of Howard Thurman* (Charlottesville: University of Virginia Press, 2021), 208–12.

23. Eisenstadt, *Against the Hounds of Hell*, 214.

24. "New Church Is Organized," *The Detroit Free Press*, May 12, 1951, 8.

25. "Central Congregational Holds First Services in New Edifice," *Detroit Tribune*, September 28, 1957, Detroit, MI, 8.

26. Ward, *Prophet*, 7–8.

27. Albert B. Cleage Jr., interview by Scott Morrison, *Mutual News*, WOR-AM, New York, November 1968.

28. Kimathi Nelson, "The Theological Journey of Albert B. Cleage Jr.: Reflections from Jaramogi's Protégé and Successor," *Albert Cleage Jr. and the Black Madonna and Child*, ed. Jawanza Clark (New York: Palgrave MacMillan, 2016), 29.

29. James Cone, *Said I Wasn't Gonna Tell Nobody* (Maryknoll, NY: Orbis, 2018), 7.

30. James Cone, *Black Theology and Black Power* (1969; repr., Maryknoll, NY: Orbis, 1997), ix.

31. Marvin A. McMickle, *Encyclopedia of African American Christian Heritage* (Valley Forge, PA: Judson, 2002), 95.

32. James Cone, *God of the Oppressed*, rev. ed. (Maryknoll, NY: Orbis, 1997), 123–25.

33. Cone, *God of the Oppressed*, 125.

34. Cone, *Said I Wasn't Gonna Tell Nobody*, 21.

35. Shirley Chisholm was not the first Black woman to run for president. That distinction goes to Charlene Mitchell, who was the presidential nominee for the American Communist Party ticket in 1968.

36. Debra Michals, "Shirley Chisholm," National Women's History Museum, https://www.womenshistory.org/education-resources/biographies/shirley-chisholm.

37. Shirley Chisholm, *Unbought and Unbossed* (1970; repr., New York: Amistad, 2022), 55.

38. Chisholm, *Unbought and Unbossed*, 14.

39. Chisholm, *Unbought and Unbossed*, 18.

40. Chisholm, *Unbought and Unbossed*, 27.

41. Chisholm, *Unbought and Unbossed*, 80.

42. Robert McClory, "Rep. Shirley Chisholm Announces Candidacy for Top Office Tuesday," *Pittsburgh Courier*, January 29, 1972, 1A.

43. McClory, "Rep. Shirley Chisholm," 1A.

44. Julie Gallagher, "Waging 'the Good Fight': The Political Career of Shirley Chisholm, 1953–1982," *Journal of African American History* 92, no. 3 (2007): 408, http://www.jstor.org /stable/20064206.

45. Gallagher, "Waging 'the Good Fight,'" 408.

46. Marian Christy, "The Fire Inside Rep. Chisholm," *The Boston Globe*, July 9, 1982, 36.

47. Chisholm, *Unbought and Unbossed*, 104.

48. Carol Cannon, "Younger Members Want Bigger Role in Running NAACP," *The Akron Beacon Journal*, November 11, 1991, 16.

49. Steven A. Holmes, "Leader Used N.A.A.C.P. Money to Settle a Sex Harassment Case," *New York Times*, July 29, 1994, 1A.

50. Don Terry, "N.A.A.C.P. Audit Shows Lavish Spending, Members Say," *New York Times*, July 13, 1995, 21A.

51. Robin B. Bennefield, "Only for You, Myrlie Evers-Williams, Only for You," *The Crisis* (July 1998): 74.

52. Bennefield, "Only for You, Myrlie Evers-Williams," 74.

53. Myrlie B. Evers and William Peters, *For Us, the Living* (1967; repr., Oxford: University of Mississippi Press, 1996), 35.

54. Evers and Peters, *For Us, the Living*, 37.

55. Evers and Peters, *For Us, the Living*, 43.

56. Evers and Peters, *For Us, the Living*, 47.

57. Evers and Peters, *For Us, the Living*, 54.

58. Myrlie Evers and Melinda Blau, *Watch Me Fly: What I Learned on the Way to Becoming the Woman I Was Meant to Be* (New York: Little, Brown, 1999), 59.

59. Myrlie Evers-Williams and Manning Marable, *The Autobiography of Medgar Evers: A Hero's Life and Legacy Revealed through His Writings, Letters, and Speeches* (New York: Basic Civitas, 2005), 10.

60. Evers-Williams and Marable, *The Autobiography of Medgar Evers*, 12.

61. Evers-Williams and Marable, *The Autobiography of Medgar Evers*, 13.

62. Evers and Blau, *Watch Me Fly*, 79.

63. Evers and Peters, *For Us, the Living*, 303.

64. Evers and Peters, *For Us, the Living*, 78.

65. Evers and Peters, *For Us, the Living*, 79.

66. Evers and Peters, *For Us, the Living*, 1.

67. For a detailed accounting of the decades-long endeavor to convict Byron De La Beckwith of Medgar Evers's murder, see Jerry Mitchell, *Race against Time: A Reporter Reopens the Unsolved Murder Cases of the Civil Rights Era* (New York: Simon & Schuster, 2021).

68. Evers and Blau, *Watch Me Fly*, 9.

69. Staff, "Evers Named to LA Board of Public Works," *Jackson Clarion-Ledger*, May 30, 1987, 2.

70. "Medgar and Myrlie Evers Home National Monument," National Park Foundation, https:// www.nationalparks.org/explore/parks/medgar-and-myrlie-evers-home-national-monument.

71. Evers and Blau, *Watch Me Fly*, 221.

72. Thea Bowman, "Address to US Conference of Catholic Bishops," speech, June 1989, South Orange, NJ, https://www.usccb.org/issues-and-action/cultural-diversity/african-american /resources/upload/Transcript-Sr-Thea-Bowman-June-1989-Address.pdf.

73. Bowman, "Address to US Conference of Catholic Bishops."

74. Bowman, "Address to US Conference of Catholic Bishops."

75. Bowman, "Address to US Conference of Catholic Bishops."

76. Bowman, "Address to US Conference of Catholic Bishops."

77. Cecilia A. Moore, "Writing Black Catholic Lives: Black Catholic Biographies and Autobiographies," *U.S. Catholic Historian* 29, no. 3 (2011): 53, http://www.jstor.org/stable /41289660.

78. Charlene Smith and John Feister, *Thea's Song: The Life of Thea Bowman* (Maryknoll, NY: Orbis, 2009), loc. 451, Kindle.

79. Smith and Feister, *Thea's Song*, loc. 515, Kindle.

80. "Sister Thea Bowman (1937–1990)," Thea Bowman AHANA and Intercultural Center, Boston College, https://www.bc.edu/content/bc-web/offices/student-affairs/sites/ahana/about /baic-history/sr--thea-bowman.html.

81. Smith and Feister, *Thea's Song*, loc. 4271, Kindle.

Chapter 10: The Next Justice Generation

1. Jack Jenkins (@jackmjenkins), "In case you doubted the that [*sic*] people who raided the Capitol invoked God as they did so, here are Proud Boys kneeling in prayer before approaching the Capitol on Wed, clipped from the stream linked in the embedded tweet below. Among other things, the prayer decries socialism," video embedded, X, formerly known as Twitter, 4:50 p.m., January 9, 2021, https://twitter.com/jackmjenkins/status/1348024379502972932?s=20.

2. Jenkins, tweet, 4:50 p.m., January 9, 2021.

3. "Jury Convicts Four Leaders of the Proud Boys of Seditious Conspiracy Related to U.S. Capitol Breach," Office of Public Affairs, US Department of Justice, May 4, 2023, https://www.justice .gov/opa/pr/jury-convicts-four-leaders-proud-boys-seditious-conspiracy-related-us-capitol-breach.

4. "Proud Boys," Southern Poverty Law Center, https://www.splcenter.org/fighting-hate /extremist-files/group/proud-boys.

5. Jack Jenkins, "The Insurrectionists' Senate Floor Prayer Highlights a Curious Trumpian Ecumenism," *Religion News Service*, February 25, 2021, https://religionnews.com/2021/02/25 /the-insurrectionists-senate-floor-prayer-highlights-a-curious-trumpian-ecumenism/.

6. Jemar Tisby, "What Is White Christian Nationalism with Dr. Jemar Tisby," video, Jemar Tisby (YouTube channel), uploaded November 16, 2022, YouTube, https://www.youtube.com /watch?v=5ZGR7TAgA3w.

7. "Col. Simmons Begins Defense of the Klan," *New York Times*, March 19, 1922, https://timesmachine.nytimes.com/timesmachine/1922/03/19/103582854.pdf?pdf _redirect=true&ip=0.

8. Portions of the proceeding originally appeared in an article titled "A Virtual Roundtable on the Threat of Christian Nationalism, Part 2 of 4 by Jemar Tisby," https://jemartisby.substack.com /p/a-virtual-roundtable-on-the-threat.

9. Philip S. Gorski and Samuel L. Perry, *The Flag and the Cross: White Christian Nationalism and the Threat to American Democracy* (New York: Oxford University Press, 2022), 4–5.

10. "Barack Obama Celebrates His Victory at Grant Park," *Chicago Tribune*, October 26, 2012, https://www.chicagotribune.com/news/chi-081104-obama-rally-grant-park-photogallery -photogallery.html.

11. ABC News, "How Donald Trump Perpetuated the 'Birther' Movement for Years," *ABC News*, September 16, 2016, https://abcnews.go.com/Politics/donald-trump-perpetuated-birther -movement-years/story?id=42138176.

12. Vanessa Williamson, Theda Skocpol, and John Coggin, "The Tea Party and the Remaking of Republican Conservatism," *Perspectives on Politics* 9, no. 1 (2011): 26, http://www.jstor.org /stable/41622724.

13. NAACP, "Resolution: The Tea Party Movement," 2010, https://naacp.org/resources/tea-party -movement.

14. NAACP, "Resolution: The Tea Party Movement."

15. Geoffrey Kabaservice, "The Forever Grievance: Conservatives Have Traded Periodic Revolts for a Permanent Revolution," *Washington Post*, December 4, 2020, https://www .washingtonpost.com/outlook/2020/12/04/tea-party-trumpism-conservatives-populism/.

16. Jemar Tisby, *The Color of Compromise: The Truth about the American Church's Complicity in Racism* (Grand Rapids: Zondervan Reflective, 2019), 177.

17. Tobin Grant, "InterVarsity Leaders Back Black Lives Matter Efforts during Student Conference," *The Christian Century*, February 3, 2016, https://www.christiancentury.org /article/2015-12/intervarsity-calls-support-blacklivesmatter.

18. Mark Oppenheimer, "Some Evangelicals Struggle with Black Lives Matter Movement," *New York Times*, January 22, 2016, https://www.nytimes.com/2016/01/23/us/some-evangelicals -struggle-with-black-lives-matter-movement.html.

19. Amanda Tyler, testimony, December 13, 2022, Hearing on Confronting White Supremacy, pt. 7, House Oversight Committee's Subcommittee on Civil Rights and Civil Liberties, 12, https://oversightdemocrats.house.gov/sites/democrats.oversight.house.gov/files/Tyler%20 Testimony.pdf.

20. "Christians against Christian Nationalism," Christians against Christian Nationalism, Baptist Joint Committee for Religious Liberty, https://www.christiansagainstchristiannationalism.org /statement.

21. "Christian Nationalism and the January 6, 2021 Insurrection," Christians against Christian Nationalism, https://www.christiansagainstchristiannationalism.org/jan6report.

22. I contributed to the "Christian Nationalism and the January 6, 2021 Insurrection" report.

23. "What and Why," Vote Common Good, https://www.votecommongood.com/what-and-why/.

24. Eliza Griswold, "Teaching Democrats to Speak Evangelical," *New Yorker*, October 19, 2019, https://www.newyorker.com/news/on-religion/teaching-democrats-to-speak-evangelical.

25. RNS Staff, "Faithful America Announces New Campaigns Director to Lead Its Social-Justice Advocacy," *Religion News Service*, July 30, 2019, https://religionnews.com/2019/07/30/faithful -america-announces-new-campaigns-director-to-lead-its-social-justice-advocacy/.

26. "Resisting Christian Nationalism: FAQ and Resources," Faithful America, https://act .faithfulamerica.org/signup/christian-nationalism-resources/.

27. "Sandra Maria Van Opstal," Chasing Justice, https://chasingjustice.com/sandra-van-opstal/.

28. Lisa Fields, interview by Jasmine Holmes, "Rethinking Apologetics for the Black Church," *Christianity Today*, July 18, 2018, https://www.christianitytoday.com/ct/2018/july-web-only /rethinking-apologetics-for-black-church.html.

29. "Our Founder," Jude 3 Project, https://jude3project.org/our-founder.

30. Layla Abbas, "Asian Americans Report Influx of Racist Attacks Since Coronavirus Pandemic, Data Finds," NBC Los Angeles, April 7, 2020, https://www.nbclosangeles.com/news/local /asian-americans-report-influx-of-racist-attacks-since-coronavirus-pandemic-data-finds /2327045.

31. "By, For, and About Asian American Christians," Asian American Christian Collaborative, https://www.asianamericanchristiancollaborative.com/vision.

32. Ben Pope, "Asian American Churches Hold March through Chinatown, Calling for Unity with Black Communities," *Chicago Sun Times*, June 28, 2020, https://chicago.suntimes.com/news /2020/6/28/21306401/chinatown-march-black-lives-matter-chinese-christian-union-church -progressive-baptist-aacc.

33. "About," The New Jim Crow, https://newjimcrow.com/about.

34. Avi Holzman and Jimmy Hu, "Civil Rights Activist Michelle Alexander Discusses Structural Racism," *Student Life*, Washington University in St. Louis, March 1, 2023, https://www .studlife.com/news/2023/03/01/civil-rights-activist-michelle-alexander-discusses-structural -racism.

35. Cole Arthur Riley, *This Here Flesh: Spirituality, Liberation, and the Stories That Make Us* (New York: Convergent, 2022), 7.

36. Garrison Hayes, TikTok, https://www.tiktok.com/@garrisonhayes.

37. "Mother Jones Hires Popular TikTok Creator Garrison Hayes," Press Release, Mother Jones, November 17, 2022, https://www.editorandpublisher.com/stories/mother-jones-hires-popular -tiktok-creator-garrison-hayes,240928.

38. Nika White, "How Danielle Coke's Art Activism Helps Businesses Message DEI,"

Entrepreneur, March 24, 2022, https://www.entrepreneur.com/leadership/how-danielle-cokes
-art-activism-helps-businesses-message/420998.

39. "Danielle Coke: Oh Happy Dani Collection," Target.com, https://www.target.com/p/danielle
-coke-oh-happy-dani-collection/-/A-85445452.

40. Elwyn Lopez, "Artist Pushes Conversations about Racial Issues through Her Work," CNN,
August 3, 2020, https://www.11alive.com/article/news/local/local-artist-teaches-racial-issues
-through-her-art/85-68ac0c8e-633f-445c-8d0f-c60f1f6aef07.

41. André Henry, *All the White Friends I Couldn't Keep: Hope—and Hard Pills to Swallow—about
Fighting for Black Lives* (New York: Convergent, 2022), 84.

42. André Henry, Instagram, https://www.instagram.com/theandrehenry/.

43. "What We Do," Love beyond Walls, https://www.lovebeyondwalls.org/lovesinksin/.

44. Tyler Burns and Jemar Tisby, "Young Christian Professionals with Stanley Frankart," *Pass
the Mic*, podcast, October 10, 2022, https://podcasts.apple.com/us/podcast/young-christian
-professionals-with-stanley-frankart/id1435500798?i=1000582179828.

45. Burns and Tisby, "Young Christian Professionals with Stanley Frankart."

46. Stanley Frankart is a recipient of the inaugural Witness Fellowship that awards $100,000 over
two years and provides fellows with leadership training and a cohort experience to prepare the
next generation of Black civil rights leaders. I was part of the committee that selected Frankart
for the fellowship.

47. "About," Common Hymnal, https://commonhymnal.com/about.

48. Malcolm du Plessis, "Praise and Protest," Common Hymnal, https://commonhymnal.com
/blog/praise-and-protest.

49. "Walk with Me (Otis' Dream)," Common Hymnal, https://commonhymnal.com/songs/walk
-with-me-otis-dream.

Chapter 11: The Spirit of Justice Speaks

1. "The General Rules of the Methodist Church," *The Book of Discipline of the United Methodist
Church* (Nashville: United Methodist Publishing House, 2016), https://www.umc.org/en
/content/the-general-rules-of-the-methodist-church.

2. Courtney Pace, *Freedom Faith: The Womanist Vision of Prathia Hall* (Athens: University Press
of Georgia, 2019), 200.

3. Kate Clifford Larson, *Bound for the Promised Land: Harriet Tubman, Portrait of an American
Hero* (New York: One World, 2004), 140.

4. Marcus Mosiah Garvey, *Philosophy and Opinions of Marcus Garvey* (Glasgow: Good, 2022), 25.

5. Jens Manuel Krogstad and Kiana Cox, "For Black History Month, a Look at What Black
Americans Say Is Needed to Overcome Racial Inequality," Pew Research Center, January 20,
2023, https://www.pewresearch.org/short-reads/2023/01/20/for-black-history-month-a-look
-at-what-black-americans-say-is-needed-to-overcome-racial-inequality/.

6. Jemar Tisby, *How to Fight Racism: Courageous Christianity and the Journey toward Racial Justice*
(Grand Rapids: Zondervan Reflective, 2021), 14–15.

7. Civil Rights in Mississippi Digital Archive, "Fannie Lou Hamer Recalls the Mississippi Voter
Registration Campaign," SHEC: Resources for Teachers, https://shec.ashp.cuny.edu/items
/show/983.

INDEX